It isn't surprising materialists deny
deny the existence of me! (an
beautiful circularity about all
subjective 'I' is an 'illusion' sou
madness. 'The fool says in his

The ontological argument (I think) fails because it posits 'existence' as an aspect of greatness. Contra this, I think existence is a humble property of material things which have only a derivative reality in the mind or consciousness.

Put another way – the ontological argument can only establish the existence of something 'at the top of the material heap.' It can't establish the existence of something beyond the heap.

Maybe it does establish the existence of a kind of personal god, a psychological entity.

Thou, who hast given me eyes to see
And love this sight so fair,
Give me a heart to find out thee
And read thee everywhere

John Keble

Maximal God

Maximal God

A New Defence of Perfect Being Theism

Yujin Nagasawa

OXFORD
UNIVERSITY PRESS

OXFORD
UNIVERSITY PRESS

Great Clarendon Street, Oxford, OX2 6DP,
United Kingdom

Oxford University Press is a department of the University of Oxford.
It furthers the University's objective of excellence in research, scholarship,
and education by publishing worldwide. Oxford is a registered trade mark of
Oxford University Press in the UK and in certain other countries

© Yujin Nagasawa 2017

The moral rights of the author have been asserted

First Edition published in 2017

Impression: 2

All rights reserved. No part of this publication may be reproduced, stored in
a retrieval system, or transmitted, in any form or by any means, without the
prior permission in writing of Oxford University Press, or as expressly permitted
by law, by licence or under terms agreed with the appropriate reprographics
rights organization. Enquiries concerning reproduction outside the scope of the
above should be sent to the Rights Department, Oxford University Press, at the
address above

You must not circulate this work in any other form
and you must impose this same condition on any acquirer

Published in the United States of America by Oxford University Press
198 Madison Avenue, New York, NY 10016, United States of America

British Library Cataloguing in Publication Data
Data available

Library of Congress Control Number: 2017936761

ISBN 978–0–19–875868–6

Links to third party websites are provided by Oxford in good faith and
for information only. Oxford disclaims any responsibility for the materials
contained in any third party website referenced in this work.

For Sylwia and Kazan, with love

Acknowledgements

I read parts of this book, at various stages of development, at conferences and workshops, including: the Belief and Metaphysics Conference in Granada; the Eighth Biannual Conference of the British Society for the Philosophy of Religion at Lady Margaret Hall, Oxford; the Fourth Annual Philosophy of Religion Conference at Baylor University; the Metaphysics and Philosophy of Religion Workshop at the University of Texas at San Antonio; the Ontological Proofs Today Conference at Kazimierz Wielki University; and the Philosophical Theology Workshop at King's College, London. They were also read at seminars at many universities including the University of Barcelona; the University of Birmingham; the University of Cambridge; the University of Edinburgh; the University of Heidelberg; Heythrop College, the University of London; the University of Liverpool; the University of Nottingham; Oriel College, the University of Oxford; Oxford Brookes University; the University of Reading; the State University of New York at Stony Brook; the University of Texas, Austin; and the University of York.

I would like to thank the following people for helpful comments and suggestions: Robert Adams, Keith Allen, Michael Almeida, Nader Alsamaani, Maria Rosa Antognazza, Helen Beebee, Toby Betenson, John Bishop, Einar Bohn, Lisa Bortolotti, Joshua Brown, Andrei Buckareff, Elizabeth Burns, Darragh Byrne, David Cheetham, Sarah Coakley, John Cottingham, Ben Curtis, Dorothea Debus, Jamie Dew, Petr Dvořák, Eric Eck, John Edge, Nikk Effingham, David Efird, Marius Felderhof, Peter Forrest, Philip Goff, Tyron Goldschmidt, John Haldane, Douglas Hedley, John Hick, Daniel Hill, Robert Koons, Klaas Kraay, Robert Lawrence Kuhn, Jonathan Kvanvig, Iain Law, Brian Leftow, Gary Mar, Tim Mawson, Chad Meister, Thaddeus Metz, Peter Millican, Dan O'Brien, David Oderberg, Graham Oppy, Ken Perszyk, Alexander Pruss, Michael Rea, Michael Ridge, Constantine Sandis, Martin Smith, Eric Steinhart, Tom Stoneham, Bart Streumer, Scott Sturgeon, Richard Swinburne, Emily Thomas, Patrick Todd, Nick Trakakis, Joss Walker, and Ed Wierenga. I am particularly indebted to the following people for detailed written comments: William Barnett, Tom Flint, Joseph Jedwab, Ian Logan, Peter Millican, Graham

Oppy, James Orr, Edward Wierenga, and anonymous readers for Oxford University Press. Apologies to those I may have omitted.

This book project was supported by a summer stipend offered by the Classical Theism Project at the University of St. Thomas directed by Gloria Frost and Tim Pawl and funded by the John Templeton Foundation. I am grateful for their generous support. I would also like to thank the University of Birmingham for allowing me to complete this book on my sabbatical. I am also grateful to Matthias Butler, Peter Momtchiloff, and their team at the Oxford University Press for their impeccable editorial support.

Several parts of this book draw upon previously published material of mine: 'Millican on the Ontological Argument', *Mind* 116, 2007, pp. 1027–40; 'A New Defence of Anselmian Theism', *Philosophical Quarterly* 58, 2008, pp. 577–96; 'The Ontological Argument and the Devil', *Philosophical Quarterly* 60, 2010, pp. 72–91; 'Anselmian Theism', *Philosophy Compass* 6, 2011, pp. 564–71; 'Is There a Shallow Logical Refutation of the Ontological Argument?', *European Journal for Philosophy of Religion* 4, 2012, pp. 87–99; and 'Models of Anselmian Theism', *Faith and Philosophy* 30, 2013, pp. 3–25. I would like to thank the publishers of these journals for allowing me to use the material here.

Finally, a word of thanks should also go to my family and friends for their love and support.

Contents

List of Figures xiii

Introduction 1

Part I. Perfect Being Theism

1. Conceptual, Historical, and Cognitive Roots of Perfect Being Theism 7
   - 1.1. Introduction 7
   - 1.2. Perfect Being Theism vs. Atheism, Polytheism, Pantheism, and Panentheism 11
   - 1.3. Historical Origins 15
   - 1.4. Cognitive and Developmental Origins 24
   - 1.5. The Merits of Perfect Being Theism 27
   - 1.6. Arguments for Perfect Being Theism 35
   - 1.7. Arguments Against Perfect Being Theism 36
   - 1.8. Conclusion 38
2. Perfect Being Theism and the Great Chain of Being 40
   - 2.1. Introduction 40
   - 2.2. The Great Chain of Being 42
   - 2.3. Some Preliminaries 46
   - 2.4. The Linear Model 49
   - 2.5. The Radial Model 52
   - 2.6. The Comprehensive Greatness View 63
   - 2.7. Objections to the Comprehensive Greatness View 64
   - 2.8. Reconsidering the Linear Model 70
   - 2.9. A Knock-Down Objection to the Linear Model? 72
   - 2.10. Conclusion 76

Part II. The Maximal God Refutation of Arguments Against Perfect Being Theism

3. Maximal God and Arguments Against Perfect Being Theism I 79
   - 3.1. Introduction 79
   - 3.2. The Perfect Being Thesis and the Omni God Thesis 80
   - 3.3. Three Types of Argument Against Perfect Being Theism 82

3.4. The Case-by-Case Approach to Arguments Against Perfect Being Theism 88
3.5. The Maximal God Thesis 90
3.6. Maximal God and Epistemically Possible Scenarios 94
3.7. Conclusion 102

4. Maximal God and Arguments Against Perfect Being Theism II 103
4.1. Introduction 103
4.2. Objections Concerning God's Great-Making Properties 104
4.3. Objections Concerning the Monotheistic Aspect of Perfect Being Theism 109
4.4. Objections Concerning Evil 113
4.5. Objections Concerning Methodological Issues 116
4.6. Conclusion 120

Part III. The Maximal God Defence of the Ontological Argument for Perfect Being Theism

5. A Partial Defence of the Classical Ontological Argument I 123
5.1. Introduction 123
5.2. Anselm Invented the Classical Ontological Argument 124
5.3. Why the Classical Ontological Argument Persists 131
5.4. The Theory of Natures 134
5.5. Millican's Objection to the Classical Ontological Argument 138
5.6. Initial Response to Millican's Objection 139
5.7. Further Response to Millican's Objection 142
5.8. Response to Millican's Rejoinder 145
5.9. Conclusion 150

6. A Partial Defence of the Classical Ontological Argument II 152
6.1. Introduction 152
6.2. Gaunilo's Island Parody 154
6.3. Responses to Gaunilo's Island Parody 156
6.4. The Virtues of the Parody Objection 157
6.5. Millican's AntiGod Parody 160
6.6. Response to Millican's AntiGod Parody 163
6.7. Chambers's Devil Parody 169
6.8. Objection to Chambers's Devil Parody 172
6.9. A Hypothesis Concerning the Parody Objection 174
6.10. Conclusion 178

7. Maximal God and the Modal Ontological Argument 180
7.1. Introduction 180
7.2. The Modal Ontological Argument 181

7.3. Existing Arguments for the Possibility Premise 186
7.4. The Maximal God Argument for the Possibility Premise 202
7.5. Conclusion 205
Conclusion 207

References 209
Index 223

List of Figures

2.1 The linear model. 52

2.2 Extensive equality. 57

2.3 Extensive superiority. 57

2.4 Intensive equality. 58

2.5 Intensive superiority. 58

2.6 The radial model. 62

2.7 Broad's first scenario. 74

2.8 Broad's second scenario. 74

3.1 Scenario S_1. 96

3.2 Scenario S_2. 97

3.3 Scenario S_3. 100

See, through this air, this ocean, and this earth,
All matter quick, and bursting into birth.
Above, how high, progressive life may go!
Around, how wide! how deep extend below?
Vast chain of being! which from God began,
Natures ethereal, human, angel, man,
Beast, bird, fish, insect, what no eye can see,
No glass can reach; from Infinite to thee,
From thee to nothing.—On superior powers
Were we to press, inferior might on ours;
Or in the full creation leave a void,
Where, one step broken, the great scale's destroy'd:
From Nature's chain whatever link you strike,
Tenth or ten thousandth, breaks the chain alike.

—Alexander Pope, *Essay on Man*

Introduction

I do not remember how it happened, but when I was around fifteen years old I suddenly became fascinated by the existence of concepts, ideas, and thoughts. These elements of mental life are intangible—you cannot see or touch them. Yet they have 'power' to make people happy, sad, and even angry. They could make a couple get married but they could just as easily cause a war between countries. This seemed to me to be a mystery. I then wondered: Among uncountably many concepts, which one is the greatest? I wanted to find out the answer because I thought that I would feel comforted in conceiving such a concept. Is the greatest concept love, truth, or beauty? My tentative conclusion then was that whatever it is, it must be the concept of something that is truly incredible.

One day a mathematics teacher told me that there are proofs not only in mathematics but also in philosophy, and that there are indeed such things as philosophical proofs of the existence of God. I was excited to hear this—I did not know that the existence of God could be proved in the way that mathematical statements are proved. I went home and looked this up in an encyclopaedia. It turned out that what my teacher called proofs of the existence of God were not exactly proofs with mathematical precision, but *arguments* for the existence of God. (In defence of the teacher, Immanuel Kant and many other philosophers have used the term 'proof' in this context.) Among various arguments for the existence of God introduced in the encyclopaedia, I was particularly impressed by the ontological argument, which was originally introduced by Anselm of Canterbury in the eleventh century. The ontological argument is based on the concept of God as 'the being thing than which no greater is conceivable', which seemed to me to be the greatest concept—the very concept that I had been looking for. By appealing to this concept, Anselm develops a purely a priori argument for the existence of God. If Anselm's argument is sound, then we do not need any scientific investigation or empirical observation to derive the existence of God. We can sit down in an armchair and demonstrate through a mental exercise alone that God, as the being than which no greater is conceivable, exists in reality. I found it astonishing. I thought this could possibly be humanity's greatest discovery and, hence, I was puzzled as to why people do not talk about it all the time. (And I am still puzzled!) I had thought that if I could pinpoint the greatest concept, that would be a significant achievement. Anselm has not only discovered such a concept but also claims to have invented an argument for the existence of the very thing to which the concept refers.

The encyclopaedia I consulted also discussed an objection to the ontological argument. According to the objection, it is impossible that the existence of anything can be proved merely by analysing its concept. It is impossible, for example, to prove that there is a £20 note in your pocket by analysing the concept of a £20 note. Yet I speculated that perhaps God is an exception because, as the being than which no greater is conceivable, He might have a unique property that other beings lack. Schopenhauer says cynically that the ontological argument is only a 'charming joke', but there was something about the argument that made me not want to dismiss it as a philosophical joke. I thought it would be worth investigating this argument. Looking back now, that was when my long journey with perfect being theism began.

Perfect being theism is a form of theism based on Anselm's concept of God. According to perfect being theism, God, as the being than which no greater is conceivable or metaphysically possible, exists. Perfect being theism is widely accepted among Judeo-Christian-Islamic theists today. It is no exaggeration to say that nearly all the central debates over the existence and nature of God in the philosophy of religion rely on this form of theism. Even atheists and agnostics base their discussions on perfect being theism. Yet this view faces many criticisms. The aim of this book is to develop a radically new, game-changing defence of this important view. Perfect being theists typically subscribe to the 'omni God thesis', according to which God is the omniscient, omnipotent, and omnibenevolent being. I introduce an alternative to the omni God thesis, the 'maximal God thesis', according to which God is the being that has the maximal consistent set of knowledge, power, and benevolence. I argue that the maximal God thesis allows us to undermine nearly all existing arguments against perfect being theism simultaneously and, moreover, to establish a new, successful version of the modal ontological argument for the existence of God.

This book has the following structure. In Part I, I offer a detailed survey of philosophical issues concerning perfect being theism. In particular, in Chapter 1, I consider perfect being theism in relation to various forms of theism and non-theism, such as monotheism, polytheism, pantheism, panentheism, and atheism. I also address the historical, cognitive, and developmental origins of perfect being theism and explain the philosophical merits of endorsing perfect being theism. I then provide an overview of arguments for and against perfect being theism. In Chapter 2, I consider precisely how we can understand the relationship between God and other possible beings in perfect being theism by referring to the notion of the 'great chain of being', a hierarchy of all beings. I introduce and examine various formulations of perfect being theism through distinct models of the great chain of being. I defend, with some caution, what I call the 'radial model' and the 'linear model'.

In Part II, I focus on existing arguments against perfect being theism and develop a radically new, economical refutation of them. In particular, in Chapter 3, I classify existing arguments against perfect being theism into three types and offer a novel response to them using the maximal God thesis. I argue that my response undercuts nearly all the arguments against perfect being theism *all at once*. In Chapter 4, I try to strengthen my approach by responding to potential and existing criticisms. I conclude that there is no successful argument against perfect being theism.

Even if there is no successful argument against perfect being theism, critics can still question if there is a successful argument *for* perfect being theism. In Part III, therefore, I examine two versions of the ontological argument, the most prominent, direct argument for perfect being theism. In Chapters 5 and 6, I discuss the classical version of the ontological argument, which is normally attributed to the second chapter of Anselm's *Proslogion*. I believe that refuting the argument is difficult because it is cleverly designed in such a way that no matter how one approaches it, one cannot undermine it without making a significant metaphysical or epistemic assumption, one that is likely to be contentious in its own right. I therefore pay particular attention to attempts to defeat the argument without making any significant assumptions. In particular, in Chapter 5, I examine Peter Millican's attempt to refute the argument which targets only shallow, logical details of the argument. In Chapter 6, I examine various attempts to reveal the absurdity of the argument by creating its parallel parodies. I argue that none of these attempts succeeds. I conclude at that point that as far as the classical ontological argument is concerned, perfect being theists and their critics end in a draw. Although there are powerful objections to the argument, they cannot undermine it without raising issues that are controversial independently of their relationships to the argument. In Chapter 7, I focus on the modal, as opposed to the classical, ontological argument for perfect being theism. The most controversial premise of the argument is the so-called 'possibility premise' which says that it is possible that God exists. It is relatively uncontroversial that the argument goes through once this premise is shown to be true. I consider existing arguments for the possibility premise and claim that none of them is compelling. I then introduce a new way of establishing the premise that uses, again, the maximal God thesis.

I hope to show over the course of this book that we have good reason to think that perfect being theism is true, because the maximal concept of God allows us to refute arguments *against* perfect being theism while establishing a robust argument *for* it.

PART I

Perfect Being Theism

1

Conceptual, Historical, and Cognitive Roots of Perfect Being Theism

1.1 Introduction

Perfect being theism is arguably the most widely accepted form of traditional monotheism. It has been the central notion in the philosophy of religion over the last few centuries and it has always been the focus of philosophers of religion when they address the existence and nature of God. It is a view that is derived from (or at least inspired by) Anselm's *Proslogion*. In that work, Anselm proposes (or at least hints at or implies) the following definition of God:

(1) God is something than which no greater is conceivable.[1]

The term 'thinkable' is sometimes used instead of 'conceivable'. Anselm also talks about whether the being in question can 'exist in the mind (rather than in reality)'. I assume here that 'thinkable', 'conceivable', and 'can exist in the mind' all mean the same. Anselm also seems to endorse the following thesis:

(2) God is something than which no greater is metaphysically possible.

[1] Logan contends that Anselm does not intend to offer a definition of God because 'God is not susceptible of definition in the dialectical tradition in which Anselm is operating' (Logan 2009, p. 91). That is why I say Anselm at least *hints at* or *implies* this definition. Having said that, it seems puzzling to me that Anselm would have written that he tried to 'find one single argument... that by itself would suffice to prove that God really exists' if he really thought that God cannot be defined (Anselm 1965, originally 1077–8, p. 103). In any case, as I explain below, Anselm scholarship is not my primary concern in this book.

Thesis (1) is at least partly epistemic because it defines God in terms of what is *conceivable*. Thesis (2), however, is purely metaphysical because it defines God in terms of what is *metaphysically possible*. It is contentious whether (2) can be derived from (1). As I explain in detail in Chapter 7, philosophers dispute whether conceivability entails metaphysical possibility.[2] This is a broader philosophical dispute which is independent of the debate over perfect being theism. A derivation from conceivability to metaphysical possibility is a crucial step in the so-called 'conceivability argument' against physicalism in the philosophy of mind. Taking a closer look, however, it seems impossible to derive (2) from (1) on the assumption that conceivability entails metaphysical possibility. The derivation of (2) from (1) is based on the following reasoning: 'A being that is greater than God is inconceivable; therefore, a being that is greater than God is metaphysically impossible.' Thus what we need here is the assumption that *in*conceivability entails metaphysical *im*possibility, which is distinct from the assumption that conceivability entails metaphysical possibility. (The thesis that conceivability entails metaphysical possibility is logically equivalent to the thesis that metaphysical impossibility entails inconceivability, not the claim that inconceivability entails metaphysical impossibility. Hence, if conceivability entails metaphysical possibility, we can derive (1) from (2), but not (2) from (1).[3])

Notice that thesis (1) does not say that God is something than which no *equal* or greater is conceivable. Similarly, thesis (2) does not say that God is something than which no *equal* or greater is metaphysically possible. Hence, it leaves open the possibility that something that is as great as God is conceivable or metaphysically possible. That is, theses (1) and (2) appear to be compatible with a version of polytheism which says that there is more than one being than which no greater is conceivable or metaphysically possible. Some philosophers argue that there cannot be more than one such being because it is impossible to obtain a situation in which such beings compete with each other. If, for example, something than which no greater is conceivable or metaphysically possible is an omnipotent being, perhaps there cannot be more than one such being because a competition between multiple omnipotent beings that are trying to perform opposing

[2] See, for example, Chalmers (1996), Gendler and Hawthorne (2002), and Kirk (2005).

[3] The thesis that conceivability entails metaphysical possibility is directly relevant if one attempts to derive the metaphysical possibility of God from the conceivability of God.

tasks, such as pushing and pulling, could entail a contradiction.[4] Whether or not such an argument succeeds, it seems appropriate to amend (1) and (2) so that they explicitly exclude the possibility that there is more than one such being. This is because perfect being theism is standardly endorsed by Judeo-Christian-Islamic theists who do not countenance there being more than one being than which no greater is conceivable or metaphysically possible. Hence, (1) should be amended as follows:

(3) God is the being than which no greater is conceivable.

Similarly, (2) should be amended as follows:

(4) God is the being than which no greater is metaphysically possible.

The term '*the* being than which no greater' ensures that there is no being that is as great as or greater than God in terms of conceivability or metaphysical possibility. Note that 'possible beings' does not mean only *merely* possible beings. It includes actual beings, i.e. possible beings that are actual, as well as merely possible beings. It is also important to note that necessary existence is included in the notion of the being than which no greater is metaphysically possible. For God to be greater than all other metaphysically possible beings, He has to be ontologically superior to all other metaphysically possible beings. No being can be ontologically superior to all other metaphysically possible beings if it exists merely contingently. One of the main reasons to hold that God is greater than us is that, unlike us, He does not exist only contingently or accidentally. His existence is a matter of ontological necessity. Also, as I explain in detail in Chapter 2, (4) implicitly assumes that God is value commensurable with all other possible beings. Otherwise, God's greatness may turn out to be trivial. Thesis (4) does not mean to allow cases in which there are beings that are not value commensurable with God. All metaphysically possible beings are value commensurable with God and He is greater than all of them.[5] To address this point, thesis (4) can be rephrased further as follows:

(5) God is the greatest metaphysically possible being.

[4] For a relevant point see Mele and Smith (1988) and Wielenberg (2001). See also Chapter 3 of this book.

[5] In this book, following the common practice, I use the pronoun 'He' to refer to God. However, this should not be taken to imply that God has a gender. I acknowledge that any standard pronoun we might use for God (whether 'He', 'She', or 'It') is problematic.

I call (4), and equivalently (5), the 'perfect being thesis'. I also assume that the phrase 'the being than which no greater is metaphysically possible' is equivalent to the phrase 'the greatest metaphysically possible being'. Appealing to the perfect being thesis, perfect being theism can be defined as follows:

Perfect being theism: God as defined in the perfect being thesis exists.

In my earlier work (Nagasawa 2008b, 2011, 2013a, 2013b), I called the perfect being thesis the 'Anselmian thesis' because it (or a version of it) is most notably championed by Anselm. However, I have decided to call it the 'perfect being thesis' in this book for three reasons. First, it is disputable whether Anselm would endorse the perfect being thesis as presented above. In fact, it is not strictly faithful to Anselm's original texts. I do not wish to provoke an exegetical debate as my project here is primarily philosophical.[6] Second, Anselm is not the first scholar to propose the perfect being thesis. I argue in Chapter 5 that Anselm is the one who invented the ontological argument which relies on the thesis. There seems little evidence to show that anyone invented or even anticipated the ontological argument prior to Anselm. Yet, as I explain in Section 1.3, we can find many texts that were written centuries before Anselm proposing ideas that were the same as or similar to the perfect being thesis. Third, while I defend perfect being theism and the ontological argument in this book, I do not wish to give the impression that my ultimate goal is to defend the entirety of Anselm's philosophical or theological system. Anselm scholarship is not my main concern here.

This chapter has the following structure: In Section 1.2, I analyse the perfect being thesis closely by considering its compatibility and incompatibility with alternatives to traditional theism such as atheism, polytheism, pantheism, and panentheism. In Section 1.3, I consider the historical origins of perfect being theism. I argue that, as I have just noted, perfect being theism is not, contrary to what is widely believed, Anselm's invention because the view traces back to Plato and it was anticipated or presented by many other philosophers and theologians prior to Anselm. In Section 1.4, I consider the cognitive and

[6] For detailed discussions of Anselm's texts see Charlesworth (1965) and Logan (2009).

developmental origins of perfect being theism. I refer to recent research in the cognitive science of religion and explore possible reasons that perfect being theism is widespread. In Section 1.5, I consider the merits of holding perfect being theism. I focus on three main merits and explain why perfect being theism is attractive. In Section 1.6, I discuss five prominent arguments for perfect being theism. I argue that the only direct argument for perfect being theism is the ontological argument and that all others, i.e. the cosmological argument, the design argument, the moral argument, and the argument from miracles, do not, even if successful, establish perfect being theism. In Section 1.7, I discuss arguments against perfect being theism. I try to show that all arguments against perfect being theism are classified into three types. I conclude my introduction to perfect being theism in Section 1.8.

1.2 Perfect Being Theism vs. Atheism, Polytheism, Pantheism, and Panentheism

Most perfect being theists are traditional theists who hold the following theses: (i) There is only one God (monotheism) and (ii) God is ontologically distinct from the universe (the independence thesis). But can perfect being theism be adopted only by traditional theists? In this section, I address this question by contrasting traditional theism with several alternatives—atheism, polytheism, pantheism, and panentheism.

Atheism

Monotheism says that the number of Gods/gods is exactly one and atheism says that the number of Gods/gods is exactly zero. Hence, atheism is clearly incompatible with perfect being *theism*, which holds that God, as the being than which no greater is metaphysically possible, exists. Yet it appears that atheism is compatible with the perfect being *thesis*. The perfect being thesis only provides a definition of God as the being than which no greater is metaphysically possible. It therefore appears possible for atheists to claim consistently that while the perfect being thesis specifies a correct definition of God, He does not exist in reality. Here is a parallel example: one can maintain consistently that while the definition of a unicorn as a horse-like animal with a spiralling horn is correct, no such creature exists in reality. However, according to some arguments, atheists cannot make the claim about God as defined in this way consistently. According to the modal ontological argument for perfect being theism, for example, once atheists agree with the perfect being thesis that God is the being than which no greater is metaphysically possible and admit the possibility of such a being, they cannot but accept that such a God indeed exists. That is, the argument says, the mere possibility of the existence of God as defined by the perfect being thesis entails its actuality. If so, the only option left for atheists is to reject the perfect being thesis or the possibility that God as defined by the thesis exists. I discuss related issues in Chapter 7 in which I address the modal ontological argument.

Polytheism

Again, monotheism says that the number of Gods/gods is exactly one while atheism says that the number of Gods/gods is exactly zero. Polytheism disagrees with both and says that the number of Gods/gods is two or more. The perfect being thesis excludes the possibility that there is more than one God by holding that God is *the* being than which no greater is metaphysically possible. Perfect being theism therefore appears initially to exclude polytheism. One might argue, however, that perfect being theism still allows polytheism because it is compatible with the possibility that there are 'gods', divine beings that are less great than God, as well as God, the greatest metaphysically possible being. Augustine seems to anticipate this point in the following passage:

> [W]hen the one supreme God of gods is thought of, even by those who believe that there are other gods, and who call them by that name, and worship them as gods, their thought takes the form of an endeavor to reach the conception of a nature, than which nothing more excellent or more exalted exists.
>
> (Augustine 2009, originally 397, Book I, chapter 7, p. 6)

Whether or not perfect being theism is compatible with polytheism of this type depends on what sorts of beings, if any, we think deserve the term 'god' and what kind of relationship we think the gods might have with God. It seems reasonable to think that perfect being theism does not immediately exclude a version of polytheism according to which there is one *God* but there are lesser *gods*.

Pantheism and Panentheism

Again, the perfect being thesis says that God is the being than which no greater is metaphysically possible. Most perfect being theists claim that this thesis entails that God has many specific 'great-making properties'—such as omniscience, omnipotence, and omnibenevolence as well as the property of being the creator of the universe—which contribute to the greatness of its possessor.[7] (I argue in Chapter 3 that it is not obvious that the perfect being thesis entails these properties, but we can set that point aside for now.)

Pantheism and panentheism reject the abovementioned independence thesis, according to which God is ontologically distinct from the universe. They hold that the universe is identical with or part of God. Such views sound radically different from traditional theism, but I submit that we can derive them by adopting an alternative interpretation of the perfect being thesis, an interpretation that is admittedly idiosyncratic. According to this interpretation, God's greatness as expressed in the thesis should be understood in terms of encompassment rather than great-making or positivity. This means that the more encompassing a being, the higher the greatness of that being. Thus, God, as something than which no greater is metaphysically possible, is the maximally encompassing being. That is, God is the totality of all there is. It is easily overlooked but pantheists and panentheists often understand God's greatness in this way. God's complete comprehensiveness and His capacity to encompass all of reality represent His ultimate significance. God is the greatest being, according to this understanding, because He encompasses absolutely everything and there is nothing beyond God. Balbus, Cicero's character in *The Nature of Gods* who defends Stoic pantheism, says, for example, 'What could be more stupid than to deny that supreme excellence to that universal nature which embraces all things?' (Cicero 1972, originally 45 BC, p. 137).[8] This view can be

[7] Some theists might think that the property of being the creator of the universe is not a direct consequence of the perfect being thesis but rather an indirect consequence of the thesis that God is omnibenevolent and omnipotent. This is based on two ideas—that God chose to create the universe out of benevolence and that He indeed succeeded in creating it thanks to His power.

[8] An anonymous reader doubts that this quote from Cicero supports the construal of greatness in terms of encompassment. The referee contends that Balbus says only that there is something which encompasses all things and that it would be foolish not to call that thing

construed as a version of either pantheism or panentheism depending on how we define them. If we define pantheism as the thesis that God is identical with reality, then this view is a version of pantheism. However, if we define pantheism as the more limited thesis that God is identical with the universe and assume that there is something beyond the universe, then the view in question can be considered a version of panentheism, according to which the universe is only a proper part of God. Either way, the independence thesis, which is normally endorsed by traditional theists, is rejected here because pantheism and panentheism hold that God is not ontologically distinct from the universe.[9] Yet perfect being theism itself is compatible with pantheism and panentheism if God's greatness is understood in terms of encompassment.

In sum: Most perfect being theists are traditional theists who accept monotheism and the independence thesis. I have argued that perfect being theism is not compatible with atheism, even though some maintain that the perfect being thesis is. I have also argued that perfect being theism is in principle compatible with certain versions of polytheism, according to which both God and lesser gods exist. Finally, I have argued that perfect being theism is compatible with pantheism and panentheism if we adopt an idiosyncratic interpretation of God's greatness in terms of encompassment rather than great-making. I mention some versions of

great. According to the referee, that is not the same as saying that the thing is great *because* it encompasses all things.

However, if encompassment has nothing to do with greatness, it is puzzling that Bulbus uses the phrase 'that universal nature which embraces all things' rather than simply 'that universal nature'. The quote in question follows this passage, which I think supports my construal:

> The various creatures of the universe may meet with many external obstacles to their perfect development. But no obstacle can frustrate the development of the universe itself. The universe moulds and *embraces all things*. Therefore, we must admit the existence of that fourth and final stage of being, which no power can assail. This is the stage of being on which the whole of nature depends. It is thus above all things and nothing has any power against it, and is the universal dwelling-place of reason and of wisdom.
>
> (Cicero 1972, originally 45 BC, p. 137, emphasis added)

In any case, whether or not my interpretation of Cicero is correct, it is quite common for pantheists and panentheists to construe God's greatness in terms of encompassment. See Oppy (1997) and Steinhart (2004).

[9] See Nagasawa (2016a) for a critical assessment of versions of pantheism and panentheism based on the perfect being thesis.

the perfect being thesis presented by pantheists in Section 1.3, but my main focus in the rest of this book is on perfect being theism considered as an option for traditional theists.

1.3 Historical Origins

Perfect being theism is often considered Anselm's invention, but it is actually older than Anselm. The following are earlier examples of perfect being theism and its variants. Some of the texts that I quote below are relatively long because I do not wish to extract them out of context. They consist of texts referenced in Barnes (1972), Davies (2004), Leftow (2011), Logan (2009), Oppy (1995), Wierenga (2011), and Witham (2008), as well as my original findings.

As Leftow (2011) claims, the core of perfect being theism traces all the way back to Ancient Greece.

Plato (428/7 BC–348/7 BC)

In Plato's *Republic* Socrates and Adeimantus, Plato's brother, have the following exchange, which presents Plato's polytheistic view:

> Do you think that a god is a sorcerer, able to appear in different forms at different times, sometimes changing himself from his own form into many shapes, sometimes deceiving us by making us think that he has done it? Or do you think he's simply and least of all likely to step out of his own form?
>
> I can't say offhand.
>
> Well, what about this? If he steps out of his own form, mustn't he either change himself or be changed by something else?
>
> He must.
>
> But the best things are least liable to alternation or change, aren't they? For example, isn't the healthiest and strongest body least changed by food, drink, and labor, or the healthiest and strongest plant by sun, wind, and the like?
>
> Of course.
>
> And the most courageous and most rational soul is least disturbed or altered by any outside affection?
>
> Yes.
>
> And the same account is true of all artifacts, furniture, houses, and clothes. The ones that are good and well made are least altered by time or anything else that happens to them.

That's right.

Whatever is in good condition, then, whether by nature or craft or both, admits least of being changed by anything else.

So it seems.

Now, surely a god and what belongs to him are in every way in the best condition.

How could they fail to be?

Then a god would be least likely to have many shapes.

Indeed.

Then does he change or alter himself?

Clearly he does, if indeed he is altered at all.

Would he change himself into something better and more beautiful than himself or something worse and uglier?

It would have to be into something worse, if he's changed at all, for surely we won't say that a god is deficient in either beauty or virtue.

Absolutely, right. And do you think Adeimantus, that anyone, whether god or human, would deliberately make himself worse in any way?

No, that's impossible.

It is impossible, then, for gods to want to alter themselves? Since they are the most beautiful and best possible, it seems that each always and unconditionally retains his own shape.

That seems entirely necessary to me. (Plato 1992, originally 380 BC, pp. 56–7, 380d–381c)

Through the above dialogue on a god's changelessness Plato suggests that a god's nature is comparable to 'the healthiest and strongest body' and 'the most courageous and most rational soul'. He then says more explicitly that a god and his nature are 'in every way in the best condition'. According to Plato, it is impossible for a god to change into something better and more beautiful than himself because he does not lack any beauty or virtue. Yet it is impossible for a god to change into something worse or uglier too because, according to Plato, anyone who is already 'the most beautiful and best possible' would not want to become worse deliberately. Plato's term 'best *possible*' is particularly important here because it suggests that he thinks, as perfect being theists do, that a god (or God) is not only the best being that actually exists but the best being that can *possibly* exist. It should be noted that Plato's main focus above seems to be on a god's specific individual properties rather than his overall greatness. When Plato suggests that there is nothing *better* than a given god, he seems to have in mind the god's property of being virtuous rather than the god's overall greatness. Yet he contends that not only 'what belongs to him [a god]' but also the god himself is in 'every way in the best condition'.

Aristotle (384–22 BC)

Aristotle inherits Plato's view of gods. He writes:

> There are, however, certain difficulties with our account of divine thought.
>
> (a) On the one hand, it is readily agreed that thinking is the most godlike of things in our experience, but there are some problems involved in showing exactly what state it must be in to be of this kind. Suppose that it is empty of content. Where then would be its grandeur? It is in that state that it would be in if it were asleep. Alternatively, suppose that it thinks, but that its doing so is under the control of some other factor, so that what is its substance is not, now, the activation of thought but merely the potential for it. In that case, its substance would fall short of supreme excellence, since it is thinking that confers its merit on it.
> (b) And again: either potential thought or actual thinking is its substance, but in either case what does it think? Obviously, it either thinks of itself or some other thing, and either of the same objects always or different objects. Does it then make any difference, or none at all, whether it thinks of the good or of any arbitrary object whatever?
> (c) Also, are there not some objects about which it is absurd that it should ratiocinate?
>
> Well, clearly, its object is the most divine and worthy thing there is, and it is also not subject to change (for any change would be a deterioration, and such a thing is already a kind of movement.) And, if we suppose that it is not activated thinking but the potential thereof, then, first, it is plausible that the continuity of its thinking would be rather arduous for it, and, secondly, there would clearly then be something else of higher merit than the thinking, to wit the object of thought.
>
> Now indeed thinking and thought will belong even to one who thinks the worst thought. How do we get round this? (Remember that there are things it is not even better to see than not to see.) We deny that it is mere, unqualified thinking that is the best thing. That is just why it must think itself, if it is to retain supremacy, and absolute thinking is the thinking of thinking.
>
> (Aristotle 2004, originally 350 BC, pp. 382–3, Book Lambda, 9)

In the above passage, Aristotle presents his view of divine thought, a view that is based on several assumptions that seem to anticipate perfect being theism. First, he thinks that a god is a substance of 'supreme excellence', which is akin to the perfect being thesis that God is the being than which no greater is metaphysically possible. And on this assumption Aristotle infers that the 'grandeur' of thinking should be attributed to a god. Aristotle contends that, given the supreme excellence, a god's thinking must be 'absolute thinking'; that is, 'the thinking of thinking', which Aristotle considers 'the best thing'. (It is interesting to note that Aristotle seems to anticipate the contemporary debate on God's knowledge in the above passage where he addresses an instance of thinking which belongs to 'one who thinks the worst thought'. Contemporary philosophers discuss whether God can have knowledge that is linked to negative things, such as the knowledge of what it is like to be evil and what it is like to be limited.[10] Many of them try to preserve God's omniscience and claim that there are ways for God to acquire such knowledge without compromising His greatness. Aristotle's response, on the other hand, seems to be that God does not have such knowledge because otherwise He cannot preserve his supremacy.) Aristotle also writes as follows, in Fragment 16 of Book III of his lost work *On Philosophy*, which is preserved in Simplicius's commentary on *On the Heavens* (288.28–289.15): 'In things in which there is better, there is also a best; since therefore in things that exist one thing is better than another, there is a best, and this would be divine'.[11] Positing that a god is a best and that what is best is also divine seems to anticipate perfect being theism.

Zeno of Citium (334–262 BC) and Cicero (106–43 BC)

Zeno of Citium is the founder of the Stoic school of philosophy. His theological view is radically different from Plato's and Aristotle's because he is a pantheist, identifying God with the universe rather than a polytheist holding that there are many gods in the universe. His focus is, therefore, on the universe rather than on gods. Yet his view of God's (or the universe's) greatness still anticipates perfect being theism. Zeno

[10] See, for example, Alter (2002), Blumenfeld (1978), and Nagasawa (2008a).

[11] See P. G. Walsh's note 7 in Boethius (1999, originally 523), p. 140.

says, according to Cicero, 'That which has reason is more perfect than that which has not. But there is nothing more perfect than the universe: therefore the universe is a rational being'. Cicero expands on this idea:

> It can similarly be proved that the universe is wise, blessed and eternal. For beings possessed of all these qualities are superior to beings which lack them, and there is nothing superior to the universe. Hence it follows that the universe and God are one. (Cicero 1972, originally 45 BC, p. 132, Book II, 20)

Given that Zeno identifies the universe with God, his claim that 'there is nothing more perfect than the universe' seems comparable to perfect being theism. Zeno derives a specific individual property of the universe, namely reason, from this claim. As I explain in Section 1.4, perfect being theists typically adopt similar inferences to derive God's specific properties, such as omniscience, omnipotence, and omnibenevolence, from God's overall property of being the being than which no greater is metaphysically possible. Cicero also writes:

> But there cannot be anything greater than the whole universe. And it is clear that a being which is alive with sense and reason is better than one without them. It follows that the universe must be a living being, endowed with sense and mind and reason: and so by this argument too we may infer that the universe is God.
>
> (Cicero 1972, originally 45 BC, p. 141, Book II, 46)

Cicero's phrase 'there *cannot* be anything greater' implies that Cicero thinks that God is the greatest *possible* being, not just the greatest existing being.

Chrysippus (279–206 BC) and Cicero (106–43 BC)

Chrysippus was born much later than Zeno but he is sometimes considered a co-founder of Stoicism because he made significant contributions to the systematization of Zeno's philosophy. Chrysippus, like Zeno, endorses pantheism. Cicero reports that Chrysippus says as follows:

> If there is anything in nature which the human mind, which human intelligence, energy and power could not create, then the creator of such things must be a being superior to man. But the heavenly bodies in their eternal orbits could not be created by man. They must therefore be created by a being greater than man. But what is such a greater being but a god? For if no gods exist, then what is there in nature greater than man? He alone is endowed with the supreme gift

of reason. Only an arrogant fool would imagine that there was nothing in the whole world greater than himself. Therefore there must be something greater than Man. And that something must be God.

(Cicero 1972, originally 45 BC, p. 130, Book II, 16)

Cicero elaborates Chrysippus's point:

But what of that which surpasses all these, I mean reason, or, if you wish, in other words, mind, purpose, thought, wisdom? Where have we found this? Whence have we derived it? Does the universe have everything else, but yet lack this one thing, the most valuable of all? Yet beyond doubt there is nothing superior to the universe, there is nothing more excellent or more beautiful. Not only is there nothing better, but nothing better can even be imagined. But if reason and wisdom are the best of all things, they must belong to that which we confess to be the best. (Cicero 1972, originally 45 BC, p. 131, Book II, 19)

Chrysippus's claim that 'only an arrogant fool would imagine that there was nothing in the whole world greater than himself' reminds us of Anselm's use of the Bible verse, 'The fool says in his heart, "There is no God"', in presenting the ontological argument even though Chrysippus predates Anselm (Anselm 1965, originally 1077–8, II, p. 117; Psalm 14:1). Chrysippus seems to try to derive the existence of God through a hierarchical structure of being. He says that the creator of things in nature which human intelligence, energy, and power cannot create must be superior to man. Yet, he says, there is nothing in nature that is superior to man. This means that the creator of things in nature must be God. Therefore, Chrysippus concludes, there must be a God. It seems that Chrysippus has in mind the following hierarchy of being in improving order: things in nature other than man, man, and God. Cicero expands on what Chrysippus says with a claim that is even more similar to perfect being theism. He says that there is nothing superior, more excellent, or more beautiful than the universe. From this idea he infers that the universe has reason and wisdom as they are among the best properties to have. The most important claim in Cicero's passage is, '[n]ot only is there nothing better, but nothing better can even be imagined'. This coincides with Anselm's thesis that God is something than which no greater is *conceivable*. That is, God is not only the being than which no greater actually exists but the being than which no greater is conceivable even among all possible beings. Like many perfect being theists, Cicero seems to think that the inconceivability of beings greater than God entails the metaphysical impossibility of such beings.

Seneca (4 BC–65 AD)

Another Stoic philosopher, Seneca, writes:

> What is god? The intelligence of the universe. What is god? All that you see and all that you do not see. Only then is his true greatness recognised—greatness than which nothing greater can be imagined—if he alone is everything.
>
> (Seneca 2010, originally first century, pp. 138–9, Book I, 13)

Like other Stoics, Seneca seems to defend pantheism. This is apparent in his claim in the above passage that god is the 'intelligence of the universe'. However, he also seems to place god within the universe (or the world) instead of identifying god with the universe when he says that god is 'the greatest *part* of the world' (Seneca 2010, originally first century, p. 134, Book VII, 13.4, emphasis added). His phrase 'greatness than which nothing greater can be imagined' is essentially identical to what is present in Anselm's thesis that God is the being than which no greater is conceivable.

Augustine (354–430 AD)

Perfect being theism seems to be fully formed and clearly presented by the time of Augustine. Edward Wierenga (2011) goes as far as saying that all the ingredients of perfect being theism that are normally attributed to Anselm are present in the thought of Augustine. In *On Christian Doctrine*, Augustine writes:

> For when the one supreme God of gods is thought of, even by those who believe that there are other gods, and who call them by that name, and worship them as gods, their thought takes the form of an endeavor to reach the conception of a nature, than which nothing more excellent or more exalted exists. And since men are moved by different kinds of pleasures, partly by those which pertain to the bodily senses, partly by those which pertain to the intellect and soul, those of them who are in bondage to sense think that either the heavens, or the universe itself, is God of gods: or if they try to get beyond the universe, they picture to themselves something of dazzling brightness, and think of it vaguely as infinite, or of the most beautiful form conceivable; or they represent it in the form of the human body, if they think that superior to all others. Or if they think that there is no one God supreme above the rest, but that there are many or even innumerable gods of equal rank, still these too they conceive as possessed of shape and form, according to what each man thinks the pattern of excellence. Those, on the other hand, who endeavor by an effort of the intelligence to reach a conception of God, place Him above all visible and bodily natures, and even above all intelligent and

spiritual natures that are subject to change. All, however, strive emulously to exalt the excellence of God: nor could any one be found to believe that any being to whom there exists a superior is God. And so all concur in believing that God is that which excels in dignity all other objects.

(Augustine 2009, originally 397, Book I, chapter 7, p. 6)

As I mentioned earlier, perfect being theism is in principle compatible with a version of polytheism according to which God as well as lesser gods exist. Augustine agrees with this in the above passage. He also implies that perfect being theism is in principle compatible with pantheism, which holds that 'the heavens, or the universe itself, is God of gods'. Yet, he says, no matter what kind of ontological view of divinity one accepts—whether it is polytheistic or pantheistic—we would consider God as 'a nature than which nothing more excellent or more exalted exists'. How to characterize God's specific properties varies significantly depending on what conception of God one accepts, but, Augustine says, no one can believe that there is a being superior to God and everyone agrees that 'God is that which excels in dignity all other objects'.

Proclus (412–85 AD)

Proclus is a neo-Platonic idealist who postulates the One, divine unity or ultimate reality. He develops a view of the One by referring to Plato's *Parmenides*:

[E]ach thing, even the lowest grade of being you could mention, becomes god by participating in unity according to its rank. For if God and One are the same because there is nothing greater than God and nothing greater than the One, then to be unified is the same as to be deified. Just as, if the Sun and God were the same, to be illumined would be the same as to be deified; for the One gives unity, the Sun light....

Now this One, we may say, exists otherwise in the gods than in the being that comes after the gods; in the one case, it is self-sufficient, not like something existing in a substratum (for every god is god by virtue of the One, though the supreme God is one purely and simply, having no multiple aspect, while each of the others is more than unity, one thing because it has these entities dependent on it, another those; the beings that are nearer the pure One are fewer in number, those further away are more numerous, just as those nearer have a nature more akin to it and those further away are less akin; addition and plurality come about because of their descent in the scale of being.) So in the former case the One truly is, while in the latter case it exists as a character in something.

(Proclus 1992, originally fifth century, pp. 36–7, Book I, 641–2)

As I explain in Chapter 2, Proclus, like many other perfect being theists, considers God's greatness in terms of 'the scale of being'. He thinks that God sits on the top of the scale because 'there is nothing greater than God'. Yet, Proclus says, other things on the scale, including even 'the lowest grade of being you could mention', can become god by participating in the divine unity. In the above passage Proclus seems to suggest the following inference: God is such that there is nothing greater than Him. The One is also such that there is nothing greater than that. Therefore, God and the One are identical. This inference is based on the monotheistic assumption that is normally endorsed by perfect being theists: there cannot be more than one being than which no greater is metaphysically possible. Proclus also proposes an interesting view about the number of Gods/gods in the scale. He suggests that there is only one supreme God that is pure and simple, but the lower down the scale we go, the more gods we find.

The Bible

We have seen many philosophical and theological texts which anticipated or presented perfect being theism before Anselm. What about the Bible? The Bible does not explicitly define God; it is not a scholarly text. Nevertheless, we can find some verses that are reminiscent of the perfect being thesis:

> As for God, his way is perfect: The Lord's word is flawless; he shields all who take refuge in him. (2 Samuel 22:31; also Psalm 18:30)

This verse says that God's *way* is perfect and His *word* is flawless, but it is charitable to construe these claims as reflecting the idea that God Himself is perfect and flawless. The following verse is more explicit about the perfection of God Himself:

> Be perfect, therefore, as your heavenly Father is perfect. (Matthew 5:48)

The Bible talks about God's greatness as well as perfection:

> For great is the Lord and most worthy of praise; he is to be feared above all gods. (1 Chronicles 16:25)

The claim that God 'is to be feared above all gods' reminds us of Augustine's contention that even for polytheists, who believe that there are many gods, God is 'a nature, than which nothing more excellent or more exalted exists' (Augustine 2009, originally 397, Book I chapter 7, p. 6). The claim that 'he is to be feared above all gods' seems to assume implicitly that God is greater than any other beings and most likely also that He is greater than any other *possible* beings. God's superiority to other beings is implied in the following verse as well:

> Yours, Lord, is the greatness and the power and the glory and the majesty and the splendor, for everything in heaven and earth is yours. Yours, Lord, is the kingdom; you are exalted as head over all. (1 Chronicles 29:11)

It is important to note that the scope of God's greatness and power is said to be on 'everything in heaven and earth' and that God is considered 'head over all'. The following verse seems even more akin to the perfect being thesis:

> No one is like you, Lord; you are great, and your name is mighty in power. (Jeremiah 10:6)

It seems charitable to construe the phrase '[n]o one is like you, Lord; you are great' as meaning that no (possible) being is comparable to God with respect to greatness, which seems to imply the perfect being thesis.

We have seen a number of texts that anticipate or introduce perfect being theism prior to Anselm. I agree with Leftow (2011) that perfect being theism traces back to Greco-Roman philosophy and with Wierenga (2011) that at least most of the components of perfect being theism had already been presented by Augustine's time (and possibly earlier than that). Perfect being theism is also hinted at in many verses in the Bible. I conclude, therefore, that the perfect being thesis is not Anselm's invention. In Chapter 5, however, I argue that Anselm is nevertheless an outstanding figure in the history of perfect being theism because he is the one who invented the ontological argument, an argument that purports to derive the existence of God through the perfect being thesis. Some claim that the ontological argument was also presented or anticipated by philosophers earlier than Anselm, but I argue that there is no convincing evidence to support such a claim.

1.4 Cognitive and Developmental Origins

It is sometimes claimed, not only among atheists but also among theists, that perfect being theism is an unnatural, scholarly artefact. The perfect being thesis, according to which God is the being than which no greater is metaphysically possible, does not seem intuitive enough to ordinary religious believers. This corresponds to the fact that philosophers and theologians have disputed for centuries the apparent conflict between the 'God of the philosophers', the concept of God presented and discussed by philosophers, and the 'God of Abraham, Isaac, and Jacob', the image of God presented in religious experiences and biblical revelations. The God of the philosophers is developed through so-called 'natural theology', which is based primarily on an a priori and analytical enquiry into the existence and nature of God, while the God of Abraham, Isaac, and Jacob is developed through so-called 'revealed theology', which is based primarily on a posteriori and experiential religious data.[12]

The claim that the perfect being concept of God is a scholarly artefact seems to make sense particularly if, as many perfect being theists think, the perfect being thesis entails the following:

The omni God thesis: God is the omniscient, omnipotent, and omnibenevolent being.

Such complex properties as omniscience, omnipotence, and omnibenevolence seem to be derived through highly sophisticated scholarly reflections, which appear to be detached from the beliefs of ordinary religious believers.

There are many examples that show how complex the concepts of omni-properties can be. Thomas P. Flint and Alfred J. Freddoso, for example, analyse the concept of omnipotence as follows:

(D) *S* is omnipotent at *t* in *W* if and only if for any state of affairs *p* and world-type-for-*SLs* such that *p* is not a member of *Ls*, if there is a world *W** such that

(i) *Ls* is true in both *W* and *W**, and

(ii) *W** shares the same history with *W* at *t*, and

(iii) at *t* in *W** someone actualizes *p*,

then *S* has the power at *t* in *W* to actualize *p*. (Flint and Freddoso 1983, p. 99)

[12] See chapter 1 of Morris (1987b) for the distinction between the God of the philosophers and the God of Abraham, Isaac, and Jacob.

To take another example, Joshua Hoffman and Gary S. Rosenkrantz propose the following analysis of omniscience:

> S is omniscient at time t = df. (i) for any proposition *p*, if *p* is a necessary truth, or if *p* is a contingent truth that is not about the future relative to *t*, and either *p* can be grasped by different individuals, or *p* can be grasped by *S* alone, then at *t*, *S* knows *p*, and (ii) for any proposition *p*, if *p* is a contingent truth about the future relative to *t* whose truth is *causally inevitable* at *t*, and either *p* can be grasped by different individuals, or *p* can be grasped by *S* alone, then at *t*, *S* knows *p*.
>
> (Hoffman and Rosenkrantz 2002, p. 124)

Whether or not these analyses of omni-properties are coherent, we cannot but wonder if they have anything to do with the God of Abraham, Isaac, and Jacob. They seem to be products of highly sophisticated conceptual analysis. However, interestingly enough, some researchers in the emerging field of the cognitive science of religion have suggested that these omni-properties might not be unnatural artefacts after all. They maintain that people naturally form the concepts of these great-making properties in childhood.

The twentieth-century Swiss psychologist Jean Piaget hypothesized that children younger than seven years old ascribe omniscience and omnipotence to adults, especially to their parents. This makes sense because there is a survival advantage for young children in trusting adults unquestioningly. By utterly trusting adults, children can acquire knowledge and skills that are useful for securing food and shelter. Adopting a sceptical stance towards adults, on the other hand, is not beneficial to children in this respect. Piaget's hypothesis has been confirmed by recent empirical studies undertaken by cognitive scientists. These studies suggest that young children naturally first form a belief that adults are omniscient and omnipotent, and later, as they grow up, correct such a belief (Barrett 2004, pp. 77–8, 83–4).

One might wonder if children also ascribe omnibenevolence, or moral perfection, to adults. The cognitive scientist of religion Justin L. Barrett speculates that it might well be the case that, just as children overestimate the knowledge and power of adults, they might also overestimate the morality of adults (Barrett 2004, p. 86). I think it is worth speculating still further, given that there are cognitive and developmental reasons that children overestimate specific great-making properties of adults, whether they overestimate the overall greatness of adults as well. It might well be the case that children overestimate the overall greatness of adults first and then infer their omniscience and omnipotence from that estimation. Such an inference would be parallel to the inference from the perfect being thesis to the omni God thesis, which is commonly adopted by philosophers. If this hypothesis is correct, both the omni God thesis and the perfect being thesis are more natural and less artificial than is often assumed.

The cognitive science of religion is a new field; further research is needed to confirm and analyse these results. Yet philosophers have already started considering the philosophical implications of the findings in the cognitive science of religion. Some atheists argue that the findings undermine theism because they suggest that the formation of religious belief can be explained without postulating the existence of God or any other supernatural entities. Some theists, on the other hand, argue that the findings motivate theism because they suggest that we are equipped with what John Calvin calls '*sensus divinitatis*', a hypothetical epistemic module granted by God which makes humans disposed to form belief in God. Some others claim that these findings have no implications for the ontological question as to whether God exists.[13] Whichever position is correct, it is interesting to note that recent empirical data suggest that the perfect being concept of God might not necessarily be a purely scholarly artefact; it seems to have cognitive and developmental bases.

1.5 The Merits of Perfect Being Theism

The findings in the cognitive science of religion discussed above seem to suggest that perfect being theism is widespread because of our cognitive and developmental dispositions. However, at least within philosophy and theology, that is not the only reason it is widespread. Perfect being theists claim that the view is widespread and enduring because there are a number of merits in holding it. In what follows, I explain the three most important merits.

[13] For the implications of the cognitive science of religion for the philosophy of religion, see, for example, De Cruz and De Smedt (2014), Schloss and Murray (2009), Leech and Visala (2011a, 2011b, 2012), and Wood (2011).

Perfect Being Theism can Serve as a Basis of the Ontological Argument

The first merit is that perfect being theism allows one to put forward the ontological argument for the existence of God. In fact, Anselm introduces the perfect being thesis (or a thesis sufficiently similar to it) in his *Proslogion* in the course of developing the argument.

There are a number of arguments for the existence of God, such as the design argument, the cosmological argument, the moral argument, and the argument from miracles. However, the ontological argument seems to be one of very few direct arguments for the existence of God as the being than which no greater is metaphysically possible. Other arguments establish, even if they are sound, only that there is a being that has impressive individual properties, such as being very powerful or being a creator of the universe, but not the property of being the being than which no greater is metaphysically possible.

Despite the close conceptual link between the perfect being thesis and the ontological argument, perfect being theists are not required to accept the ontological argument. They could hold that while the perfect being thesis provides a correct definition of God and such a God exists, the ontological argument fails to establish His existence. I argue in later chapters of this book, however, that the ontological argument is a successful argument for the existence of God.[14] I do not think the argument is a deductive *proof* of the existence of God but I still think it is a good *argument*: the argument is formally valid and I do not see any obvious flaw in it.

There are several distinct versions of the ontological argument. Since I discuss the argument in detail in Chapters 5, 6, and 7, I provide only crude summaries of the two most prominent versions of the argument here: the classical version and the modal version. Anselm presents the classical version in Chapter 2 of the *Proslogion*. This version goes roughly as follows: Even atheists can conceive of God as the being than which no greater is metaphysically possible. That is, God exists at least in the mind. It follows that God exists either in the mind only or in the mind as well as in reality. Suppose that God can exist in the mind only. We can then

[14] To be precise, I argue that the modal version of the ontological argument, if not the classical version, is successful. See Chapters 5, 6, and 7 of this book.

conceive of a being that is greater than God; namely, the same being that exists in reality as well as in the mind. However, it is contradictory to say that a being that is greater than God—the being than which no greater is metaphysically possible—is conceivable. Therefore, God exists in reality as well as in the mind.

Philosophers had taken it for granted for centuries that, in the *Proslogion*, Anselm defends only one version, the classical version, of the ontological argument. However, Charles Hartshorne and Norman Malcolm claimed in the middle of the twentieth century that Anselm defends, or at least hints at defending, another version, the modal version, in Chapter 3 of the *Proslogion*. Hartshorne presented this version in his 1941 book but he was not explicit about the fact that it is found in Chapter 3 of the *Proslogion* until 1953, when he revealed it in his book with William L. Reese. Malcolm made the same point and addressed the argument thoroughly in his 1960 paper, which followed Hartshorne's 1961 paper on the same topic. In his two books published in 1974, Alvin Plantinga introduced a strengthened reformulation of the modal version. Plantinga's reformulated version goes roughly as follows: Necessarily, a being is maximally excellent in a given possible world only if it is omnipotent, omniscient, and omnibenevolent in that world. And, necessarily, a being is maximally great only if it is maximally excellent in every possible world. God—that is, the being than which no greater is metaphysically possible—is a maximally great being. Now it is *possible* that a maximally great being exists. This means that it is possible that, necessarily, a maximally excellent being exists. This is equivalent to saying that it is necessary that a maximally excellent being exists, which is equivalent to saying that it is necessary that an omniscient, omnipotent, and omnibenevolent being exists. Therefore, an omniscient, omnipotent, and omnibenevolent being exists in the actual world as well as in all other possible worlds.[15]

Compared with other prominent arguments for the existence of God, the ontological argument is not very popular these days. However, arguably, there is no consensus among critics as to exactly what is

[15] I assume for the sake of argument that the being than which no greater is metaphysically possible is an omniscient, omnipotent, and omnibenevolent being. That is, I assume that the perfect being thesis entails the omni God thesis. I dispute this point, however, in Chapter 3.

wrong with the ontological argument and the debate over it is still ongoing after nine centuries.[16] The perfect being thesis is a foundation of this powerful argument.

Perfect Being Theism Captures all Great-Making Properties of God

The second merit of holding perfect being theism is that it allows one to talk about God in an informed manner without listing specific individual properties that He may or may not have. As I mentioned above, perfect being theists normally assume that God has many distinctive great-making properties, such as omniscience, omnipotence, and omnibenevolence. They also commonly attribute other properties to God such as incorporeality, immutability, impassibility, timelessness (or eternity), changelessness, simplicity, necessary existence, omnipresence, independence, aseity, ineffability, and the property of being the creator of the universe. They think that God has so many unique individual great-making properties because they assume that the property of being something than which no greater is metaphysically possible subsumes or entails these great-making properties.

According to Cicero, Zeno of Citium says, 'That which reasons is superior to that which does not; nothing is superior to the world; the world, therefore, reasons' (Cicero 1972, originally 45 BC, p. 263, Book II, VII). Here Zeno seems to share the idea that the property of being the being than which no greater is metaphysically possible subsumes God's individual properties. God—which is identical with the world, according to Zeno—is the greatest possible being; reason is a great-making property; therefore God must reason too. Augustine similarly writes:

> The truest beginning of piety is to think as highly of God as possible; and doing so means that one must believe that he is omnipotent, and not changeable in the smallest respect; that he is the creator of all good things, but is himself more excellent than all of them; that he is the supremely just ruler of everything that he created; and that he was not aided in creating by any other being, as if he were not sufficiently powerful by himself. It follows that he created all things from nothing.
>
> (Augustine 1993, originally 387–9, p. 4, Book I)

[16] For recent works on the ontological argument see, for example, Szatkowski (2013) and Smith (2014). For earlier works see also Hick and McGill (1968), Oppy (1995), and Plantinga (1965).

Here Augustine seems to be suggesting that if we think of God as the greatest possible being, or, using Augustine's phrase, if we 'think as highly of God as possible', it follows that God has specific great-making properties, such as omnipotence, changelessness, the property of being the creator of all good things, the property of being the just ruler of His creation, and so on.[17]

Anselm presents the same reasoning. After introducing the perfect being thesis and the ontological argument, he writes as follows: 'What goodness, then, could be wanting to the supreme good, through which every good exists? Thus You are just, truthful, happy, and whatever it is better to be than not to be—for it is better to be just rather than unjust, and happy rather than unhappy' (Anselm 1965, originally 1077–8, p. 121). God is supremely great/good, so any individual property that is better to possess than not to possess should be possessed by God. Such properties include, according to Anselm, truthfulness and happiness. (Eadmer, a contemporary and biographer of Anselm, describes how Anselm came to write the *Proslogion*. Curiously enough Eadmer focuses on Anselm's idea that the perfect being thesis subsumes God's individual properties, rather than on his renowned ontological argument. He writes, 'Afterwards it came into his [Anselm's] mind to try to prove by one single and short argument the things which are believed and preached about God, that he is eternal, unchangeable, omnipotent, omnipresent, incomprehensible, just, righteous, merciful, true, as well as truth, goodness, justice and so on; and to show how all these qualities are united in him' (Eadmer 1962, originally 1124, p. 29). It is not clear why Eadmer focuses on this idea rather than the ontological argument itself. Perhaps he was more impressed by it than the argument, or perhaps he was not attracted to the ontological argument as the existence of God was evident to him.

[17] The following passage from Augustine also seems to present the idea that God's individual great-making properties can be derived from His property of being the being than which no greater is metaphysically possible:

> What, then, is the God I worship? He can be none but the Lord God himself, for *who but the Lord is God? What other refuge can there be, except our God?* You, my God, are supreme, utmost in goodness, mightiest and all-powerful, most merciful and most just. You are the most hidden from us and yet the most present among us, the most beautiful and yet the most strong, ever enduring and yet we cannot comprehend you. You are unchangeable and yet you change all things...
>
> (Augustine 1961, originally 398, Book I, 4, p. 23, emphasis in the original)

Richard Southern is puzzled by the fact that while it is the ontological argument 'which has given Anselm his place in the history of philosophy... Eadmer, being no philosopher, unduly neglected the first stage in the argument and, in his brief resumé concentrated on the remainder' (Eadmer 1962, originally 1124, p. 29).)

Robin Harwood, a contemporary philosopher, presents the same point as follows: The being than which no greater is metaphysically possible (or the 'Maximally Great Being', as Harwood calls it) 'is one that has all possible positive qualities to the highest possible extent and is totally devoid of negative qualities' (Harwood 1999, p. 478). So, for example, if knowledge, power, and benevolence are positive qualities (or great-making properties) while ignorance, vulnerability, and malevolence are negative qualities (or worse-making properties), then God has knowledge, power, and benevolence to the highest possible extent while totally lacking ignorance, vulnerability, and malevolence. However, when we try to focus on individual properties, we face a number of difficult questions: (i) Exactly which properties are great-making properties? (ii) How can we define each great-making property? (iii) Among the great-making properties, exactly which ones should be ascribed to God, if not all of them? (iv) Can God have 'neutral properties', which are neither great nor bad? (v) Can God have worse-making properties if, by doing so, He can have extra great-making properties that compensate for the worse-making properties? I address some of these questions in Chapter 2. The perfect being thesis is convenient because it allows us to define and talk about God without getting trapped in these difficult questions. If we accept the perfect being thesis, we can set aside God's individual properties and talk about God informatively enough by simply stating that He is the being than which no greater is metaphysically possible. Whatever individual properties might be involved, there is no metaphysically possible being which is greater than God.

There are two ways to understand the relationship between the property of being the being than which no greater is metaphysically possible and individual great-making properties. According to what I call the 'top-down view', God has the individual great-making properties by virtue of being the being than which no greater is metaphysically possible. That is, the property of being the being than which no greater is metaphysically possible is more fundamental than the individual properties. According to what I call the 'bottom-up view', on the other hand,

God has the property of being the being than which no greater is metaphysically possible by virtue of having individual great-making properties. That is, the individual great-making properties are more fundamental than the property of being the being than which no greater is metaphysically possible. Whether these two views are compatible is a matter of dispute as it depends on, for example, whether we should understand grounding relations as unitary (Bliss and Trogdon 2014). But perfect being theists typically think that God is first and foremost the being than which no greater is metaphysically possible.

Perfect Being Theism Provides an Answer to the Question 'Why is There Something Rather Than Nothing?'

The third merit of holding perfect being theism is that it automatically answers the question 'Why is there something rather than nothing?', which is arguably the most fundamental and intractable metaphysical question one can ask. There are a number of proposed answers to this question. Some argue that there is a quantum mechanical explanation for why there is something rather than nothing. Others argue that there is something rather than nothing because the concept of nothingness is self-contradictory. Yet others argue that there is something rather than nothing because, probabilistically speaking, it is most likely that one of infinitely many possible worlds that contain something is actualized rather than that the world that contains nothing is actualized.[18] All of these answers are highly disputed, but once we accept perfect being theism, we can set them aside because perfect being theism entails the following answer: God, as the being than which no greater is metaphysically possible, exists necessarily, which is equivalent to saying that God exists in all possible worlds. That is, in every single possible world there is 'something', namely God. Therefore, it is necessarily the case that there is something rather than nothing.

The perfect being thesis provides only a definition of God, so the above answer is not formulated in an ad hoc manner for the purpose of answering the question why there is something rather than nothing. Hence, it is a genuine bonus for perfect being theists to be able to answer

[18] For more on the debate over why there is something rather than nothing, see Goldschmidt (2013), Krauss (2012), Kuhn (2007), Leslie and Kuhn (2013), and Rundle (2004).

the question without developing an independent answer separately. This is perhaps the biggest bonus one can imagine for any philosophical position because, again, the question why there is something rather than nothing is arguably the most fundamental and intractable metaphysical question that one can raise.

One might argue at this point that the perfect being thesis response to the question is not satisfactory because God is not meant to fall within the scope of the question why there is something rather than nothing. The question is about ordinary objects, such as atoms, trees, rocks, planets, or animals, that occupy spatio-temporal locations, and the question asks why any of these things exists at all. I argue, however, that even on this interpretation the question loses its force once perfect being theism is accepted. The question implicitly assumes that the state of there being nothing is what we should naturally expect. That is why the actual state in which there is something is a surprise for us. It appears difficult to explain why there is something rather than nothing because it seems impossible to produce something from nothing (unless we think that the question is ill-formed or that nothingness is a necessarily impossible state of affairs to obtain). But once perfect being theism is accepted, we do not need to produce something from nothing because the existence of God, whether or not it falls within the scope of the question, is already given. God is, according to perfect being theism, an extremely powerful and extremely knowledgeable being, so He must be the right being to bring about many things, including the spatio-temporal objects that fall within the scope of the question. In sum: even if we assume that God does not qualify as 'something', the question why there is something rather than nothing still loses its force once perfect being theism is accepted.

The question why there is something rather than nothing is also sometimes construed as asking why there is *this* universe, i.e. our universe, rather than some other universe. On this construal, the question turns out to be even less pressing for perfect being theists. Whether or not it ultimately succeeds, perfect being theists can speculate about all sorts of explanations of God's choosing to create this specific universe by referring to His omnipotence and omnibenevolence. These reasons are not available to non-theists. Some perfect being theists go even further and argue that perfect being theism can not only explain why there is this universe rather than some other universe, but also, by positing the very existence of this specific universe—the fine-tuned universe rather than some other universe—it can establish the existence of God.[19]

1.6 Arguments for Perfect Being Theism

What arguments apart from the ontological argument can we give to defend perfect being theism? There are a number of arguments for the existence of God: the cosmological argument, the design argument, the moral argument, the argument from miracles, and so on. But hardly any of them is a *direct* argument for perfect being theism. Take, for example, the cosmological argument. There are many distinct versions of the cosmological argument but they all purport to derive the existence of the ultimate cause or ground of events, causation, or contingency. Proponents of the argument normally claim that such an ultimate cause or ground has to have many great-making properties that are normally attributed to God, such as significant power, significant intelligence, and necessary existence. Yet, even if the argument is sound, it does not exactly establish the existence of the being than which no greater is metaphysically possible. At best it establishes the existence of a being whose most notable properties seem to be compatible with being the being than which no greater is metaphysically possible. The same point applies to other arguments. The design argument purports to establish the existence of an intelligent designer of the universe and its inhabitants, the moral argument purports to establish the ultimate ground of morality, and the argument from miracles purports to establish the existence of a supernatural agent that can violate the laws of nature. However, none of these arguments, even if sound, directly establishes the existence of the being than which no greater is metaphysically possible. Suppose that all of these arguments are sound and that all of them lead to the existence of the same being. It then follows that there is a necessary, supernatural, very powerful, very intelligent being that is also the ultimate origin or

[19] For the fine-tuning argument for the existence of God see, for example, Barrow and Tipler (1986), Carr (2009), and Manson (2003). Atheists can at this point raise the problem of evil, asking why there is evil if God is the creator of the universe. This is a large topic that I set aside here. My point here is simply that the existence of the fine-tuned universe at least prima face motivates theism. See Chapters 3 and 4 for the relationship between the problem of evil and perfect being theism.

cause of the universe and morality. Yet it is still far from clear that such a being must be the being than which no greater is metaphysically possible. It could well be that a higher intelligence has all these impressive properties without reaching the level of the greatest metaphysically possible being.

Anselm seems to be aware of this problem. In the *Monologion* he introduced several independent arguments which he believed jointly support the existence of God. He was, however, not satisfied because he wanted to discover a *single* argument that alone is sufficient to establish the existence of God. In the preface of the *Proslogion* Anselm describes this point:

> After I had published [the *Monologion* which defends various theistic arguments]...I began to wonder if perhaps it might be possible to find one single argument that for its proof required no other save itself, and that by itself would suffice to prove that God really exists, that He is the supreme good needing no other and is He whom all things have need of for their being and well-being, and also to prove whatever we believe about the Divine Being.
>
> (Anselm 1965, originally 1077–8, p. 103)

This explains why Anselm needed the ontological argument. It is an argument purporting to derive through purely a priori reasoning the existence of God as defined in the perfect being thesis. It is the most direct argument for perfect being theism in the following two senses: (i) there is no gap between the concept of God defined in the perfect being thesis and the being whose existence the argument purports to establish—that is, if the argument is sound, then it establishes the existence of the very being defined in the perfect being thesis; (ii) it is an a priori argument, so there are no contentious premises or assumptions about our observations of the external world. That is, if there is any flaw in the argument, it is a purely conceptual flaw. In this sense, again, the ontological argument is the most directly relevant argument to perfect being theism. Hence, I focus on this argument throughout this book and particularly in Chapters 5, 6, and 7.

1.7 Arguments Against Perfect Being Theism

There are literally dozens of arguments against perfect being theism and many works have been produced on each of them. It is, however, frequently overlooked that most of them focus on the omni God thesis, namely that God is an omniscient, omnipotent, and omnibenevolent being, rather than the perfect being thesis, namely that God is the being than which no greater is metaphysically possible. They focus on the omni God thesis because it is more specific than the perfect being thesis. There are many arguments of this kind but I submit that nearly all of them fall into one of the following three types. (I merely sketch these types in this chapter; I discuss them in detail in Chapters 2, 3, and 4.)

Type A: Arguments that Purport to Show the Internal Incoherence of God's Individual Properties

Type-A arguments are meant to show that at least one of God's properties specified in the omni God thesis—omniscience, omnipotence, or omnibenevolence—is internally incoherent. From the internal incoherence of at least one of the properties, opponents of the omni God thesis deduce that there cannot exist an omniscient, omnipotent, and omnibenevolent being. Given opponents' contention that the perfect being thesis entails the omni God thesis and that there cannot exist an omniscient, omnipotent, and omnibenevolent being, the arguments conclude that perfect being theism is false. Type-A arguments include: (i) the paradox of the stone, which purports to show the incoherence of omnipotence by considering the possibility of an omnipotent being's creating a stone which that being itself cannot lift (Mavrodes 1963); and (ii) the Cantorian argument against omniscience, which purports to show the incoherence of omniscience by demonstrating that there is no set of all truths (Grim 1984, 1986, 1990, 1991, 2000, 2007).

Type B: Arguments that Purport to Show the Mutual Inconsistency Between God's Properties

Type-B arguments are meant to show that even if each of God's properties specified in the omni God thesis is internally coherent, at least some of them are mutually inconsistent. If some of the properties are mutually inconsistent, then, again, there cannot exist an omniscient, omnipotent, and omnibenevolent being and perfect being theism is false. Type-B arguments include: (i) the argument from God's inability to sin, which purports to show the inconsistency between omnipotence and omnibenevolence by claiming that an omnibenevolent being cannot be omnipotent because it cannot perform a morally wrong action (Morriston 2001a, 2001b; Pike 1969); and (ii) the argument from experience, which purports to derive the inconsistency between omniscience and omnipotence by showing that an omnipotent being cannot be omniscient because it fails to know fully what fear and frustration are (Blumenfeld 1978).

Type C: Arguments that Purport to Show the Mutual Inconsistency Between the Set of God's Properties and a Certain Fact About the Actual World

Type-C arguments are meant to show that, even if God's properties specified in the omni God thesis are internally coherent and mutually consistent, the set of properties is mutually inconsistent with a certain fact about the actual world. If that is true, then, again, the omni God thesis is false and perfect being theism is also false. Type-C arguments include: (i) the argument from evil, which purports to show the inconsistency between the existence of an omniscient, omnipotent, and omnibenevolent being and the fact that there is evil in the actual world (Mackie 1982); and (ii) the argument from divine hiddenness, which purports to show the inconsistency between the existence of an omniscient, omnipotent, and omnibenevolent being and the fact that the existence of such a being is not manifest to everyone in the actual world (Schellenberg 1993).

In Chapter 3, I critically discuss these arguments and defend perfect being theism from them.

1.8 Conclusion

In this chapter, we have overviewed perfect being theism by focusing on its core, the perfect being thesis, according to which God is the being than which no greater is metaphysically possible. We have seen that the perfect being *thesis* appears to be compatible with atheism even though perfect being theism is not. We have also seen that a certain version of perfect being theism is in principle compatible with polytheism, pantheism, and panentheism, even though I focus in the rest of this book on traditional monotheism. I have also discussed the historical origins of perfect being theism. I have argued that perfect being theism was anticipated or presented by many philosophers and theologians before Anselm. I have also considered possible developmental and cognitive origins of perfect being theism as well as the philosophical merits of holding perfect being theism. And, finally, I have discussed arguments for and against perfect being theism. I have claimed that none of the prominent theistic arguments except the ontological argument is a direct argument for perfect being theism, and I have also explained that nearly all arguments against perfect being theism fall into one of three types.

In Chapter 2, I offer a more detailed analysis of perfect being theism by investigating exactly what perfect being theists mean when they say that God is the being than which no greater is metaphysically possible.

2

Perfect Being Theism and the Great Chain of Being

2.1 Introduction

We saw in Chapter 1 that the core of perfect being theism is the following:

The perfect being thesis: God is the being than which no greater is metaphysically possible.

Again, this thesis has been widely accepted among Judeo-Christian-Islamic theists and it has for several hundred years been a central notion in the philosophy of religion. Whenever philosophers—whether they are theistic, atheistic, or agnostic—debate the existence and nature of God, they reference this thesis as their starting point. Ironically, however, philosophers have rarely analysed the concept expressed in the perfect being thesis itself.[1] Instead, as I explained in Chapter 1, they focus most of their attention on the omni God thesis, according to which God is the omniscient, omnipotent, and omnibenevolent being, without considering God's greatness in general. It remains unclear, therefore, exactly what greatness in the perfect being thesis is and what it means to say that God is that than which no *greater* is metaphysically possible. Anselm himself is silent about these questions in the *Proslogion*. While he does touch on them in his earlier work the *Monologion*, his answers are not very clear:

[1] Aquinas's *Summa Theologica* might be one of very few exceptions that addresses God's perfection in general even though Aquinas does not talk about God's *greatness* in general or analyse the perfect being thesis itself. His primary focus, like that of most other scholars, is on God's nature in relation to His individual great-making properties (Aquinas 1967, originally 1485).

> We have found, then, that there is something supremely good (because all good things are good through some one thing, namely that which is good through itself). But in the same way we arrive at the necessary conclusion that there is something supremely great, since whatsoever is greater is great through some one thing, namely that which is great through itself. I do not mean great in terms of size, like some sort of body; but something which, the greater it is, the better or more valuable it is, like wisdom. And since only that which is supremely good can be supremely great, it is necessary that there is something that is best and greatest—i.e. of everything that exists, the supreme.
>
> (Anselm 1998, originally 1076, p. 13)

In this passage Anselm offers a paradigm example of a type of greatness that is relevant, namely wisdom, and a paradigm example of a type of greatness that is not relevant, namely size. However, he does not say exactly what sorts of conditions God must satisfy for Him to be that than which no greater is metaphysically possible. Anselm hints, however, that the respective greatnesses of God and other beings can be understood in terms of a hierarchy. Again, in the *Monologion*, rather than in the *Proslogion*, he writes:

> [I]f one considers the nature of things, one cannot help realizing that they are not all of equal value, but differ by degrees. For the nature of a horse is better than that of a tree, and that of a human more excellent than that of a horse, and to doubt it is simply not human. It is undeniable that some natures can be better than others. None the less reason argues that there is some nature that so overtops the others that it is inferior to none.
>
> (Anselm 1998, originally 1076, pp. 14–15)

Anselm does not, however, say what sort of structure must be present in the hierarchy to render the perfect being thesis coherent.

The aim of this chapter is thus to specify exactly what the perfect being thesis means by providing rigorous, systematic models of its structure and content. A hierarchy of all beings is often called the 'great chain of being', the 'ladder of life', or '*Scala Naturae*'. There are many versions of the great chain of being but the one that most intuitively characterizes the perfect being thesis is a single linear ranking of all possible beings in which God occupies the top link in the chain. I call the model of the perfect being thesis that is based on this type of hierarchy the 'linear model'. It is widely agreed among contemporary philosophers, however, that the linear model does not succeed because it does not seem to make sense to say that there can be a single objective scale of value that ranks *all* possible beings.

In the central part of this chapter, therefore, I explore alternatives to the linear model by systematically analysing God's properties. I argue that what I call the 'radial model' is the most plausible alternative, even though the model faces a powerful objection. I argue, however, that the linear model should also be taken seriously as a backup option for perfect being theists because (i) it is not vulnerable to the objection that the radial model faces and (ii) what is widely regarded as a knock-down objection to the linear model is not as compelling as some have claimed.[2]

This chapter has the following structure: In Section 2.2, I explain how the concept of the great chain of being underlies the perfect being thesis by tracing its history. In Section 2.3, I explain some preliminaries for discussing distinct models of the great chain of being. In Section 2.4, I introduce the linear model and raise a potential problem for it. In Sections 2.5 through 2.7, I introduce an alternative to the linear model, the radial model, and defend it from possible objections. In Sections 2.8 and 2.9, I revisit and defend the linear model as a backup option for perfect being theists. I conclude in Section 2.10.

2.2 The Great Chain of Being

I noted above that we can understand the perfect being thesis by analysing it in terms of a hierarchy, the great chain of being. Let us consider briefly the historical background of this notion.[3]

As Arthur O. Lovejoy (1936) remarks, Plato's theory of forms can be understood as one of the oldest theories concerning the hierarchy of beings (Lovejoy 1936, p. 24). Plato divides reality into the realm of non-material forms, which he considers to be superior and fundamental, and the realm of material things, which he considers to be inferior and less fundamental. One could argue that this theory anticipates the hierarchical way of understanding reality on which the great chain of being is based.

Aristotle, in his work on natural history (1883, originally fourth century BC), presents a more fine-grained taxonomy or scale of being

[2] In my 2013a paper I identified the linear model with the great chain of being. But I now think that it is more appropriate to consider the linear model only as a version of the great chain of being while considering other models as alternative versions of the chain.

[3] For historical accounts of the great chain of being see Arthur O. Lovejoy (1936) and E. M. W. Tillyard (1972, originally 1942).

which places humans at the highest rank and then ranks the rest roughly in the following order: other higher animals (such as mammals, birds, reptiles, and fish), lower animals (such as insects, spiders, and jellyfish), higher and lower plants, and finally inanimate matter. It is important to note that Aristotle's scale is not presented in terms of evolution. That is, none of the organisms on the scale has developed from others lower on the scale. Their positions are fixed and they all remain where they are. If we present a similar scale of being in terms of evolution, we can obtain what we call today the 'phylogenetic tree'. The phylogenetic tree illustrates evolutionary relationships between distinct species by identifying their common ancestors.

Aristotle focuses on beings in nature, so his scale terminates with humans at the top. However, the great chain that we are concerned with here includes beings higher than humans and places God, as the being than which no greater is metaphysically possible, at the top. Let us see what philosophers say about such a chain that goes beyond humans. Cicero, for example, writes as follows:

> What could be more stupid than to deny the supreme excellence to that universal nature which embraces all things? And if it is supreme in excellence, must it not be conscious, endowed with reason and purpose, and finally with wisdom? How else can it be supreme? For if it were like a plant or an animal, there would be reason to rate it at the bottom rather than at the top of the scale. And if it is endowed with mind, but has been without wisdom from the beginning, its state will be lower than that of Man. A man can become wise. But if the universe has been devoid of wisdom through all the infinity of past time, then obviously it will never acquire any now. So it will be inferior to Man. But this is absurd and we must therefore conclude that the universe was endowed with wisdom from eternity and is itself divine. There is nothing, other than the universe as a whole, that lacks nothing and is complete and perfect throughout in every part.
> (Cicero 1972, originally 45 BC, pp. 137–8, Book II, 37)

As I mentioned in Chapter 1, Cicero talks about the universe instead of God as his focus is on pantheism. Cicero says that the universe should be placed higher than a plant, an animal, and a man because it is 'supreme in excellence'. This means, Cicero contends, that the universe has consciousness, reason, purpose, and wisdom.

Sextus Empiricus reports Cleanthes arguing as follows:

> One animal, however, is better than another, as (say) the horse than the tortoise, and the bull than the ass, and the lion than the bull. And of all the terrestrial

> animals Man is the highest and best in respect of the disposition of both body and soul; therefore a certain best and most excellent animal will exist. Yet Man cannot be absolutely the best animal...
>
> (Sextus Empiricus 1936, originally second century, p. 49, Book I, 89–90)

Proclus defends an unusual view that any being can move up the scale of being by participating in the One, which Proclus identifies with God:

> [E]ach thing, even the lowest grade of being you could mention, becomes god by participating in unity according to its rank. For if God and One are the same because there is nothing greater than God and nothing greater than the One, then to be unified is the same as to be deified. Just as, if the Sun and God were the same, to be illumined would be the same as to be deified; for the One gives unity, the Sun light.... Now this One, we may say, exists otherwise in the gods than in the being that comes after the gods; in the one case, it is self-sufficient, not like something existing in a substratum (for every god is god by virtue of the One, though the supreme God is one purely and simply, having no multiple aspect, while each of the others is more than unity, one thing because it has these entities dependent on it, another those; the beings that are nearer the pure One are fewer in number, those further away are more numerous, just as those nearer have a nature more akin to it and those further away are less akin; addition and plurality come about because of their descent in the scale of being.) So in the former case the One truly is, while in the latter case it exists as a character in something.
>
> (Proclus 1992, originally fifth century, pp. 36–7, Book I, 641–2)

It is interesting to note that Proclus suggests that there are fewer and fewer beings as we move up the hierarchy and there is only a single One at the top.

As Edward Wierenga says, hierarchical thinking is present in Augustine's view of God as well (Wierenga 2011, pp. 141–2). Augustine writes:

> There is a nature which is susceptible of change with respect to both place and time, namely, the corporeal. There is another nature which is in no way susceptible of change with respect to place, but only with respect to time, namely the spiritual. And there is a third Nature which can be changed neither in respect to place nor in respect to time: that is, God. Those natures of which I had said that they are mutable in some respect are called creatures; the Nature which is immutable is called Creator.... [Y]ou cannot fail to distinguish, in this classification of natures, which exists in the highest possible manner, and which occupies the lowest place, yet is within the range of existence, and which occupies the middle place, greater than the lowest, but coming short of the highest. That highest is essential blessedness; the lowest, that which cannot be either blessed or wretched; and the intermediate nature lives in wretchedness when it stoops

towards that which is lowest, and in blessedness when it turns towards that which is highest. (Augustine 1974, originally 390, pp. 45–6)

Such hierarchical thinking allows us to classify, according to Augustine, all beings into three categories—i.e., the corporeal, the spiritual, and God—and rank them accordingly. Augustine does not state explicitly that there can be finer-grained hierarchies within the corporeal and the spiritual but, given the diversity of beings in these categories, it seems sensible for him to hold such a view.

All of the hierarchies that we have seen are proposed on the assumption that beings can be ranked in accordance with their relevant properties. We might reason as follows: Plants rank higher than inorganic matter because they have life, which inorganic matter lacks. Animals rank higher than plants because they have will, which plants lack. Humans rank higher than animals because they have reason, which animals lack. Angels rank higher than humans because they have immortality, which humans lack. God ranks higher than angels because He has perfection, which angels lack. This can be schematized as follows:[4]

God: life, will, reason, immortality, perfection
Angels: life, will, reason, immortality
Humans: life, will, reason
Animals: life, will
Plants: life
In organic matter: none

This is indeed a hierarchy that is often assumed implicitly by philosophers and theologians when they discuss the perfect being thesis. God sits atop the chain because He exemplifies the highest or best possible instance of every property including existence, life, will, reason, immortality, and perfection. Such a hierarchical view of God seems to be present in the biblical verses we addressed in Chapter 1:

Yours, Lord, is the greatness and the power and the glory and the majesty and the splendor, for everything in heaven and earth is yours. Yours, Lord, is the kingdom; you are exalted as head over all. (1 Chronicles 29:11)

[4] See Tillyard (1972, originally 1942), p. 35.

Also:

For great is the LORD and most worthy of praise; he is to be feared above all gods.
(1 Chronicles 16:25)

In human society, perhaps such a hierarchy is most clearly present in monarchy. It makes sense therefore that God is analogized with the monarch in the above verses.

The great chain of being originated in Ancient Greece and was widespread from the Middle Ages to the early modern period in religious, philosophical, and political discourse. It is also present in scientific discourse, particularly in relation to the theory of evolution established by Charles Darwin. The above hierarchy and its variants are often implicitly assumed in Western culture. Yet, as Tillyard remarks, it is 'one of those accepted commonplaces, more often hinted at or taken for granted than set forth' (Tillyard 1972, originally 1942, p. 34). In what follows, I make the hierarchical thinking associated with the great chain of being more explicit and provide a rigorous analysis of the perfect being thesis in relation to it.

2.3 Some Preliminaries

Before proceeding with our discussion, let us note two points. First, in the rest of this chapter, I use the terms in the following pairs interchangeably: (i) property/attribute; (ii) greater/superior; (iii) worse/inferior. This is not very elegant but it is unavoidable because the literature mixes up the terms in each pair. Second, since the aim of this chapter is to *model*, rather than to defend, the perfect being thesis—according to which God is the being than which no greater is metaphysically possible—I set aside attempts to refute the thesis itself. I discuss these attempts in detail in Chapter 3.

One of the most important questions about the great chain of being is that of determining what sorts of beings should be included in it. In our context, the great chain has to include not only beings in nature but also beings beyond nature. This assumption is necessary as our aim is to develop a model of the perfect being thesis, which is concerned with God as a being beyond nature. The great chain of being that we address here is, therefore, distinct from Aristotle's scale or the phylogenetic tree, which are limited to organic and inorganic matter in nature. Also, again, in our context, the great chain of being has to include all *possible* beings, not just all *actual* beings. This is because our concern is with God as the being than which no greater is metaphysically *possible*. This entails the thesis that the great chain of being exhausts all possible beings; there are no possible beings (in a relevant sense) that escape the chain. Lovejoy calls a thesis similar to this the 'principle of plenitude' (Lovejoy 1936, p. 52). According to this principle, all conceptual possibilities are (or will be) realized in actuality. This is, however, distinct from the thesis that I have in mind here. The great chain of being we discuss here does not require such a specific thesis. It requires only that all possible beings, whether they remain merely possible or are actual, are included in the great chain of being. This thesis entails that the chain exhibits continuity. Given that the chain includes all possible beings, there is no logical gap between one being and the next in the chain. The chain is, therefore, a very long one—possibly an infinitely long one—that is smooth and continuous. Borrowing David Lewis's phrase to describe modal realism, we could say that the great chain of being is a 'maximally abundant' scale of beings (Lewis 1986).

The fourteenth-century Benedictine monk Ranulf Higden makes a related point in his chronicle *Polychronicon*:

> In the universal order of things the top of an inferior class touches the bottom of a superior; as for instance oysters, which, occupying as it were the lowest position in the class of animals, scarcely rise above the life of plants, because they cling to the earth without motion and possess the sense of touch alone. The upper surface of the earth is in contact with the lower surface of water; the highest part of the waters touches the lowest part of the air, and so by a ladder of ascent to the outermost sphere of the universe. So also the noblest entity in the category of bodies, the human body, when its humours are evenly balanced, touches the fringe of the next class above it, namely the human soul, which occupies the lowest rank in the spiritual order.[5]

If, as Higden implies, the hierarchy of being is meant to be smooth and continuous, then it has to include all possible beings. Conversely, if it includes only a limited class of beings (e.g., beings that exist in the actual world), then there will be gaps in the hierarchy. Lovejoy quotes the following passage, which is attributed to Leibniz:[6]

> All the different classes of beings which taken together make up the universe are, in the ideas of God who knows distinctly their essential gradations, only so many

[5] This is Tillyard's own translation in Tillyard (1972, originally 1942), p. 36.

[6] The authenticity of the passage is disputed but it does not matter in this context who in the seventeenth or eighteenth century wrote it.

> ordinates of a single curve so closely united that it would be impossible to place others between any two of them, since that would imply disorder and imperfection. Thus men are linked with the animals, these with the plants and these with the fossils, which in turn merge with those bodies which our senses and our imagination represent to us as the absolutely inanimate. And, since the law of continuity [i.e., 'Natura non facit saltum'] requires that when the essential attributes of one being approximate those of another all the properties of the one must likewise gradually approximate those of the other, it is necessary that all the orders of natural beings form but a single chain, in which the various classes, like so many rings, are so closely linked one to another that it is impossible for the senses or the imagination to determine precisely the point at which one ends and the next begins. (Lovejoy 1936, pp. 144–5)

One might wonder at this point if abstract objects, such as sets, numbers, and propositions, should also be included in the chain. This is a difficult question to answer because philosophers have disputed for a long time how to demarcate abstract objects and concrete objects. According to some, God and angels are abstract objects because they are not spatio-temporal objects. According to others, however, they are concrete objects because they are agents with free will, knowledge, and morality (Mawson 2008, p. 36). We certainly do need to include God in the great chain of being but, fortunately, we do not need to decide what criteria for distinguishing abstract objects and concrete objects are tenable. We also do not need to decide whether sets, numbers, and propositions should be included in the great chain of being. This is because none of the claims I present here depend on this issue.

Another crucial question about the great chain of being is whether the chain is meant to rank *types* or *tokens* of possible beings. In the quoted passage above, Anselm compares the *nature* of a horse, the *nature* of a tree, and the *nature* of a human, rather than a specific horse, a specific tree, or a specific human (Anselm 1998, originally 1076, pp. 14–15). It is unclear exactly what natures are, but in discussing the ontological argument Anselm and Gaunilo use the term when they intend to refer to a being without presupposing its existence. Hence, it might not be far-fetched to interpret this to mean that Anselm considers the great chain of being in terms of types rather than tokens. Cicero compares a plant and an animal with the universe, rather than the plant type, the animal type, or the universe type, so it seems that he has in mind a ranking of distinct tokens (Cicero 1972, originally 45 BC, pp. 137–8, Book II, 37). Proclus is vague about his focus but insofar as he talks about the participation of things in unity, it may be reasonable to assume that he has in mind individual tokens rather than types (Proclus 1992, originally fifth century, pp. 36–7, Book I, 641–2). Augustine classifies and ranks three distinct natures—i.e., the corporeal, the spiritual, and God—so it seems that he has in mind a ranking of types with God representing what might be called the divine type (Augustine 1974, originally 390, pp. 45–6).

It is important to note that an attempt to rank types of beings is compatible with an attempt to rank tokens of beings. One might consistently maintain, for example, that while there is a ranking of types, including the divine type, the human type, the animal type, and so on, there is also a ranking of tokens within each type. (It could also be the case that within each type there is a ranking of subtypes. For example, within the animal type there might be a ranking in order of the mammal subtype, the bird subtype, the reptile subtype, etc., and within each subtype there might be a ranking of tokens of that type.) I believe, however, that it is better to consider the great chain of being in terms of tokens rather than types for two reasons. First, it is contentious whether there are clear types. One might argue that types are not natural kinds. Second, there might be borderline or vague cases in which we cannot decide to which type a given token belongs. For example, there are organisms in nature such as Bacteria and Archaea that are on the borderline of living and non-living things. This problem is particularly manifest in the current context because the great chain of being includes all *possible* beings, not just all beings that happen to exist in nature. Third, there might be complex cases in which a certain superior token in a lower type is deemed greater than a certain inferior token in a higher type. We can set aside these complications by focusing on individual tokens rather than types. Having said that, nearly everything I say in the remainder of this chapter is applicable to a ranking by types as well.

2.4 The Linear Model

The most straightforward model of the great chain of being, which I call the linear model, holds that God is the being than which no greater is metaphysically possible by virtue of occupying the top link in a single chain of being, while all other possible beings occupy other links lower in the chain. The chain in question is a linear ranking of all beings, both actual and merely possible, which is established in accordance with a single objective scale of value and presented as a potentially infinitely long chain. The ranking tells us, for any pair of possible beings x and y, whether x is as great as y, greater than y, or less great than y.

It should be noted that it is not always easy to individuate beings on the chain. There might be cases where it is unclear how many beings exist if they are not clearly spatio-temporally isolated from each other. In such cases, we might have to take into account all possible combinations to individuate the beings in question. There might also be cases in which the same being has varying degrees of greatness in distinct possible worlds. Such a being has the relevant properties at their respective intensity only contingently. This means that the same being might occupy multiple links in the great chain of being if we take into account possible worlds. Suppose, for example, I am more powerful and more knowledgeable in W_1 than in W_2. In this case, I occupy a higher link in the ranking in W_1 than in W_2. Here we can treat a being in one possible world (e.g., me in W_1) and the same being in another possible world (e.g., me in W_2) as if they are two distinct beings, provided that the degree of greatness differs in these possible worlds. (My claims here need to be amended accordingly if one maintains that there can only be a *counterpart* of a given being in distinct possible worlds instead of there being the same being in distinct possible worlds.) Perfect being theists hold that whatever beings exist in distinct possible worlds, God (or His counterpart) remains the greatest being in every possible world.[7]

Thomas Morris says that the linear model is committed to 'universal value commensurability', which he defines as the thesis that 'every possible being is value commensurable' (Morris 1984, pp. 15–16). This thesis needs to be slightly amended as follows to avoid a possible confusion:

Universal value commensurability: Every possible being is overall value commensurable.

The phrase 'overall' is added to make it explicit that the overall greatness of every possible being is commensurable. It should be distinguished

[7] Another way to construct a linear ranking of all possible beings is to rank all possible beings in accordance with their greatnesses across all possible worlds. Even in this case, according to perfect being theists, God sits at the top of the chain.

from the weaker thesis that every possible being is value commensurable in a more specific respect.[8] In our discussion, I define value commensurability as follows:

Value commensurability: *x* and *y* are value commensurable if and only if the greatness of *x* can be shown to be (i) equal to, (ii) greater than, or (iii) worse than the greatness of *y* by a common measure.[9]

According to universal value commensurability, we can compare the greatness of any two beings and locate them on the great chain of being. If we have access to the great chain of being, we can easily demonstrate that God is the being than which no greater is metaphysically possible. We need only look at the chain and confirm that God, and only God, occupies the top link. Having this in mind, the linear model can be formulated as follows:

The linear model: God is the being than which no greater is metaphysically possible by virtue of occupying the top link in the great chain of being (Figure 2.1).[10]

Despite its intuitive appeal, the linear model is not taken seriously today because most philosophers reject the universal value commensurability on which the model relies. C. D. Broad, for example, says that universal value commensurability is false because a correct analysis of relevant properties does 'not allow us, even in theory, to arrange everything in a single scale of perfection' (Broad 1939, p. 177). Morris, to take another example, claims that universal value commensurability is 'a position which is clearly false' (Morris 1984, p. 19).[11] He elaborates his point as follows:

It is argued that the notion of a greatest possible being makes sense only if there is some single, all-encompassing objective scale of value on which every being, actual and possible, can be ranked, with God at the top. But surely, it is insisted,

[8] Thanks to an anonymous reader for this point.

[9] For a useful discussion of commensurability and incommensurability in value theory, see Chang (1997).

[10] The distances between the links in the chain in Figure 2.1 do not correspond to the degrees of difference between the greatnesses of the corresponding beings. It might be the case, for instance, that there is an infinite gap between the greatness of God and the greatness of the second-best possible being. The same point applies to other relevant figures throughout this chapter. Thanks to an anonymous reader for this point.

[11] For related criticisms, see Maitzen (2005) and Rogers (1993).

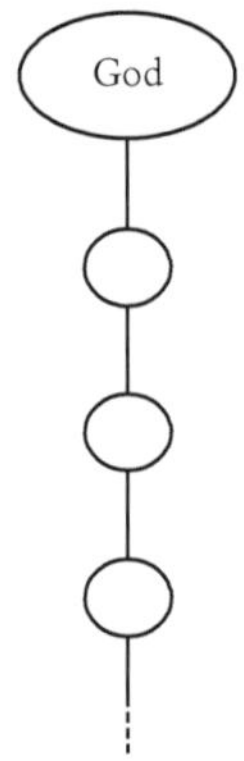

Figure 2.1 The linear model.

not all things are commensurable with respect to value. It just makes no sense to ask which is of greater intrinsic value, an aardvark or an escalator.

(Morris 1984, p. 15)

What Morris presents above is widely regarded as a knock-down objection to universal value commensurability, the thesis on which the linear model is based.

In Sections 2.8 and 2.9, I argue that the linear model is more plausible than it is often thought to be. However, before doing so, I consider whether there can be an alternative model of the perfect being thesis, a model that does not rely on universal value commensurability.

2.5 The Radial Model

Suppose, for the sake of simplicity, that there are only three possible beings: an aardvark, an escalator, and God. How can God be the greatest possible being among them on the assumption that an aardvark and an escalator are not value commensurable? Under this circumstance God can be the greatest possible being only if He is overall value commensurable with an aardvark and an escalator, individually and independently. This example suggests that once universal value commensurability is given up, the following has to be true for God to be the being than which no greater is metaphysically possible:

Universal divine value commensurability: Every possible being is overall value commensurable with God.

In fact, this is what Morris seems to endorse even though he does not explicate it in detail.[12] The idea is that while such beings as an aardvark and an escalator might not be overall value commensurable with one another, God is overall value commensurable with, and greater than, each of them. We can thus maintain that God is the being than which no greater is metaphysically possible. Universal divine value commensurability is more modest than universal value commensurability because it is entailed by universal value commensurability, but not *vice versa*.

What I call the radial model is an alternative to the linear model. The radial model says that there are multiple local chains of being instead of a single chain of being. God is the being than which no greater is metaphysically possible because, according to this model, He occupies the top link in each of the local chains. The radial model is not a single model but a model-type, because there are a number of sub-models, ranging from a sub-model that includes only two local chains to a more complex sub-model that includes a large number of local chains.[13]

To proceed with our discussion of the radial model, we need to introduce and explore in detail several additional terms. I have already discussed omniscience, omnipotence, and omnibenevolence as paradigm examples of great-making properties without defining precisely what great-making properties are. The notion of a great-making property can be defined as follows:

Great-making property: Property p is a great-making property if, all else being equal, it contributes to the greatness of its possessor.

For example, being knowledgeable is, according to many philosophers, a great-making property because, all else being equal, the property of being knowledgeable makes a being that possesses it greater than otherwise. As intuitively clear as that example is, it does not explain exactly what makes great-making properties great. I submit that there are at least four distinct senses of greatness:

A. Great for oneself: For example, the property of being smart is great for a criminal to have because it benefits the criminal.
B. Great for the world and others: For example, the property of being smart is great for a well-intentioned inventor to have (but not great

[12] See Morris (1984), p. 16.

[13] Thanks to an anonymous reader for this point.

for a criminal to have) because it is beneficial to the world and others.

C. Great in one's character/capacity: For example, the property of being sharp is great for a knife to have *qua* knife.
D. Great intrinsically: For example, the properties of being knowledgeable, powerful, benevolent, beautiful, and so on are great in themselves, regardless of their greatness in the above three senses.[14]

Anselm makes a related point:

> Different good things may none the less appear to be called good through different things. Thus a horse may appear to be called good through one thing, because it is strong, and through something else, because it is swift. For it seems to be called good through strength and good through speed, and yet strength and speed do not seem to be the same thing. And if the horse is good because it is strong and swift, how come the thief that is swift and strong is bad? Rather, it is the case that the swift and strong thief is bad because he does harm, and the strong and swift horse is good because it is beneficial. (And indeed ordinarily nothing is thought to be good except on the grounds either of what is beneficial, e.g., health and what makes for it—or of what is excellent, e.g., beauty and what contributes to it.) Now, the reasoning above is irrefutable. Necessarily, therefore, everything beneficial or excellent is, if it is truly good, good through that same one thing, through which all good things necessarily are good, whatever that thing may be. And who would doubt that that through which all things are good is a great good?
>
> Because, then, it is that through which every good thing is good, it is good through itself. It therefore follows that all the other good things are good through something other than what they themselves are, while this thing alone is good through itself. But nothing that is good through something other than itself is equal to or greater than that good which is good through itself. The one thing, therefore, that is good through itself is the one thing that is supremely good. For the supreme is that which so overtops the others that it has no equal and no superior. But what is supremely good is also supremely great. There is therefore one thing that is supremely good and supremely great, and this is of all the things that exist, the supreme. (Anselm 1998, originally 1076, p. 12)

Anselm seems to address senses B (great for the world and others) and D (great intrinsically) in the above passage. The strength and swiftness of a horse are great because they are beneficial to others. The strength and

[14] I am grateful to Philip Goff for his comments on this classification.

swiftness of a thief are not, on the other hand, because they are harmful to others. Intrinsic greatness, which Anselm calls excellence here, is supremely great because it is good through itself rather than through some other thing. Anselm seems to think that intrinsic greatness represents God's greatness.

Perfect being theists rarely discuss the nature of God's greatness itself but they seem to assume intrinsic greatness implicitly when they formulate their views.[15] Thus in what follows I adopt sense D and assume that great-making properties are *intrinsically* great properties that, all else being equal, contribute to the greatness of their possessors. I shall focus on the three individual great-making properties that are most commonly attributed to God: knowledge, power, and benevolence. I set aside other candidates for God's great-making properties, such as simplicity, timelessness, incorporeality, and immutability. In this way, I can avoid unnecessary complexity in my discussion and set aside further disputes over God's individual great-making properties.

One might claim that to determine the greatnesses of beings, we need to consider 'worse-making properties' as well; that is, properties that undermine the greatness of their possessors. For example, a being that has two great-making properties G_1 and G_2 but no worse-making properties might be judged superior to another being that has two great-making properties G_1 and G_2 as well as a worse-making property W_1, where W_1 partly undermines, say, G_1. In an extreme scenario, a certain worse-making property is so bad that it might cancel out all great-making properties that one has. I set this point aside for the sake of simplicity as there are so many (perhaps infinitely many) possible combinations of great-making properties and worse-making properties. We can assume that when I talk about great-making properties, this kind of calculation has already been made.

[15] There are questions about what the source of the intrinsic value of great-making properties is and whether it could have been otherwise than it is. If great-making properties are intrinsically valuable due to God and it could have been otherwise than it is, then it seems to entail that God is not necessarily the being than which no greater is metaphysically possible. On the other hand, if the value could not have been otherwise than it is, then one might wonder if God's power is limited. I set aside these issues as they involve controversial topics that run beyond our scope, such as the nature of omnipotence, the divine command theory, and divine aseity. Thanks to an anonymous reader for raising this point.

Let me introduce several additional terms.

Extensive equality: *x* is extensively equal to *y* if and only if both of the following are true: (i) *x* has all the great-making properties that *y* has; and (ii) neither *x* nor *y* has any other great-making property.

When we talk about the extensity of the great-making properties of possible beings, we are not concerned with their intensity. We are concerned only with whether these beings share the same great-making properties, regardless of their intensity. For example: Suppose that being *A* has only two great-making properties *G1* and *G2* and that another being *B* also has only the same great-making properties *G1* and *G2*. Regardless of the intensity of each of the great-making properties that these beings have, *A* and *B* are extensively equal. They are represented by the same number and types of bars (Figure 2.2).

Extensive superiority: *x* is extensively superior to *y* if and only if both of the following are true: (i) *x* has all the great-making properties that *y* has; and (ii) *x* has some great-making properties that *y* does not have.[16]

For example: Suppose that *A* has two great-making properties *G1* and *G2* while *B* has only one great-making property *G1*. Regardless of the intensity of each of the great-making properties these beings have, *A* is extensively superior to *B* (Figure 2.3).

The following should be obvious:

Extensive inferiority: *x* is extensively inferior to *y* if and only if *y* is extensively superior to *x*.

The extensity of great-making properties is not the only measure of a being's greatness. To measure a being's overall greatness, we need to examine the intensity of great-making properties as well:

Intensive equality: *x* is intensively equal to *y* if and only if both of the following are true: (i) *x* is extensively equal to *y*; and (ii) great-making properties are present in *x* at the same degree of intensity as in *y*.

For example: Suppose that *A* has only two great-making properties *G1* and *G2* and that *B* has also only two great-making properties *G1* and *G2*. Suppose further that *A* and *B* have these two great-making properties at

[16] I borrow the terms 'extensive superiority' and 'intensive superiority' from Broad (1939), p. 177.

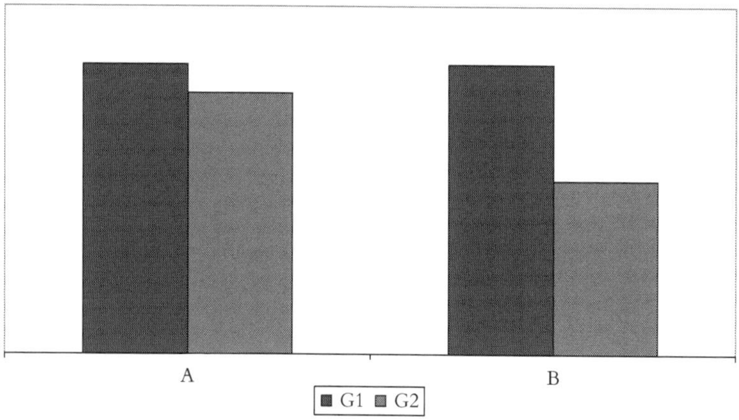

Figure 2.2 Extensive equality.

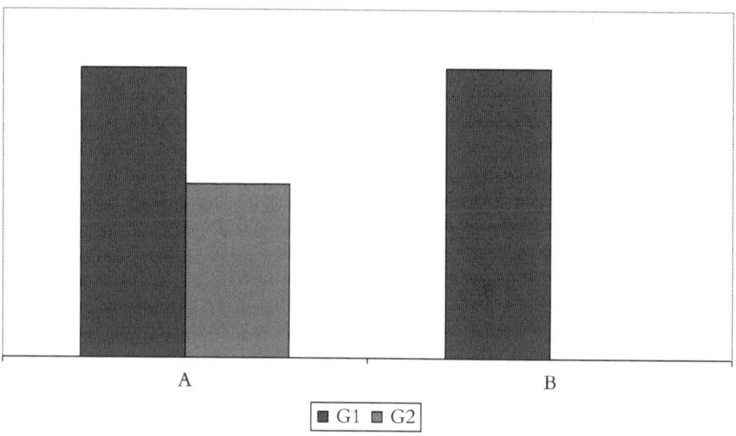

Figure 2.3 Extensive superiority.

the exact same degree of intensity. In this case *A* and *B* are intensively (and also extensively) equal (Figure 2.4).

Intensive superiority: *x* is intensively superior to *y* if and only if all of the following are true: (i) *x* is either extensively equal to or extensively superior to *y*; (ii) one or more of the great-making properties that are common to both are present in *x* at a higher degree of intensity than in *y*; and (iii) none of the great-making properties that is common to both is present in *y* at a higher degree of intensity than in *x*.

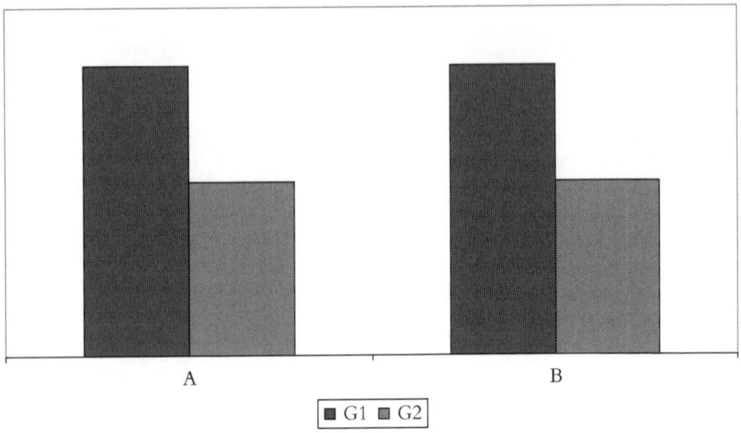

Figure 2.4 Intensive equality.

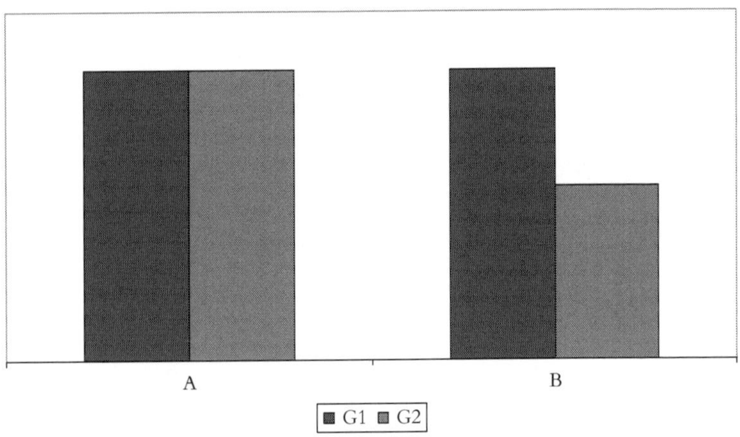

Figure 2.5 Intensive superiority.

For example: Suppose that *A* has only two great-making properties *G1* and *G2* and that *B* also has only two great-making properties *G1* and *G2*. However, while *G1* is present in both *A* and *B* at the exact same degree of intensity, *G2* is present in *A* at a higher degree of intensity than in *B*. In this case *A* is intensively superior to *B* (even though they are extensively equal; Figure 2.5).

One might argue at this point that this analysis is dubious because it seems to assume that all great-making properties play an equal role in determining the overall axiological status of a being. Suppose, for example, that the following are all true: (i) benevolence is significantly more important than other great-making properties; (ii) *A* and *B* do not possess all the same great-making properties; (iii) apart from benevolence, the great-making properties that *A* and *B* have play a relatively negligible role; and (iv) *A* is significantly more benevolent than *B*. One might claim that *A* should be deemed intensively superior to *B* in this case.[17]

My response to the above criticism is this: If a certain great-making property is significantly more important than others, then we can take that into account when we evaluate their overall greatnesses and amend a corresponding figure accordingly. For example, if benevolence is ten times more important than power, then that should be reflected in the calculation of the overall greatnesses of *A* and *B* and alter how relevant graphs are presented. Having said that, I admit that there are possible scenarios in which *A* seems to be overall superior to *B* even though *A* is not intensively superior to *B* on the criteria included in the above definition of intensive superiority. As I explain in Sections 2.8 and 2.9, this observation motivates us to reconsider the linear model.[18]

The following should be obvious:

Intensive inferiority: *x* is intensively inferior to *y* if and only if *y* is intensively superior to *x*.

With these terms in mind, consider the following thirteen combinations of relationships between *x* and *y*.

(1) *x* is extensively equal and intensively equal to *y*.
(2) *x* is extensively equal and intensively superior to *y*.
(3) *x* is extensively equal and intensively inferior to *y*.
(4) *x* is extensively superior and intensively equal to *y*.
(5) *x* is extensively superior and intensively superior to *y*.
(6) *x* is extensively superior and intensively inferior to *y*.
(7) *x* is extensively inferior and intensively equal to *y*.
(8) *x* is extensively inferior and intensively superior to *y*.
(9) *x* is extensively inferior and intensively inferior to *y*.

[17] Thanks to an anonymous reader for raising this criticism.

[18] Another possible scenario that motivates us to reconsider the linear model is the following: *A* and *B* share, say, one hundred great-making properties. *A* has ninety-nine of them significantly more intensively than *B* does, and *B* has the remaining great-making property only slightly more intensively than *A* does. In this case it seems reasonable to say that *A* is overall greater than *B* without satisfying condition (iii) in the definition.

(10) *x* is neither extensively superior, equal, nor inferior to *y*.
(11) *x* is extensively superior to *y* and the great-making properties that *x* and *y* share are present in *x* at the same degree of intensity as in *y* (in this case *x* is neither intensively superior, equal, nor inferior to *y*).
(12) *x* is extensively inferior to *y* and the great-making properties that *x* and *y* share are present in *y* at the same degree of intensity as in *x* (in this case *x* is neither intensively superior, equal, nor inferior to *y*).
(13) Other cases than (11) and (12) in which *x* is either extensively superior, equal, or inferior to *y* but *x* is neither intensively superior, equal, nor inferior to *y*.

In case (1) *x* and *y* are *genuinely equal*, which means that the greatnesses of *x* and *y* are overall equal. In case (2) *x* is *genuinely superior* to *y*, which means that *x* is overall superior to *y*. In case (3) *x* is *genuinely inferior* to *y*, which means that *x* is overall inferior to *y*. Case (4) is impossible to obtain because if *x* is intensively equal to *y*, then *x* has to be extensively equal to *y* as well. In case (5) *x* is *genuinely superior* to *y*. Case (6) is impossible to obtain because if *x* is intensively inferior to *y*, then *x* has to be either extensively equal or extensively inferior to *y*. Case (7) is also impossible to obtain because if *x* is intensively equal to *y*, then *x* has to be extensively equal as well. Case (8) is, again, impossible to obtain because if *x* is intensively superior to *y*, then *x* has to be either extensively equal or extensively superior to *y*. In case (9) *x* is *genuinely inferior* to *y*. In case (10) *x* and *y* are value incommensurable. In case (11) *x* is *genuinely superior* to *y* because *x* has all the great-making properties that *y* has at the same degree of intensity and, moreover, *x* has some extra great-making properties that *y* does not have. In case (12) *x* is *genuinely inferior* to *y* because *y* has all the great-making properties that *x* has at the same degree of intensity and, moreover, *y* has some extra great-making properties that *x* does not have. In case (13) *x* and *y* are value incommensurable.

Let us return to the radial model, which says that God is the being than which no greater is metaphysically possible by virtue of occupying the top link in all local chains of being. To establish the radial model, we first need to assume, minimally, universal divine value commensurability, according to which every possible being is overall value commensurable with God. With this thesis in hand, we can show that God is the being than which no greater is metaphysically possible because every possible being is overall value commensurable with and genuinely inferior to God. Yet we have also seen above that there seem to be possible cases, such as instances of (1), (2), (3), (5), (9), (11), and (12), in which two non-divine possible beings—that is, possible beings other than God—are value commensurable. The linear model seems to be untenable because universal value commensurability—the thesis that every possible being is value commensurable—seems too strong. But there seem to be many cases in which certain non-divine possible beings are value commensurable. This observation suggests the following thesis:

Partial non-divine value commensurability: Some non-divine possible beings are overall value commensurable with one another.

Partial non-divine value commensurability entails that even if universal value commensurability is false, some non-divine possible beings remain overall value commensurable with one another. One might say, perhaps, that while an aardvark and an escalator are not value commensurable, an aardvark and a hedgehog are value commensurable.

An interesting question concerning partial non-divine value commensurability is whether there is a non-divine possible being such that it is not overall value commensurable with any other non-divine possible being. The answer seems to be 'no' because it is reasonable to think that for any non-divine possible being, there is at least one non-divine possible being with which it jointly satisfies either (1), (2), (3), (5), (9), (11), or (12). (To see this, consider the following: For any non-divine possible being we can always conceive of a duplicate of that being with respect to great-making properties or another non-divine possible being that is genuinely slightly inferior or slightly superior.) This means that there is no local chain of being that contains God and only one non-divine possible being. Thus any local chain of being will always include God and multiple non-divine possible beings. This observation suggests the following thesis:

Universal partial non-divine value commensurability: Every non-divine possible being is overall value commensurable with one or more other non-divine possible beings.

Partial non-divine value commensurability remains true but universal partial non-divine commensurability, which is more specific, is also true. Given universal partial non-divine commensurability, we can conclude

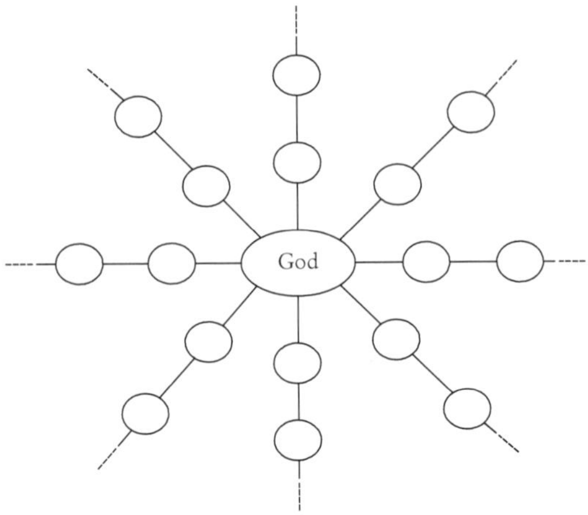

Figure 2.6 The radial model.

that there are many local chains of being such that (i) every possible being occupies a link in at least one such chain, (ii) each of the chains contains multiple non-divine possible beings, and (iii) God occupies the top link in all of the chains. The radial model can therefore be defined as follows:

The radial model: God is the being than which no greater is metaphysically possible by virtue of occupying the top link in all local chains of being, each of which contains multiple non-divine possible beings (Figure 2.6).[19]

Figure 2.6 represents only a version of the radial model. This version consists of eight local chains but alternative versions could have more or fewer local chains. There can also be alternative versions with the same number of local chains if their local chains include distinct possible beings or rank possible beings differently. It is interesting to note that while we have attempted to avoid the linear model, which is based on the infamous thesis of universal value commensurability, we have settled on something that is not very dissimilar to that model. Instead of having a

[19] In my 2013a paper I called this model the 'extended radial model' and called the following more basic thesis the 'radial model': God is the being than which no greater is metaphysically possible by virtue of occupying the top link in all local chains of being, each of which contains only one non-divine being. I now think that the latter thesis is a non-starter as there is no local chain of being that contains God and only one non-divine possible being. In this book, therefore, I drop it and simply call what I used to call the extended radial model the radial model.

potentially infinitely long single chain of being with God at the top, the radial model allows for many local chains of being, some or all of which might be infinitely long, with God at the top of each. In fact, the linear model is a special version of the radial model, a version in which universal partial non-divine value commensurability coincides with universal value commensurability and there is only one 'local' chain.

One might wonder at this point why we need to talk about these models in the first place. The differences between the models arise from how they treat commensurability between non-divine possible beings, rather than commensurability between God and non-divine possible beings. All God needs to be is, one might point out, greater than all non-divine possible beings.[20] However, it is indeed necessary to discuss these models to fully understand the perfect being thesis. Consider an illustrative example: For University *X* to be the best university, it needs only to satisfy the condition that it is better than all other universities. However, it is not helpful merely to assert, 'However other universities are compared and ranked, University *X* is the best university because it is better than all other universities'. To understand fully what it means to say that University *X* is the best university, we need to know by what criteria all universities are compared and on what basis University *X* is ranked as the best university.

2.6 The Comprehensive Greatness View

We have seen so far that once we give up the linear model, which relies on universal value commensurability, the radial model allows for the perfect being concept of God as the being than which no greater is metaphysically possible. The radial model is, however, still incomplete because it does not tell us exactly how God manages to occupy the top link in all local chains. In particular, the model does not tell us what sort of relationship God has with other possible beings. I address this issue here and in the following sections.

In Section 2.5 we saw that for x to be genuinely superior to y, x needs to satisfy one of the following conditions:

(2) x is extensively equal and intensively superior to y.
(5) x is extensively superior and intensively superior to y.

[20] Thanks to an anonymous reader for this point.

(11) x is extensively superior to y and the great-making properties that x and y share are present in x at the same degree of intensity as in y (in this case x is neither intensively superior, equal, nor inferior to y).

This means that for God to be genuinely superior to any other possible being, He needs to satisfy one of the above three conditions jointly with each one of every possible being except Himself. This observation suggests the following view:

The comprehensive greatness view: God occupies the top link in all local chains of being because, for every non-divine possible being y, God is either: (i) intensively superior to y or (ii) extensively superior to y and the great-making properties that God and y share are present in God at the same degree of intensity as in y.

The view is named as such because to satisfy either (i) or (ii) God must, first, be either extensively equal or extensively superior to all possible beings. This means that God has to have all great-making properties that at least one possible being has; that is, all possible great-making properties *simpliciter*. With this view in hand, the radial model can be advanced as follows: God has all the great-making properties that other possible beings have and, moreover, He is genuinely superior to each one of every possible being. That is why He occupies the top link in all local chains of being, which is equivalent to saying that He is the being than which no greater is metaphysically possible.

2.7 Objections to the Comprehensive Greatness View

The comprehensive greatness view is plausible at first sight and it seems compatible with perfect being theism. For example, it seems to match what Leibniz, a proponent of perfect being theism, says in his *Discourse on Metaphysics*: 'God is an absolutely perfect being . . . there are many different kinds of perfection, all of which God possesses, and each one of them pertains to him in the highest degree' (Leibniz 2012, originally 1686, p. 59). However, the comprehensive greatness view faces two major objections, which I call the 'extensity objection' and the 'intensity objection'. In this section I address these objections. I argue that while we can successfully refute the extensity objection, the refutability of the intensity objection remains controversial.

The Extensity Objection

Again, the comprehensive greatness view requires that God possess all possible great-making properties. However, the extensity objection says that there are many great-making properties that God cannot have. As I mentioned earlier, property *p* is a great-making property if, all else being equal, it contributes to the greatness of its possessor. So, for example, one might say that having a healthy heart is a great-making property because it contributes to the greatness of a person who possesses it. All else being equal, a person would be greater with a healthy heart than otherwise. To take another example, one might say that being a fast typist is a great-making property because, again, it contributes to the greatness of a person who possesses it. All else being equal, a person would be greater as a fast typist than otherwise. However, God surely does not have these great-making properties. Therefore, the comprehensive greatness view seems wrong in saying that God has all possible great-making properties. This is the extensity objection.

It is questionable whether such properties as having a healthy heart and being a fast typist are relevant to perfect being theism because they do not seem to be intrinsically great. However, I assume, in favour of the extensity objection, that they *are* intrinsically great. Fortunately, proponents of the comprehensive greatness view have an effective response to the extensity objection. This response relies on the distinction between what I call 'relative great-making properties' and 'absolute great-making properties':

Relative great-making property: Property *p* is a relative great-making property if its instantiation would improve the greatness of some beings but would worsen the greatness of some other being.

Absolute great-making property: Property *p* is an absolute great-making property if its instantiation would improve the greatness of some beings and would not worsen the greatness of any other being.

In *Against the Physicists*, Sextus Empiricus makes a similar point in reporting Zeno's exchange with Alexinus:

> [Alexinus says,] 'The poetic is better than the non-poetical and the grammatical than the non-grammatical, and the artistic product of the other arts than the inartistic; but nothing is better than the Universe; therefore the Universe is poetical and grammatical.' But in answer to this counter-argument the Stoics say that, whereas Zeno has chosen what is absolutely better—that is, the rational

than the non-rational, and the intelligent than the non-intelligent and the animate than the non-animate,—Alexinus has not done so; for the poetic is not absolutely better than the non-poetic or the grammatical than the non-grammatical. So that we observe a great difference between the two arguments; for notice how Archilochus who is poetical is not better than the non-poetical Socrates and Aristarchus who is grammatical is not better than the non-grammatical Plato.

(Sextus Empiricus 1936, originally second century, Book I, 108–10, p. 61)

The distinction between relative great-making properties and absolute great-making properties allows us to non-arbitrarily identify great-making properties that God should have. Consider, again, the property of having a healthy heart. This is only a relative great-making property because while its instantiation would improve the greatness of many people, it would worsen the greatness of God by undermining some of His other great-making properties. For example, it would be likely to undermine God's omnipotence and incorporeality.[21] Consider, on the other hand, the property of being, say, omnibenevolent. Assuming that omnibenevolence is a coherent notion, this is an absolute great-making property because its instantiation would improve the greatness of many beings, such as people and other non-divine possible beings, and would not worsen the greatness of any other being, including God Himself.

By appealing to the distinction between relative great-making properties and absolute great-making properties, we can claim as follows: The extensity objection fails because the mere fact that God cannot have all possible great-making properties does not undermine the comprehensive greatness view. The extensity objection needs to show, but fails to show, that God cannot have all *absolute* great-making properties.

The Intensity Objection

The second objection to the comprehensive greatness view is the intensity objection, which is potentially more troublesome than the extensity objection. The intensity objection says that the comprehensive greatness view cannot be sustained because there are powerful arguments that

[21] One might claim that it is impossible for God to have a healthy heart because, necessarily, He lacks any such organ as a heart. That is, the counterfactual 'if God were to have a healthy heart, then . . .' is always counterpossible. To avoid this complication, we can refer to another being that is only contingently omnipotent and contingently incorporeal when we determine whether the property of having a healthy heart is a relative great-making property.

purport to show that God cannot have even such *absolute* great-making properties as omniscience, omnipotence, and omnibenevolence; that is, knowledge, power, and benevolence at the highest degree of intensity, respectively. There are largely three types of such arguments and they coincide with what I introduced in Chapter 1. (For detailed discussion of these arguments, see Chapter 3.)

Type-A arguments purport to show that God cannot have the absolute great-making properties because they are internally incoherent. Type-A arguments include: (i) the paradox of the stone, which purports to show the incoherence of omnipotence by considering the possibility of an omnipotent being's creating a stone that that being itself cannot lift (Mavrodes 1963); (ii) the Cantorian argument, which purports to show the incoherence of omniscience by demonstrating that there is no set of all truths (Grim 1984, 1986, 1990, 1991, 2000, 2007).

The intensity objection, however, cannot rely on Type-A arguments. Suppose, for example, that the paradox of the stone is indeed successful and the concept of omnipotence is internally incoherent. In this case God cannot have the property of being omnipotent. However, this is not necessarily bad news for the comprehensive greatness view, because what the paradox shows is merely that being omnipotent is not an absolute great-making property. If the concept of power itself is internally coherent, it is reasonable to infer from this that something slightly weaker, or less intense, than omnipotence is an absolute great-making property. Perfect being theists can therefore maintain that since omnipotence is an incoherent notion, God needs only to be slightly less powerful than omnipotent. To undermine the comprehensive greatness view here, one has to show that God cannot even have the property of being slightly less powerful than omnipotent. However, one cannot derive such a conclusion from the paradox of the stone itself. The same point applies to all other Type-A arguments. In sum, Type-A arguments do not underpin the intensity objection. There are, however, two more types of arguments against the omni-properties that seem to support the intensity objection more effectively.

Type-B arguments purport to show that God cannot have the absolute great-making properties because they are mutually inconsistent. Type-B arguments include: (i) the argument from God's inability to sin, which purports to show the inconsistency between omnipotence and omnibenevolence by claiming that an omnibenevolent being cannot be omnipotent because it cannot perform a morally wrong action (Morriston 2001a, 2001b; Pike 1969); (ii) the argument from experience, which purports to derive the inconsistency between omniscience and omnipotence by showing that an omnipotent being cannot be omniscient because it fails to know fully what fear and frustration are (Blumenfeld 1978).

Type-C arguments purport to show that God cannot have the absolute great-making properties because the set they comprise is mutually inconsistent with a certain fact about the actual world. Type-C arguments include: (i) the argument from evil, which purports to show the inconsistency between the existence of an omniscient, omnipotent, and omnibenevolent being and the fact that there is evil in the actual world (Mackie 1982); (ii) the argument from divine hiddenness, which purports to show the inconsistency between the existence of an omniscient, omnipotent, and omnibenevolent being and the fact that the existence of such a being is not manifest to everyone in the actual world (Schellenberg 1993).

Unlike Type-A arguments, Type-B and Type-C arguments do seem to support the intensity objection to the comprehensive greatness view. Suppose, for example, that the argument from God's inability to sin is correct in saying that omnipotence and omnibenevolence are indeed mutually inconsistent. In this case, perfect being theists must compromise the intensity of either God's power or God's benevolence to maintain the existence of God as the being than which no greater is metaphysically possible. Let us assume that God's power should be compromised.[22] Here, while God is omnibenevolent, He is not really omnipotent; the intensity of His power extends only as far as it is consistent with omnibenevolence. If so, however, the comprehensive greatness view might be wrong, because being as powerful as possible consistently with omnibenevolence might not be an absolute great-making property. If there could be a non-omnibenevolent being that is fully omnipotent or very nearly fully omnipotent, then the property of being as powerful as possible consistently with omnibenevolence diminishes, rather than maintains or enhances, the greatness of the being in question. Yet, by definition, no absolute great-making property diminishes the greatness of any being. The comprehensive greatness view, therefore, appears to

[22] Bishop (1993) considers this move in response to the argument from evil and Morriston (2001a) does the same in response to the argument from God's inability to sin. See Chapter 4 for further discussion on this point.

fail. It seems impossible for God to have all absolute great-making properties.

The intensity objection is certainly more forceful than the extensity objection but defending it is not as easy as it initially appears. First, for the intensity objection to succeed, at least one of the Type-B and Type-C arguments has to be sound. However, many powerful objections have been proposed to refute these arguments. If one wants to defend the intensity objection, therefore, one has to refute conclusively all existing objections to at least one of the arguments, which is a difficult task. Second, once proponents of the comprehensive greatness view compromise one of the omni-properties, the onus of proof is on opponents of the thesis to show that the property with the compromised intensity is not an absolute great-making property. For example, once proponents of the comprehensive greatness view admit that God is not omnipotent and that He is only as powerful as possible consistently with omnibenevolence, opponents have to show, to advance the intensity objection, that the property of being as powerful as possible consistently with omnibenevolence is not an absolute great-making property. This is not an easy task either, especially, but not only, if a Type-A argument succeeds in showing that the concept of omnipotence is internally incoherent and thus that it is impossible for any being to be omnipotent in the first place. In sum: While the intensity objection is potentially a serious threat to the comprehensive greatness view, whether it ultimately succeeds remains contentious.

Our conclusion at this point is thus the following: (i) The radial model seems promising. It seems right to hold that God is the being than which no greater is metaphysically possible by virtue of occupying the top link in all local chains of being, each of which contains multiple non-divine possible beings. (ii) The comprehensive greatness view seems plausible. God occupies the top link in all local chains of being because for every non-divine possible being *y*, with respect to all absolute great-making properties, God is either extensively equal/superior and intensively superior to *y* or extensively superior to *y*, and the absolute great-making properties that God and *y* share are present in God at the same degree of intensity as in *y*. I believe that the radial model supplemented by the comprehensive greatness view allows us to characterize the perfect being thesis correctly, according to which God is the being than which no greater is metaphysically possible. However, as I have claimed in this section, the intensity objection against the comprehensive greatness view remains controversial. In what follows, therefore, I reconsider the linear model as a backup option for perfect being theists. I argue that despite its infamous reputation, the linear model should be taken seriously because it undercuts the extensity and intensity objections and, also, because what is widely regarded as a knock-down objection to the model is not as compelling as people often think.

2.8 Reconsidering the Linear Model

We have seen in Section 2.7 that the comprehensive greatness view faces two objections: (i) the extensity objection, which purports to show that there are great-making properties that God cannot have; and (ii) the intensity objection, which purports to show that God cannot have all absolute great-making properties at maximum intensity. I argue in this section that perfect being theists should keep the linear model as a backup option because it avoids both of these objections. Moreover, I argue in Section 2.9 that the model might be able to block what is widely regarded as a knock-down objection.

As I explained earlier, the linear model says that God is the being than which no greater is metaphysically possible by virtue of occupying the top link in the great chain of being. This model assumes universal value commensurability, according to which all possible beings are overall value commensurable with one another.

We also saw above that the comprehensive greatness view—which complements the radial model, an alternative to the linear model—is based on the idea that *x* is genuinely superior to *y* only in the following cases:

(2) *x* is extensively equal and intensively superior to *y*.

(5) *x* is extensively superior and intensively superior to *y*.

(11) *x* is extensively superior to *y* and the great-making properties that *x* and *y* share are present in *x* at the same degree of intensity as in *y* (in this case *x* is neither intensively superior, equal, nor inferior to *y*).

We saw, moreover, that the comprehensive greatness view is based on the idea that *x* and *y* are not value commensurable in the following cases:

(10) *x* is neither extensively superior, equal, nor inferior to *y*.

(13) Other cases than (11) and (12) in which *x* is either extensively superior, equal, or inferior to *y* but *x* is neither intensively superior, equal, nor inferior to *y*.

The linear model agrees with the comprehensive greatness view that in cases (2), (5), and (11) x and y are value commensurable and x is genuinely superior to y. However, it disagrees with the comprehensive greatness view that x and y are not value commensurable in cases (10) and (13) by advancing the following view:

The overall greatness view: The intensity and extensity of one's great-making properties can be converted into its overall greatness.

According to the overall greatness view, all possible beings are ultimately extensively equal because we can convert the intensity and extensity of individual great-making properties into the extensity of one great-making property: overall greatness. Once we determine the overall greatnesses of all possible beings, we can show that God is the being than which no greater is metaphysically possible. He occupies the top link in the great chain of being by achieving the combination of the great-making properties that yields the maximum intensity of overall greatness.

In Section 2.5, we addressed an objection to my formulation of intensive superiority, an objection according to which it is implausible to think that all great-making properties play an equal role in determining the overall axiological status of a being. The example we considered was one in which the following are all true: (i) benevolence is significantly more important than other great-making properties; (ii) *A* and *B* do not possess all the same great-making properties; (iii) apart from benevolence, the great-making properties that *A* and *B* have play a relatively negligible role; and (iv) *A* is significantly more benevolent than *B*. In such a case, it appears that, contrary to what my formulation suggests, *A* should be deemed intensively superior to *B*.

In response to this objection, I claimed that my definition excludes it as an instance of intensive superiority. Yet I also acknowledged that there is a certain degree of plausibility in this objection. If we hold the linear model and the overall greatness view, we do not need to face this objection. A is genuinely superior to B because A has a higher intensity of *overall greatness* than B. And, more importantly, if we hold the linear model and the overall greatness view, we do not need to face either the extensity objection or the intensity objection. We can undercut the extensity objection because whether there are some individual great-making properties that God cannot have does not affect the overall greatness view as long as He exhibits the maximum intensity of overall greatness. It also undercuts the intensity objection because whether God can simultaneously have all individual great-making properties at maximum intensity does not affect the model, again, as long as He exhibits the maximum intensity of overall greatness. In sum, the linear model and the overall greatness view are not vulnerable to the extensity and intensity objections because they purport to show that God is overall greater than any other possible being without directly comparing the extensity and intensity of individual great-making properties. If one takes seriously the perfect being thesis, according to which God is the being than which no greater is metaphysically possible, then, as the linear model and the overall greatness view suggest, what matters is only whether God is *overall* greater than any other possible being. Whether He is greater than any other possible being with respect to every great-making property is beside the point.

2.9 A Knock-Down Objection to the Linear Model?

As we saw in Section 2.8, the linear model, along with the overall greatness view, can undercut the extensity and intensity objections. However, as we also saw in Section 2.4, it faces an objection of its own. Morris puts forward the objection by stating, 'It just makes no sense to ask which is of greater intrinsic value, an aardvark or an escalator' (Morris 1984, p. 17). If the linear model and the overall greatness view are correct, we must be able to locate both an aardvark and an escalator on the same chain and compare their greatnesses. Morris thinks that that is clearly impossible. Again, this objection is widely regarded as a knock-down objection to the linear model. In this section, however, I argue that it is not so obvious that the objection ultimately succeeds.

As Katherin A. Rogers says, if we focus only on this specific example, we might be able to refute Morris's claim simply by saying as follows: An aardvark and an escalator *are* value commensurable (Rogers 1993, p. 64). An aardvark is clearly greater than an escalator because, unlike an escalator, it lives a sentient life, which is intrinsically great. As we saw in Section 2.2, this is what many philosophers assume too when they present the great chain of being. However, the point that Morris tries to make is not limited to this specific example. C. D. Broad makes the same point by referring to other examples: (i) the comparison of the greatnesses of a cat and a dog, where the cat can climb trees but the dog cannot, and the dog can track by scent but the cat cannot; (ii) the comparison of the greatnesses of a mathematical genius of very slight musical capacity and a musical genius of very slight mathematical capacity (Broad 1939, pp. 177–8). Broad says that it is impossible to construct the great chain of being because the beings in each pair are not value commensurable. (Neither the ability to track by scent nor the ability to climb trees seems relevant to the perfect being thesis because neither seems to be intrinsically great. However, I assume otherwise in favour of Broad.)

Consider scenario (i). Assume, for the sake of simplicity, that the cat and the dog are genuinely equal with respect to greatness, except that the cat has the property of being able to climb trees and the dog has the property of being able to track by scent. In this scenario, according to Broad, the cat and the dog are not value commensurable. If we set aside all other properties that the cat and dog have, this scenario can be illustrated as in Figure 2.7.

Consider scenario (ii). Assume, for the sake of simplicity, that the mathematical genius and the musical genius are genuinely equal with respect to greatness, except for their mathematical and musical capacities. In this scenario, according to Broad, the mathematical genius and the musical genius are not value commensurable. If we set aside all other properties that the two geniuses have, this scenario can be illustrated as in Figure 2.8.

The scenario of the cat and dog is an instance of (10) above, in which a given being is neither extensively superior, equal, nor inferior to another being. The scenario of the mathematical genius and the musical genius is an instance of (13) above, in which two beings are extensively equal but neither of them is intensively superior, equal, or inferior to the other. The linear model and the overall greatness view reject Broad's objection in saying that two beings are value commensurable even in instances of (10) and (13) because we can convert the intensity and extensity of their great-making properties into the extensity of the overall greatnesses of these beings. So, for example, perhaps the cat is greater than the dog because the calculation of their great-making properties shows that, despite the inability to track by scent, the overall greatness of the cat exceeds the overall greatness of the dog. But how can we motivate such a claim without begging the question against Broad and Morris? One

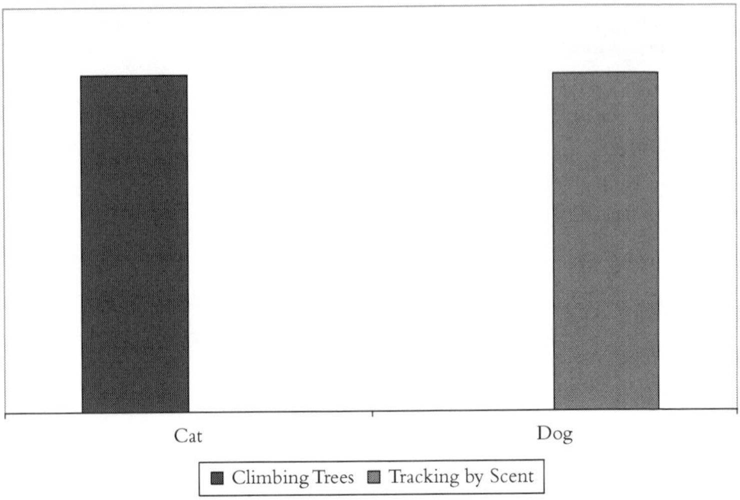

Figure 2.7 Broad's first scenario.

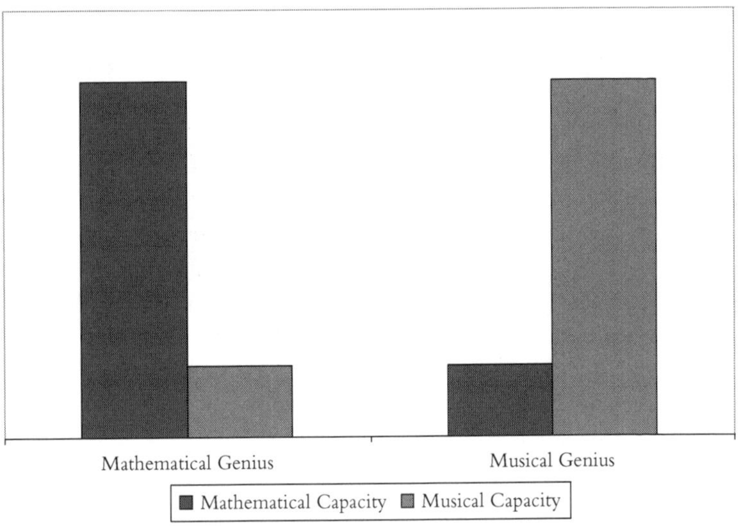

Figure 2.8 Broad's second scenario.

possible route here is to provide an instance of (10) or (13) in which two beings are clearly value commensurable.

Consider, for example, the comparison between the greatnesses of Mother Teresa and Adolf Hitler. Broad (and possibly Morris as well) would say that such a comparison is impossible because this is an instance of (10). That is, there are great-making properties that Mother Teresa has but Hitler does not and *vice versa* (i.e., they are not extensively equal). Even if we assume that Mother Teresa and Hitler do share the exact same great-making properties (i.e., they are extensively equal), it is still impossible to compare their greatnesses because while there are great-making properties that are present in Mother Teresa at a higher degree of intensity than in Hitler (e.g., benevolence), there are also great-making properties that are present in Hitler at a higher degree of intensity than in Mother Teresa (e.g., power). That is, if this is not an instance of (10), it is still an instance of (13). Nevertheless, it does not seem unreasonable to say that Mother Teresa is overall greater than Hitler because she is significantly more benevolent than Hitler. This example seems to suggest that there are instances of (10) and (13) in which two beings are value commensurable.

Broad might respond to this point as follows: The above example shows only that there are *some* instances of (10) and (13) in which two beings are value commensurable. However, to construct the great chain of being, we need to show that in *all* instances of (10) and (13) two beings are value commensurable. Morris tries to show that there are indeed instances of (10) and (13) in which two beings are not value commensurable, again, when he asserts, 'It just makes no sense to ask which is of greater intrinsic value, an aardvark or an escalator'.

The most obvious interpretation of Morris's assertion is that, since an aardvark and an escalator are so fundamentally different, they are not overall value commensurable with each other. However, there seem to be at least two possible interpretations that *are* consistent with the linear model. The first interpretation says that it does not seem to make sense to compare the greatnesses of an aardvark and an escalator (or, taking Broad's example, the greatnesses of the cat and the dog, or the greatnesses of the mathematical genius and the musical genius) because of our intellectual limitations. That is, we cannot confidently compare the greatnesses of these beings because it is extremely difficult for us to list all the great-making properties (or all the worse-making properties) that they have and perform a highly complex calculation of their overall greatnesses. But this means only that an aardvark and an escalator are not value commensurable *to us*, which is just an epistemic, not a metaphysical, problem. The second interpretation of Morris's assertion says that it does not make sense to ask which is greater, an aardvark or an escalator, because, while they are value commensurable, neither is greater than the other. That is, their overall greatnesses are equal. Contrary to what Morris's assertion implies, the great chain of being does not demand that for any pair of beings one has to be greater than the other. It demands only that for any pair of beings one has to be greater than *or equal to* the other. If it is impossible for us to tell which one is greater between an aardvark and an escalator, it might be reasonable to conclude that their overall greatnesses are equal.

2.10 Conclusion

Over the course of this chapter I have discussed two models of the perfect being thesis. First, I defended the radial model according to which God is the being than which no greater is metaphysically possible by virtue of occupying the top link in all local chains of being, each of which contains multiple non-divine possible beings. This model is based on universal divine value commensurability, partial non-divine value commensurability, and universal partial non-divine value commensurability, and supplemented by the comprehensive greatness view. Second, I considered, as a backup option for perfect being theists, the infamous linear model, according to which God is the being than which no greater is metaphysically possible by virtue of occupying the top link in the great chain of being. This model is based on universal value commensurability and supplemented by the overall greatness view. I argued that this model is more attractive than many philosophers have characterized it because it undercuts both the extensity and intensity objections. Moreover, I argued that it might be able to respond to what is widely regarded as a knock-down objection.

The perfect being thesis is a foundation of perfect being theism. I hope our discussion in this chapter helps us achieve a better understanding of this thesis.

PART II

The Maximal God

Refutation of Arguments Against Perfect Being Theism

3

Maximal God and Arguments Against Perfect Being Theism I

3.1 Introduction

We have discussed what perfect being theism is in Part I of this book. At this point we face two crucial questions: (i) Is there a successful argument *against* perfect being theism? (ii) Is there a successful argument *for* perfect being theism? In the rest of this book, I address these questions. Here in Part II, which includes this chapter and Chapter 4, I answer question (i) negatively. I develop a novel, unified response to all arguments against perfect being theism by appealing to what I call the maximal concept of God. In Part III, which includes Chapters 5, 6, and 7, I answer question (ii) positively. Using the maximal concept of God, I propose a new way of constructing the modal ontological argument, which I believe successfully demonstrates the existence of God according to perfect being theism.

As we have seen, the core of perfect being theism is the following thesis:

The perfect being thesis: God is the being than which no greater is metaphysically possible.

As I explained in Chapter 1, most perfect being theists think that the perfect being thesis entails the following:

The omni God thesis: God is an omniscient, omnipotent, and omnibenevolent being.

The idea is that if God is the being than which no greater is metaphysically possible, then He is not merely knowledgeable, powerful, and benevolent; He is knowledgeable, powerful, and benevolent *to the greatest possible extent*. Critics of perfect being theism have spent the better part of nine hundred years trying to undermine this view by introducing numerous distinct arguments against the existence of an omniscient, omnipotent, and omnibenevolent God. In response to these arguments, perfect being theists have attempted to provide objections on a case-by-case basis. That is, they have examined each of the arguments independently and in every case they have maintained that the argument in question fails to refute the existence of an omniscient, omnipotent, and omnibenevolent God. This approach seems, however, to have further complicated the debate over perfect being theism. It has caused endless disputes, with opponents and proponents exchanging objections, counter-objections, counter-counter-objections, and so on. If one's ultimate goal is to defend perfect being theism, it is particularly uneconomical to spend one's time disputing each argument one by one.

My aim in this chapter is quite ambitious. I try to establish a radically new and significantly more economical defence of perfect being theism, a defence that undercuts existing arguments against it *all at once*. The chapter has the following structure. In Section 3.2, I identify key assumptions about, and offer clarifications of, both the perfect being thesis and the omni God thesis. In Section 3.3, I classify existing arguments against perfect being theism into three types. In Section 3.4, I focus on the case-by-case approach to perfect being theism and explain its inefficiency. In Section 3.5, I introduce a new defence of perfect being theism that undercuts all the arguments at once by appealing to the maximal concept of God. In Section 3.6, I examine epistemically possible scenarios in which, consistently with perfect being theism, God is not an omniscient, omnipotent, and omnibenevolent being. I conclude in Section 3.7.

3.2 The Perfect Being Thesis and the Omni God Thesis

Before addressing arguments against perfect being theism, I identify several key assumptions about both the perfect being thesis and the omni God thesis, and address some related issues.

Consider the perfect being thesis first. As I explained in Chapter 1, while this thesis is most commonly attributed to Anselm's *Proslogion*, it is not his invention. Several philosophers and theologians anticipated or defended the thesis prior to Anselm. In earlier work (Nagasawa 2008b, 2011) I called this thesis the 'Anselmian thesis', but here I call it the 'perfect being thesis' primarily to avoid giving the wrong impression that I aim to defend the entirety of Anselm's theological system. It might well be the case that what I argue for here is inconsistent with Anselm's overall view. This is not a problem as the aim of this book is to defend perfect being theism, which is based on the perfect being thesis, rather than Anselm's particular theological system.

Consider now the aforementioned omni God thesis. This thesis specifies three of God's great-making properties: omniscience, omnipotence, and omnibenevolence. The thesis does not imply that these are God's only properties. God must have many trivial or obvious properties such as the property of being self-identical or the property of being greater than human beings. Moreover, virtually all proponents of the omni God thesis agree that God has many other unique great-making properties, which might include independence, timelessness, incorporeality, immutability, omnipresence, and others. Yet, in this chapter, for the sake of simplicity, I focus on omniscience, omnipotence, and omnibenevolence and set aside other great-making properties. It should be noted that most proponents of the omni God thesis hold, in addition, that God is *necessarily* omniscient, *necessarily* omnipotent, and *necessarily* omnibenevolent because a being that has these properties necessarily is greater than a being that has them only contingently or by accident. Being omniscient, omnipotent, and omnibenevolent in all possible worlds makes one greater than being omniscient, omnipotent, and omnibenevolent in only a limited number of possible worlds.[1] Hence, in this chapter, I assume that God's main properties are all necessary, even though I omit the word 'necessary' when I talk about them.

Following the majority of perfect being theists, I assume in addition that the overall greatness of any being corresponds to the greatness of that being's individual great-making properties. This entails that the overall greatness of God, as the being than which no greater is metaphysically possible, also corresponds to His individual great-making

[1] Davis (1983) is among a small number of philosophers who reject the necessity of God's properties. Pike (1969) also considers the idea that God is omnipotent in the actual world but not in all possible worlds.

properties, such as knowledge, power, and benevolence. This assumption links the perfect being thesis to the omni God thesis.

3.3 Three Types of Argument Against Perfect Being Theism

How can one construct an argument against perfect being theism? The most effective way would be to analyse properties that perfect being theists ascribe to God and try to show that there cannot exist a being that has them. Thus, Anthony Kenny writes:

> [A]nyone who is interested in the question of the existence of God has to study first of all the divine attributes; for to say that God exists is to say that there is something that has the divine attributes; and if 'God exists' is to be true, the divine attributes must at least be coherent and jointly compatible. The coherence of the notion of God, as possessor of the traditional divine attributes, is a necessary, though of course not sufficient, condition for God's existence.
>
> (Kenny 1979, p. 5)

The perfect being thesis is not, however, very informative; it says only that God is the being than which no greater is metaphysically possible. It does not specify exactly which individual great-making properties God has. That is why opponents of perfect being theism typically pay more attention to the omni God thesis, which is more informative.

There are literally dozens of existing arguments against perfect being theism and numerous scholarly works have been produced on each of them. Yet it should be acknowledged that all of these arguments target God's great-making properties, and nearly all of them fall into one of three types. We touched on this point briefly in Chapters 1 and 2, but it is important to discuss it in greater detail here. The three types of arguments are as follows.

Type A: Arguments that Purport to Show the Internal Incoherence of God's Individual Properties

Type-A arguments purport to show that at least one of God's properties as specified in the omni God thesis is internally incoherent. From the internal incoherence of at least one of the properties, the opponents of the omni God thesis deduce that God cannot exist. Based on the thesis that the perfect being thesis entails the omni God thesis and the thesis that there cannot exist an omniscient, omnipotent, and omnibenevolent God, the arguments conclude that perfect being theism is false.

The paradox of the stone purports to show the internal incoherence of omnipotence. Either God can create a stone that He cannot lift or He cannot create a stone that He cannot lift. If He can create a stone that He cannot lift, then He is not omnipotent. If He cannot create a stone that He cannot lift, then, again, He is not omnipotent. Hence, the concept of omnipotence is internally incoherent; no one, not even God, can be omnipotent. If God cannot be omnipotent, then the omni God thesis is false, and, accordingly, perfect being theism is false.[2]

Patrick Grim's Cantorian argument purports to show the internal incoherence of omniscience. Suppose, for the sake of *reductio ad absurdum*, that there is a set T of all truths; $P(T)$ is its powerset. There exists then a unique truth corresponding to each element s_i of $P(T)$. For example, to each s_i there corresponds a unique truth as follows:

$$s_i \in P(T)$$

This means that there are at least as many elements in T as there are elements in $P(T)$. This contradicts Cantor's theorem, according to which the powerset of any set contains more elements than the set itself. Hence, the argument says, there is no set of all truths. Given that omniscience corresponds to the set of all truths, the argument concludes that the concept of omniscience is internally incoherent. If this is true, then the omni God thesis is false, and, accordingly, perfect being theism is false.[3]

What I call the 'argument from moral admiration' purports to show the internal incoherence of omnibenevolence. An omnibenevolent being is morally admirable because it is morally perfect. A morally admirable being is a being such that while it has the power to perform a morally wrong action, it chooses to perform a morally right action instead. However, a morally perfect being *cannot* perform a morally wrong action. That is, such a being cannot choose to perform a morally right action. Hence, an omnibenevolent being cannot be morally admirable,

[2] For discussions of the paradox of the stone, see, for example, Frankfurt (1964), Mavrodes (1963), Savage (1967), and Sobel (2004).

[3] For Grim's defence of the Cantorian argument against omniscience, see Grim (1984, 1986, 1990, 1991, 2000, 2007). For discussions of the argument, see also Abbruzzese (1997), Beall (2000), Cartwright (1994), Lembke (2012b), Mar (1993), Plantinga and Grim (1993), and Simmons (1990).

which entails that the concept of omnibenevolence is internally incoherent. Therefore, the omni God thesis is false and, accordingly, perfect being theism is false.[4]

Type B: Arguments that Purport to Show the Mutual Inconsistency Between God's Properties

Suppose that perfect being theists can refute all Type-A arguments and succeed in demonstrating that omniscience, omnipotence, and omnibenevolence are all internally coherent. Does that mean that perfect being theism is thereby secured? The answer is 'Not entirely'. Type-B arguments attempt to show that even if each of God's properties specified in the omni God thesis is internally coherent, at least some of them are mutually inconsistent. If some of God's properties are mutually inconsistent, then, again, the omni God thesis is false and, accordingly, perfect being theism is false.

The so-called 'argument from God's inability to sin' purports to show that omnipotence and omnibenevolence are mutually inconsistent.[5] Suppose that God is omnibenevolent. He should then be unable to perform morally wrong or sinful actions, such as killing hundreds of innocent children. Still, if God is omnipotent, He must be able to perform such an action; after all, even we can do so in principle. Therefore, God cannot be omnipotent and omnibenevolent at the same time. Therefore, the omni God thesis is false and, accordingly, perfect being theism is false.

The 'argument from experience', as I call it, purports to show that omniscience and omnipotence are mutually inconsistent. If God is omniscient, then He must understand fully what fear and frustration are. The argument says, however, that given a modest form of concept empiricism—according to which one must have a relevant experience to grasp any concept fully—an omnipotent God cannot understand fear and frustration fully because He, who is omnipotent, cannot experience what it is like to suffer fear and frustration. Therefore, the argument

[4] The argument from moral admiration is not widely discussed but some variations of it are addressed by Hoffman and Rosenkrantz (2002, pp. 156–9).

[5] For discussions of the argument from God's inability to sin, see, for example, Mawson (2002), Morriston (2001a, 2001b, 2003), and Pike (1969).

concludes, the omni God thesis is false and, accordingly, perfect being theism is also false.[6]

The argument from experience can be formulated as an argument against the mutual consistency of omniscience and omnibenevolence as well. If God is omniscient, then He must understand fully what evil is. The argument says, however, that given a modest form of concept empiricism, an omnibenevolent God cannot understand evil fully because He, who is omnibenevolent, cannot experience what it is like to be evil. Therefore, the argument concludes, the omni God thesis is false and, accordingly, perfect being theism is also false.[7]

Type C: Arguments that Purport to Show the Mutual Inconsistency Between the Set of God's Properties and a Certain Fact About the Actual World

Suppose that theists can refute all Type-A and Type-B arguments and thereby demonstrate that omniscience, omnipotence, and omnibenevolence are all internally coherent and mutually consistent. Does that mean that perfect being theism is thereby secured? The answer is, again, 'Not entirely'. Type-C arguments purport to show that, even if God's properties as specified in the omni God thesis are internally coherent and mutually consistent, the set of the omni-properties is mutually inconsistent with a certain fact about the actual world. If that is true, then, again, the omni God thesis is false and perfect being theism is also false.[8]

The argument from evil, which is probably *the* most prominent argument against the existence of God, purports to show the mutual inconsistency between the set of the omni-properties and the fact that

[6] For defences of the argument from experience and its variants, see, for example, Blumenfeld (1978), Bringsjord (1989), Martin (1974, 1990, 2000), and Lachs (1963a, 1963b). For discussions of these arguments, see Alter (2002), Beaty and Taliaferro (1990), Nagasawa (2008a), and Prior (1963).

[7] Alter (2002) and Nagasawa (2008a) discuss the specific version of the argument from experience that focuses on God's knowledge of evil.

[8] By the term the 'set of the omni-properties' I mean the possession of the omni-properties by a single being, such as God. It might well be the case that the fact about the actual world in question is not mutually inconsistent with the existence of, say, three distinct beings which are omniscient (but not omnipotent or omnibenevolent), omnipotent (but not omniscient or omnibenevolent), and omnibenevolent (but not omniscient or omnipotent), respectively. Yet, according to the problem of evil, the fact is mutually inconsistent with the existence of a single being that is simultaneously omniscient, omnipotent, and omnibenevolent.

there is evil in the actual world.[9] We can observe many forms of evil, such as wars, murders, and rapes, in the actual world. If God is omniscient, then He must know how to eliminate them from the actual world. If God is omnipotent, then He must be able to eliminate them from the actual world. If He is omnibenevolent, then He must be willing to eliminate them from the actual world. Therefore, the argument concludes, given that there is evil in the actual world, an omniscient, omnipotent, and omnibenevolent God does not exist and, accordingly, perfect being theism is false.[10]

The argument from evil is often presented as an objection to theism in general, but that is not correct. The argument is directed specifically against a version of theism which accepts the omni God thesis, or theses that are sufficiently similar to it. J. L. Mackie, one of the most well-known proponents of the argument from evil, makes this point by saying, 'The problem of evil, in the sense in which I shall be using the phrase, is a problem only for someone who believes that there is a God who is both omnipotent and wholly good' (Mackie 1955, p. 200). Similarly, Michael Martin, another opponent of perfect being theism, writes, '[T]he problem of evil presumably does not show that God does not exist when "God" refers to some being that is either not omnipotent or not completely benevolent' (Martin 1974, p. 232).

The argument from divine hiddenness purports to show the mutual inconsistency between the set of the omni-properties and the fact that God is hidden in the actual world. It seems obvious that God is hidden from nonculpable nonbelievers. Even though they would be willing to embrace theistic belief if God were to reveal Himself to them, He simply does not do it. If God is omniscient, then He must know how to reveal Himself to them. If God is omnipotent, then He must be able to reveal Himself to them. If God is omnibenevolent, then He must be willing to

[9] According to Daniel Hill, more than 3,600 articles and books were written on the argument from evil between 1960 and the late 1990s (Hill 1998, p. 32).

[10] For critical assessments of the argument from evil, see, for example, Adams and Adams (1990), Mackie (1982), Meister and Dew (2013), Peterson (1992), Plantinga (1974a), and Rea (2015). There are generally two versions of the argument from evil: the logical version and the evidential version. I set aside the evidential version because my focus here is on deductive arguments against perfect being theism. It is often assumed that the logical version of the argument from evil has been successfully refuted by Plantinga's free defence, but that is far from obvious. See Almeida (2012), Oppy (2006), and Sobel (2004) for recent attempts to revive the logical version.

reveal Himself to them (so He can have a personal relationship with them). Therefore, the argument concludes, given divine hiddenness in the actual world, an omniscient, omnipotent, and omnibenevolent God does not exist and, accordingly, perfect being theism is false. While the argument from evil and the argument from divine hiddenness bear a certain resemblance to one another, they can be presented as distinct arguments. For example, in a world in which God is not hidden but there is evil, the argument from evil stands while the argument from divine hiddenness does not. Similarly, in a world in which God is hidden but there is no evil, the argument from divine hiddenness stands even though the argument from evil does not.[11]

What I call the 'argument from the imperfection of the actual world' purports to show the mutual inconsistency between the set of the omni-properties and the fact that the actual world is not the best possible world.[12] We can easily conceive of a world that is better than the actual world. For example, we can conceive of a world that is identical to the actual world except that a certain minor mishap in the actual world does not take place in that world. This shows that the actual world is not the best possible world. If God is omniscient, then He must know how to create the best possible world. If God is omnipotent, then He must be able to create the best possible world. If He is omnibenevolent, then He must be willing to create the best possible world. Therefore, the argument concludes, given that the actual world is not the best possible world, an omniscient, omnipotent, and omnibenevolent God does not exist and, accordingly, perfect being theism is false.[13] Notice that this argument is distinct from the argument from evil because it is not necessarily concerned with the existence of evil in the actual world. In fact, the argument would stand even if the actual world had been completely free from evil, so long as the actual world was not the best possible world.

[11] For critical assessments of the argument from divine hiddenness, see, for example, Green and Stump (2016), Howard-Snyder and Moser (2002), Rea (2015), and Schellenberg (1993, 2015). For the relationship between the argument from divine hiddenness and the argument from evil, see Nagasawa (2016b), Schellenberg (2009, 2010), and van Inwagen (2002).

[12] Leibniz famously bites the bullet and contends that, assuming that God is the creator of the world and is also the greatest possible being, the actual world *is* the best possible world. However, few philosophers agree with him. See Leibniz (1985, originally 1710).

[13] For critical assessments of the argument from the imperfection of the actual world, see, for example, Adams (1972), Kraay (2008), Langtry (2008), and Rowe (2004).

3.4 The Case-by-Case Approach to Arguments Against Perfect Being Theism

As I noted in Section 3.1, perfect being theists, including Anselm himself, have for centuries responded to Type-A, Type-B, and Type-C arguments on a case-by-case basis.[14] That is, they have tried to analyse each of the arguments independently and explain exactly how it fails. For example, in response to the paradox of the stone, some have tried to show that the paradox can be blocked by limiting the scope of our ordinary definition of omnipotence (Mavrodes 1963), while others have tried to show that the paradox is based on a misinterpretation of the second horn of the dilemma (Savage 1967). In response to Grim's argument against omniscience, some have maintained that the argument does not work if we adopt an alternative set theory (Mar 1993), while others have claimed that the argument is self-defeating (Abbruzzese 1997). In response to the argument from moral admiration, some have tried to show that the ordinary sense of moral admirableness, which applies to people, who have to overcome their immoral impulses, does not apply to God, who can effortlessly and unfailingly intend to perform the morally right action in every situation (Hoffman and Rosenkrantz 2002), while others have claimed that moral perfection should be understood as a contingent, rather than necessary, property of God (Guleserian 1985). In response to the argument from God's inability to sin, some have tried to show that the inability to perform morally wrong actions is not a limit on power (Anselm 1965, originally 1077–8), while others have claimed that the argument fails once the distinction between strong actualization and weak actualization is introduced (Flint and Freddoso 1983). In response to the argument from experience, some have tried to show that the argument is based on an unreasonably narrow understanding of God's epistemic capability (Alter 2002; Zagzebski 2013), while others have maintained that the version of concept empiricism on which the argument relies is vulnerable to counterexamples (Nagasawa 2008a).

In response to the argument from evil, some have tried to show that the argument fails once we acknowledge that God had to create free humans that are capable of performing both morally right actions and morally wrong actions (Plantinga 1974a), while others have claimed that the

[14] For Anselm's case-by-case approach see Leftow (2004), pp. 150–3.

argument is unsuccessful once we acknowledge our epistemic limitations with respect to knowing God's purposes (Wykstra 1984). In response to the argument from divine hiddenness, some have tried to show that the argument overlooks God's purpose in maintaining an epistemic distance between Himself and humans to allow humans to cultivate their spirituality spontaneously (Hick 1966), while others have claimed that the argument is based on cognitive idolatry, which posits an unreasonable demand on God (Moser 2002). In response to the argument from the imperfection of the actual world, some have tried to show that God's grace entails that He does not have to create the best possible world (Adams 1972), while others have claimed that the argument rests on the incorrect assumption that this world (or the universe) is the only one that God has created (Kraay 2010). This is only a very brief summary of a few important moves in the vast literature.

The most obvious problem with the case-by-case approach is that, whether or not the individual responses to these arguments ultimately succeed, it is not very efficient as a defence of perfect being theism. The history of the debate over the cogency of perfect being theism has been an endless exchange of arguments and counterarguments between opponents and proponents of the view. A paradigm example can be found in the debate over the coherence of omnipotence. When opponents of perfect being theism introduce a Type-A argument against the coherence of omnipotence (or a Type-B argument against the consistency of omnipotence with another great-making property), proponents typically respond to it by introducing a revised definition of omnipotence that they believe renders the argument irrelevant. Opponents then construct a new argument that undermines even the revised definition, and proponents then respond to it by providing a further revision of the revised definition of omnipotence, and so forth. As the debate advances, the definition becomes more and more complex and both proponents and opponents of perfect being theism tend to move away from the original aim of the debate, namely to evaluate the cogency of perfect being theism.[15] Observing this situation, Wes Morriston remarks as follows:

> In recent years, definitions of omnipotence have become more and more complicated. Indeed, they frequently employ so much technical apparatus and

[15] See Chapter 1 for examples of highly complex definitions of omnipotence and omniscience.

contain so many subordinate clauses and qualifications, that it is natural to wonder whether they have much to do with what an ordinary person might mean by saying that God is all-powerful. (Morriston 2002, p. 358)

I do not wish to say that the case-by-case approach fails. It might well be the case that it eventually yields successful individual objections to all Type-A, Type-B, and Type-C arguments against perfect being theism. I also do not wish to claim that the case-by-case approach is *always* inefficient. In some cases, especially when an argument is clearly fallacious, it is efficient to provide a specific objection to eliminate the argument straight away. However, if one's ultimate goal is to defend perfect being theism, the approach is not economical. Instead of settling the debate, the approach only invites a seemingly endless cycle of objections and counter-objections. It also does not preclude critics from developing further arguments against perfect being theism.

In what follows, I try to develop a radically new and more economical response to perfect being theism, one that aims to eliminate the force of the existing arguments against it *all at once* and block any further arguments. In the course of defending the new response, I propose what I call the 'maximal God thesis', according to which God is the being that has the maximal consistent set of knowledge, power, and benevolence. I suggest that this thesis should replace the omni God thesis, according to which God is an omniscient, omnipotent, and omnibenevolent being.

3.5 The Maximal God Thesis

In Section 3.4, I extracted the general structures of many arguments against perfect being theism and classified them into three types. To establish a new response that undercuts all types of arguments at once, it would be necessary to extract an even more general structure that is common to these arguments. I submit that all the arguments among the three types share the following basic structure:

(1b) If perfect being theism is true, then the perfect being thesis is true.
(2b) If the perfect being thesis is true, then the omni God thesis is true.
(3b) If the omni God thesis is true, then God is an omniscient, omnipotent, and omnibenevolent being.
(4b) There cannot be an omniscient, omnipotent, and omnibenevolent being.

(5b) Therefore, the omni God thesis is false.
(6b) Therefore, the perfect being thesis is false.
(7b) Therefore, perfect being theism is false.

The argument is formally valid and the first three premises appear innocuous. Premise (1b) expresses merely the commitment of perfect being theism to the perfect being thesis. Premise (2b) asserts the common assumption that the perfect being thesis entails the omni God thesis. Premise (3b) imparts the content of the omni God thesis. Thus, premise (4b) appears to be the only contentious premise in this formulation. We have seen a range of arguments advanced in the effort to establish premise (4b). Type-A arguments try to establish premise (4b) by showing that at least one member of the property set comprising omniscience, omnipotence, and omnibenevolence is internally incoherent. Type-B arguments try to establish premise (4b) by showing that some of these properties are mutually inconsistent. Type-C arguments try to establish premise (4b) by showing that the property set is mutually inconsistent with a certain fact about the actual world. We have also seen that perfect being theists have tried to defend their view by showing that each of these arguments fails to establish premise (4b). This means that both proponents and opponents in these disputes have concentrated their efforts solely on the cogency of premise (4b). What I think is more crucial to consider is, however, whether the arguments against perfect being theism really go through if premise (4b) *is* true. I contend that that is far from obvious, for there is no obvious reason to accept premise (2b).

As I have noted, premise (2b) is based on the assumption that the perfect being thesis entails the omni God thesis. This assumption is widely accepted among philosophers of religion. For instance, Daniel J. Hill defends the view that 'possession of [the property of being maximally great] implies possession of the traditional properties of a divine being: omnipotence, omniscience, omnipresence, perfect goodness, eternity, maximal beauty, as well as possession of some properties that divine beings share with many other beings' (Hill 2005, p. 246). To take another example, Thomas V. Morris writes, 'Standardly employed, perfect being theology issues in a conception of God as a necessarily existent being who has such properties as omnipotence, omniscience, perfect goodness, eternity, and aseity as essential properties' (Morris 1987b, p. 25). He also writes, '[I]t is a commitment of many Anselmians that the divine perfections are all necessarily coexemplified' (Morris 1986, p. 83).

The claim that the perfect being thesis entails the omni God thesis seems, however, ungrounded. First, as far as I know, there is no compelling philosophical argument that supports the entailment. Both proponents and opponents of perfect being theism have generally taken it for granted without troubling to argue for it. Second, the entailment lacks support from the religious canon. The Bible talks about God's knowledge, power, and benevolence as though God has these properties to a significant extent, but nowhere does it say explicitly that God is omniscient, omnipotent, and omnibenevolent in a philosophically strict sense. For example, the Bible says, concerning God's epistemic capacity, '[God's] understanding has no limit' (Psalm 147:5) and 'If our hearts condemn us, we know that God is greater than our hearts, and he knows everything' (1 John 3:20). But it would be uncharitable to construe these verses as making the scholarly claim that God's epistemic capacity corresponds exactly to whatever philosophers define as omniscience. Similarly, the Bible says, concerning God's power, 'Great is our Lord and mighty in power' (Psalm 147:5) and 'Jesus looked at them and said, "With man this is impossible, but with God all things are possible"' (Matthew 19:26). The Bible also says, concerning God's moral character, 'The Lord is righteous in all his ways and faithful in all he does' (Psalm 145:17) and 'No one who is born of God will continue to sin, because God's seed remains in them; they cannot go on sinning, because they have been born of God' (1 John 3:9). But, again, it would be uncharitable to construe these verses as making the scholarly claim that God's power and moral character correspond exactly to whatever philosophers define as omnipotence and omnibenevolence.

My new response to the arguments against perfect being theism is to replace the omni God thesis with the following thesis:

The Maximal God thesis: God is the being that has the maximal consistent set of knowledge, power, and benevolence.

The maximal God thesis suggests that, while God is certainly very knowledgeable, very powerful, and very benevolent, He might or might not be omniscient, omnipotent, and omnibenevolent. Given the maximal God thesis, we can say that the arguments against perfect being theism that we have seen all fail at premise (2b) because while the perfect being thesis does entail the maximal God thesis, it has not been shown that it entails the omni God thesis as well. Although the maximal God thesis is consistent with the omni God thesis, it does not imply that God is unquestionably an omniscient, omnipotent, and omnibenevolent being. I believe that the crucial mistake perfect being theists make is that they commonly commit themselves to a claim that is unnecessarily specific: God is the being than which no greater is metaphysically possible and, *moreover*, God is an omniscient, omnipotent, and omnibenevolent being. The second part of this claim, which corresponds to the omni God thesis, invites critics to attack perfect being theism through Type-A, Type-B, and Type-C arguments. If perfect being theists do not make the unnecessary commitment to the omni God thesis, they do not need to face these arguments in the first place. Given that there is no argument for the claim that the perfect being thesis entails the omni God thesis rather than the maximal God thesis, perfect being theists can conclude that Type-A, Type-B, and Type-C arguments fail to refute perfect being theism, or at least that there is no reason to think that the arguments can be used to refute perfect being theism. If the arguments show anything at all, they show merely that God according to perfect being theism, i.e. the being than which no greater is metaphysically possible, is not an omniscient, omnipotent, and omnibenevolent being, which is, given the maximal God thesis, consistent with perfect being theism. This new response is applicable to all the arguments against perfect being theism that we have seen.

It is important to emphasize that I am not *rejecting* the omni God thesis here. What I am saying is that perfect being theists do not need to worry about the cogency of the omni God thesis. They can maintain perfect being theism by holding the maximal God thesis, which is more modest than the omni God thesis. The omni God thesis might turn out to be true or it might turn out to be false. Either way, by holding the maximal God thesis, perfect being theists can retain their view that God, as the being than which no greater is metaphysically possible, exists. I cannot emphasize this point strongly enough because my view is often misinterpreted. I do not claim that God is definitely omniscient, omnipotent, and omnibenevolent, but, equally, I do not claim that God is definitely *not* omniscient, omnipotent, and omnibenevolent. I claim that this is an open question, on which the cogency of perfect being theism does not hinge.

At this point, opponents of perfect being theism might say that perfect being theists are not justified in replacing the omni God thesis with the maximal God thesis, because it is analytically true that the perfect being thesis entails the omni God thesis. That is, the being than which no greater is metaphysically possible *is*, by definition, an omniscient, omnipotent, and omnibenevolent being. In what follows, I argue that this is far from obvious, because there are many epistemically possible scenarios in which, while the perfect being thesis and the maximal God thesis are true, the omni God thesis is false. Proponents of the arguments against perfect being theism must reject these scenarios to defend their arguments.

3.6 Maximal God and Epistemically Possible Scenarios

Let us compare the greatness of God with the greatness of *X*, the second greatest possible being. In this comparison we focus only on their three main great-making properties, knowledge, power, and benevolence, to avoid unnecessary complications.

In Chapter 2, we saw that, according to the radial model, *x* is genuinely superior to *y* in the following three cases:

(2) *x* is extensively equal and intensively superior to *y*.

(5) *x* is extensively superior and intensively superior to *y*.

(11) *x* is extensively superior to *y* and the great-making properties that *x* and *y* share are present in *x* at the same degree of intensity as in *y* (in this case *x* is neither intensively superior, equal, nor inferior to *y*).

We can set aside cases (5) and (11) because we assume here that God and *X* are extensively equal; they both have three great-making properties—knowledge, power, and benevolence—and we ignore other properties they have for the sake of simplicity. We assume here that God and *X* are only intensively unequal.

By the term 'epistemically possible scenarios' I mean scenarios such that it is not immediately obvious that they are metaphysically impossible, even though they might in fact be metaphysically impossible. I use the phrase 'epistemically possible' instead of 'conceivable' here because some philosophers claim that conceivability entails metaphysical possibility.[16] I also use the word 'scenario' instead of 'world' because claims about a specific scenario could have implications that bear on more than one world.

Consider, for example, the following hypothesis: an arbitrary angle can be divided into three equal angles using only a compass and an unmarked straightedge. This hypothesis is necessarily false (and hence it is metaphysically impossible for it to be true), but it is still epistemically possible at least for many of us; that is why mathematicians disputed the hypothesis for more than 2,000 years, until 1837 when Pierre Laurent Wantzel proved its falsity. Therefore, there are epistemically possible scenarios in which an arbitrary angle can be divided into three equal angles using only a compass and an unmarked straightedge.

Now consider various epistemically possible scenarios in which the perfect being thesis is true. In the first set of such scenarios, God is (i) omniscient, omnipotent, and omnibenevolent, (ii) intensively superior to X, the second greatest possible being, with respect to at least one of knowledge, power, and benevolence, and (iii) at least intensively equal to X with respect to the remaining properties. In these scenarios, God is the greatest possible being because He is genuinely superior to X. One of the scenarios in this set, S_1, is illustrated in Figure 3.1.

Proponents of the Type-A, Type-B, and Type-C arguments against perfect being theism assume that if perfect being theism is true, then a scenario comparable to S_1 must be not only epistemically possible but also actual. That is, they assume that perfect being theists are committed to the idea that there is a being, God, that is omniscient, omnipotent, and omnibenevolent and, moreover, that there is no other possible being that is intensively equal or superior to God.[17] Proponents of the argument assume that if they establish that there cannot be an omniscient, omnipotent, and omnibenevolent God, perfect being theism is false.

Yet scenarios like S_1 are not the only epistemically possible scenarios in which the perfect being thesis is true. That is, scenarios such as S_1 are not the only epistemically possible scenarios in which God and X jointly

[16] See, for example, Chalmers (1996) and Gendler and Hawthorne (2002).

[17] We talk only about *intensive* equality and superiority here because, again, we focus on scenarios in which God and X have knowledge, power, and benevolence while setting aside other properties they have or lack.

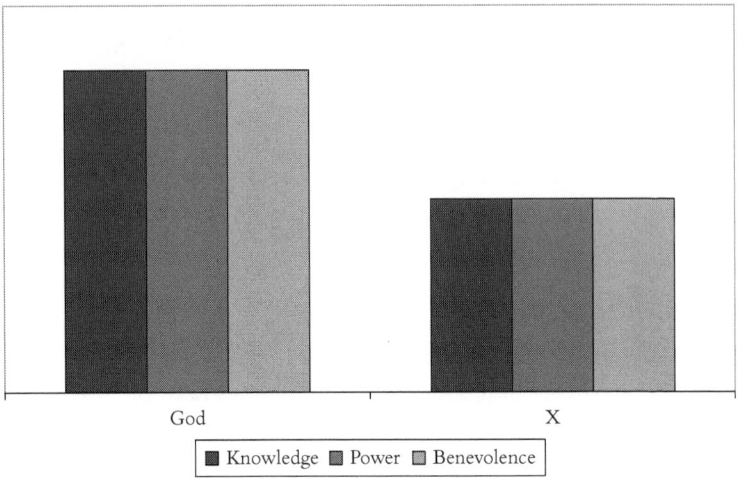

Figure 3.1 Scenario S_1.

satisfy (5), i.e. in which God is extensively superior and intensively superior to *X*. Consider another set of scenarios in which God is (i) less than omniscient, omnipotent, and/or omnibenevolent, (ii) intensively superior to *X* with respect to at least one of knowledge, power, and benevolence, and (iii) at least intensively equal to *X* with respect to the remaining properties. In this scenario too, God and *X* jointly satisfy (5).

In one of the scenarios in this set, S_2, shown in Figure 3.2, God is very knowledgeable but not quite omniscient because, say, there is one true proposition that it is metaphysically impossible for Him to know. (I focus on knowledge only as an example; my claims apply equally to power and benevolence.) Still, *X* is even less knowledgeable than God because there are two propositions that it is impossible for *X* to know. (Here I assume what I call the 'quantitative account of knowledgeableness', according to which the more propositions one knows, the more knowledgeable one is. Some might disagree with this account and advance the qualitative account instead. According to the qualitative account, for example, a being that possesses only one proposition *p* could be more knowledgeable than another being that possesses two propositions *q* and *r* if *p* is, in a relevant sense, more valuable to know than the sum of *q* and *r*. I set aside the qualitative account here. It should be noted, however, that my defence of perfect being theism can be

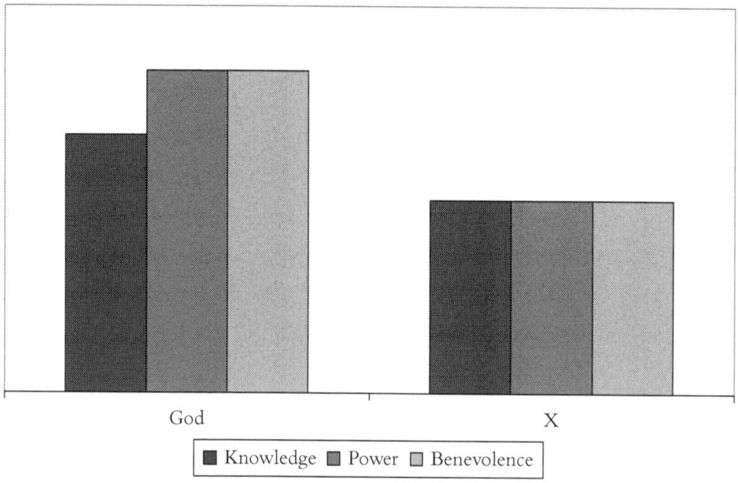

Figure 3.2 Scenario S_2.

formulated in accordance with the qualitative account as well.) In S_2, while the perfect being thesis is true, the omni God thesis is *false*.

There are two versions of S_2. In the first version, call it S_{2A}, the true proposition that God cannot know is something that no being can possibly know. In the second version, call it S_{2B}, the true proposition in question is something that some being, say, *X*, can know even though God cannot. However, in both S_{2A} and S_{2B} God is still more knowledgeable than *X* and every other being. (It seems coherent to say that God is more knowledgeable than *X* even if He does not know a certain proposition that *X* knows because, in general, the statement that *A* is more knowledgeable than *B* does not entail that *A* knows *everything* that *B* knows. For example, the claim that Jessica is more knowledgeable than her small child John does not exclude the possibility that John knows some proposition that Jessica does not know, e.g. that his teacher gave him two assignments today. Parallel reasoning seems to apply to power and benevolence.) In S_{2B} any possible being that knows the proposition in question is less knowledgeable than God. Thus, if God were to change the scope of His knowledge so that He can know the proposition in question, then His overall knowledge would diminish and He would cease to be the most knowledgeable being and, accordingly, the being than which no greater is metaphysically possible.[18] Since these scenarios are epistemically possible, critics who defend premise (2b) of the arguments against perfect being theism—i.e. if the perfect being thesis is true, then the omni God thesis is true—must show them to be metaphysically impossible. Until then, perfect being theists are justified in rejecting (2b) by saying that it is not obvious that God is an omniscient, omnipotent, and omnibenevolent being.

One might claim at this point that God in S_{2A} and S_{2B} is not the being than which no greater is metaphysically possible because it *is* possible to think of a greater being, namely an omnipotent, omnibenevolent being whose knowledge extends further than the limit of God's knowledge as illustrated in Figure 3.2. This objection fails, however, to account for the relevant notion of possibility. What this objection really says is that God *in* S_{2A} and S_{2B} is not the being than which no greater is metaphysically possible *in* S_{2A} and S_{2B}, because the scope of His knowledge in these scenarios is not the greatest possible *in another epistemically possible scenario*, for instance S_1 (rather than in S_{2A} and S_{2B}). In S_1 God's knowledge extends up to omniscience, because in S_1 we assume that it is possible for a being to be omniscient. However, in S_{2A} and S_{2B} we assume that no being can be omniscient. It is illegitimate to complain that God in S_{2A} and S_{2B}, for which it is stipulated that the extent of acquirable knowledge does not reach omniscience, is not maximally knowledgeable, by referring to S_1, for which it is stipulated that the extent of acquirable knowledge does reach omniscience, unless it is shown that S_{2A} and S_{2B} are metaphysically impossible.

Here is another interesting observation. In S_{2A} and S_{2B}, it is metaphysically impossible for any being to be omniscient, omnipotent, and omnibenevolent simultaneously. Hence, to demand that God be an omniscient, omnipotent, and omnibenevolent being as well as the being than which no greater is metaphysically possible in these scenarios means to demand that God be non-existent. However, this goes against the spirit of perfect being theism because, according to perfect being theism, existence (or necessary existence) is regarded as one of the most

[18] This is only an illustrative example. In reality, few perfect being theists would think that God can change the scope of His knowledge because they believe that it is necessarily impossible for God to diminish His knowledge.

essential properties or features of the being than which no greater is metaphysically possible.

The final set of epistemically possible scenarios is perhaps more radical than the second set. In scenarios in this set God is (i) slightly less than omniscient, omnipotent, and omnibenevolent, (ii) intensively inferior to *X* with respect to at least one of knowledge, power, and benevolence, (iii) at least intensively equal to *X* with respect to the remaining properties, and (iv) greater than *X* overall. As we saw in Chapter 2, God is greater than *X* overall in this scenario if the overall greatness view, i.e. the view that the intensity and extensity of one's great-making properties can be converted into its overall greatness, is assumed. God is not greater than *X* overall if we hold the comprehensive greatness view, which holds the following: God occupies the top link in all local chains of being because, for every non-divine possible being *y*, God is either: (i) intensively superior to *y* or (ii) extensively superior to *y*, and the great-making properties that God and *y* share are present in God at the same degree of intensity as in *y*.

In one of the scenarios in this set, S_3, shown in Figure 3.3, God is less knowledgeable than *X*. Still, assuming the overall greatness view, He is, overall, greater than *X* as well as every other possible being. God remains, in S_3, the being than which no greater is metaphysically possible because the limit on His knowledge is compensated for by His other great-making properties. In S_3, assuming that the overall greatness view is correct, again, while the perfect being thesis is true, the omni God thesis is *false*.

We have considered four epistemically possible scenarios. In S_1, God is omniscient, omnipotent, and omnibenevolent; He is, overall, greater than any other possible being and greater than any other possible being with respect to each of knowledge, power, and benevolence. In this scenario, both the perfect being thesis and the omni God thesis are true. However, in three other scenarios, while the perfect being thesis is true, the omni God thesis is false. More specifically, in S_{2A} and S_{2B}, God is not omniscient, omnipotent, and omnibenevolent but He is still, overall, greater than any other possible being and greater than any other possible being with respect to each of knowledge, power, and benevolence. In S_3, God is not omniscient, omnipotent, and omnibenevolent and not as great as *X* with respect to knowledge, but He is still, overall, greater than any other possible being.

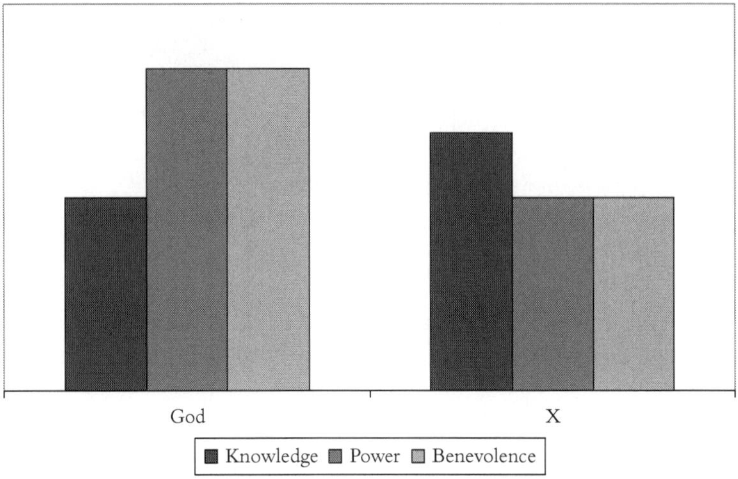

Figure 3.3 Scenario S_3.

Given the epistemic possibilities pertaining to scenarios such as S_{2A}, S_{2B}, and S_3, which are consistent with the perfect being thesis but inconsistent with the omni God thesis, perfect being theists can leave open the possibility that God, as the being than which no greater is metaphysically possible, is not an omniscient, omnipotent, and omnibenevolent being. They are therefore justified in endorsing the maximal God thesis instead of the omni God thesis and in questioning premise (2b) of the basic formulation of the arguments against perfect being theism, a premise according to which if the perfect being thesis is true, then the omni God thesis is true. They do not necessarily need to say that premise (2b) is false; they can say that there is no reason to accept (2b) because it has not been shown to be true; the onus of proof is on proponents of the arguments to establish the truth of the premise.

Let us apply what we have seen to examples of Type-A, Type-B, and Type-C arguments. Consider, for example, the paradox of the stone, a Type-A argument. What the paradox essentially purports to show is that no being can be omnipotent. In response to it, perfect being theists can simply maintain, by appealing to the perfect being thesis and the maximal God thesis, that *if* the paradox is cogent at all, it teaches us only that God, as the being than which no greater is metaphysically possible, is not an omnipotent being. This is fine for them because it has not been shown

that God must be omnipotent. It would be problematic if the paradox showed that God is not very powerful but it does not even pretend to show that.

Consider, to take another example, the argument from God's inability to sin, a Type-B argument. The argument essentially purports to show that no being can be omnipotent and omnibenevolent simultaneously. In response to it, perfect being theists can simply maintain, by appealing to the perfect being thesis and the maximal God thesis, that *if* the argument is cogent at all, it teaches us only that God, as the being than which no greater is metaphysically possible, is not a being that is simultaneously omnipotent and omnibenevolent. This is fine for them because it has not been shown that God *must* be a being that is simultaneously omnipotent and omnibenevolent. It would be problematic if the argument showed that God is not very powerful or not very benevolent but it does not even pretend to show that.

Consider, finally, the argument from evil, a Type-C argument. What the argument essentially purports to show is that, given the existence of evil in the actual world, no being can be simultaneously omniscient, omnipotent, and omnibenevolent. In response to it, perfect being theists can simply maintain, by appealing to the perfect being thesis and the maximal God thesis, that *if* the argument is cogent at all, it teaches us only that God, as the being than which no greater is metaphysically possible, is not a being that is simultaneously omniscient, omnipotent, and omnipotent. This is fine for them because it has not been shown that God must be simultaneously omniscient, omnipotent, and omnibenevolent. It would be problematic if the argument showed that God is not very powerful, not very knowledgeable, or not very benevolent but it does not even pretend to show that.

Hence, for critics to refute perfect being theism, it is not sufficient for them to show, as they ordinarily do, that there cannot be an omniscient, omnipotent, and omnibenevolent being. They need to show further that perfect being theists must be committed to the claim that God is an omniscient, omnipotent, and omnibenevolent being or that the perfect being thesis entails the omni God thesis. In other words, they need to show that scenarios such as S_{2A}, S_{2B}, and S_3 are metaphysically impossible. To show that S_3 is metaphysically impossible, it needs to be shown minimally that God, as the being than which no greater is metaphysically possible, has to be greater than any other possible being with respect to each of knowledge, power, and benevolence. To show that S_{2A} and S_{2B} are metaphysically impossible, it needs to be shown not only that God has to be greater than any other possible being with respect to each of knowledge, power, and benevolence, but also that He has to be omniscient, omnipotent, and omnibenevolent. These are not easy tasks.

3.7 Conclusion

We have seen in this chapter that perfect being theists can undercut nearly all Type-A, Type-B, and Type-C arguments against perfect being theism by replacing the omni God thesis with the maximal God thesis. I have not proved that such scenarios as S_{2A}, S_{2B}, and S_3 *are* metaphysically possible. Thus, again, I do not claim here that if the perfect being thesis is true, the omni God thesis is false. In other words, I do not maintain that God is definitely not an omni-being. My claim is a much more modest one: perfect being theists should be neutral with respect to the truth or falsity of the omni God thesis. Perhaps the omni God thesis is true but perhaps not. This is fine for perfect being theists because the truth or falsity of this particular thesis is not crucial to the cogency of perfect being theism. It is essential for perfect being theists to hold that the perfect being thesis and the maximal God thesis are true, but whether the omni God thesis is true is a further issue on which the truth or falsity of perfect being theism does not hinge. The core of perfect being theism is the perfect being thesis but, perplexingly enough, perfect being theists and their critics have been preoccupied for centuries with the omni God thesis, which is not directly relevant to the tenability of perfect being theism.

I believe that what I have defended in this chapter is the most economical and efficient response to nearly all arguments against perfect being theism. In Chapter 4, I try to strengthen my approach by addressing numerous objections to it.

4

Maximal God and Arguments Against Perfect Being Theism II

4.1 Introduction

In Chapter 3, I developed a radically new defence of perfect being theism through the maximal concept of God. I argued that we can undercut nearly all Type-A, Type-B, and Type-C arguments against perfect being theism by appealing to the maximal God thesis, according to which God is the being that has the maximal consistent set of knowledge, power, and benevolence, instead of the omni God thesis, according to which God is an omniscient, omnipotent, and omnibenevolent being. I call this approach to defending perfect being theism the 'maximal God approach'. In this chapter, I try to strengthen the approach by addressing numerous possible and existing objections to it.

I classify the objections into four categories and advance my discussion as follows. In Section 4.2, I respond to objections that suggest that the maximal God approach entails unwelcome consequences for God's great-making properties. In Section 4.3, I respond to objections that suggest that the approach undermines the monotheistic aspect of perfect being theism. In Section 4.4, I respond to objections that suggest that the approach fails to refute certain versions of the argument from evil. In Section 4.5, I respond to objections that suggest that the approach faces methodological difficulties. I conclude in Section 4.6.

4.2 Objections Concerning God's Great-Making Properties

The objections in the first set raise worries about the implications of the maximal God approach for God's great-making properties.

Objection 1: Maximal God is not Worshipworthy

Again, the maximal God approach leaves the possibility open that God is not omniscient, omnipotent, and omnibenevolent. This seems to mean that the approach also allows the possibility that God is not worshipworthy, because God's worshipworthiness is considered to be based on His greatness. Robert Adams, for example, contends that our worship of God involves the acknowledgment, 'not just of God's benefits to us, but of [God's] supreme degree of intrinsic excellence' (Adams 1999, p. 14). Few perfect being theists would be willing to accept the maximal God approach if it can entail that God is not worshipworthy.

Call the view that God's worshipworthiness is based on His maximal degree of intrinsic excellence the 'maximal excellence account'. This account seems to be untenable. Suppose that *X* is nearly omniscient, omnipotent, and omnibenevolent, but not quite. Assume that *X* is omnipotent and omnibenevolent but only nearly omniscient insofar as there is one true proposition that it does not know: *p*. If the maximal excellence account is correct and the phrase 'maximal degree of intrinsic excellence' presupposes omniscience, omnipotence, and omnibenevolence, then whether or not *X* knows *p*, *however trivial that proposition is*, determines whether or not *X* is worthy of worship. As soon as *X* comes to know *p*, *X* suddenly becomes worthy of worship, which seems absurd.[1]

It is important to note that the maximal excellence account is not the only account of God's worshipworthiness; there are many alternatives to it. For example, some argue that God is worshipworthy because we owe our thanks to Him for our existence. Others argue that God's worshipworthiness is not grounded on anything because it is a primitive property. Still others argue that we should worship God for pragmatic

[1] I argued elsewhere with Tim Bayne for this claim. See Bayne and Nagasawa (2006, 2007). See also Cray (2011), Crowe (2007), Danaher (2012), Gwiazda (2011), and Smuts (2012).

reasons.[2] However, even if the maximal excellence account *is* right, it remains unclear why the term 'maximal degree of intrinsic excellence' has to refer to the set of omniscience, omnipotence, and omnibenevolence. If no possible being can achieve the set of omniscience, omnipotence, and omnibenevolence, then the term should refer to a set of properties that falls somewhat short of omniscience, omnipotence, and omnibenevolence. This seems to suggest that it makes more sense to define the maximal degree of intrinsic excellence in terms of the maximal consistent set of knowledge, power, and benevolence, which is compatible with the maximal God approach.

One might respond at this point that worshipworthiness is not an 'all-or-nothing' property. If so, one might say, maximal God is *less* worshipworthy than omni God, which seems to make the maximal God approach uncompelling.[3] I do not think, however, that this response succeeds. According to the maximal God approach, if it is possible for an omniscient, omnipotent, and omnibenevolent being to exist, then maximal God *is* omni God. On the other hand, if it is not possible for an omniscient, omnipotent, and omnibenevolent being to exist, then maximal God is not omni God but He still achieves the maximal consistent set of knowledge, power, and benevolence. Hence, my maximal God approach does not entail any situation in which maximal God is less worshipworthy than another possible being.

Objection 2: There is No Single Unique Combination of Knowledge, Power, and Benevolence That Defeats All Arguments Against Perfect Being Theism

One might reject my maximal God approach by saying that it is unreasonable to think that there is a single combination of knowledge, power, and benevolence that undermines all Type-A, Type-B, and Type-C arguments against perfect being theism. For example, it might be the case that perfect being theists need God to have more knowledge and less power in response to one argument but more power and less knowledge in response to another.[4]

[2] See Bayne and Nagasawa (2006) for these views.

[3] Thanks to an anonymous referee for raising this objection.

[4] Thanks to an anonymous referee for raising this objection.

This objection does not refute the maximal God approach, for several reasons. First, it is not supported by any specific example. It is important to note that the maximal God approach is an attempt to shift the burden of proof from perfect being theists to their critics. If perfect being theists pursue the omni God approach, which is based on the claim that God is perfectly omniscient, omnipotent, and omnibenevolent, then critics can present Type-A, Type-B, or Type-C arguments to show that God cannot be omniscient, omnipotent, and omnibenevolent. Here the burden of proof is on perfect being theists to show that these arguments fail to undermine the omni God thesis. But once perfect being theists pursue the maximal God approach and replace the omni God thesis with the perfect being thesis, the burden of proof remains on critics to show that these arguments establish that God is not the being that has the maximal consistent set of knowledge, power, and benevolence. A similar dialectical situation takes place with respect to the objection in question. With the maximal God thesis in hand, perfect being theists hold that God is the being that has the maximal consistent set of knowledge, power, and benevolence. Critics who raise the objection in question say that God *might* require more knowledge than power in some cases and more power than knowledge in other cases. But the problem is, this *might not* be the case. So the burden of proof remains on the critics to specify such examples. What this objection says essentially is that there is no such thing as the maximal consistent set of knowledge, power, and benevolence because two potential candidates for the maximal being are such that while they are extensively equal with respect to knowledge and power, neither of them is intensively superior, equal, or inferior to the other. This is structurally parallel to the comparison of the mathematical genius and the musical genius discussed in Chapter 2. Yet, again, critics have not shown that comparable examples arise for maximal beings. Second, this example does not undermine the maximal God approach if the overall greatness view—as opposed to the comprehensive greatness view—is adopted because the overall greatness view allows for the comparison of the greatnesses of distinct beings, even if one of them is not intensively equal, superior, or inferior to the other.[5] In sum, perfect being theists do not need to worry about this objection unless specific

[5] See Chapter 2 for the overall greatness view and the comprehensive greatness view.

examples are provided. And even if specific examples *are* provided, they do not need to worry about it if they accept the overall greatness view.

Objection 3: The Maximal God Approach Fails as There Are Great-Making Properties That Improve Indefinitely

Einar Bohn (2012) argues that the maximal God approach is untenable because the notion of God as the being than which no greater is metaphysically possible is incoherent.[6] The maximal God approach seems to be based on the assumption that the overall greatness of any being supervenes on the greatness of its individual properties such as knowledge, power, and benevolence. This assumption entails that if the greatness of any of knowledge, power, and benevolence is indefinitely extensible, overall greatness is indefinitely extensible as well. And Bohn claims that these great-making properties are indeed indefinitely extensible. This means that, according to him, for any possible being, there is always another being that is greater. Hence, he concludes, the notion of God as the being than which no greater is metaphysically possible is incoherent.

The first point that I should note is that this objection is not directed at the maximal God approach per se but at the more general perfect being thesis that God is the being than which no greater is metaphysically possible. This means that the objection applies to the omni God approach as well as to the maximal God approach. Responding to this objection is important not only for defending perfect being theism but also for defending the classical ontological argument. In Chapter 6 I address Gaunilo's criticism, which aims to undermine the argument by appealing to the Lost Island parody argument. I argue there that the Lost Island argument is not exactly parallel to the classical ontological argument because while there are intrinsic maxima of God's properties, such as knowledge, power, and benevolence, there are no intrinsic maxima of properties that the Island can have, such as the number of palm trees or pleasant beaches. I argue that proponents of the classical ontological argument, who are committed to the assumption that there are intrinsic maxima of God's properties, are not committed to the assumption that there are intrinsic maxima of the Island's properties as well. What the objection in question suggests is that, like the Island's

[6] See Oppy (2011) for a similar objection.

properties, God's properties, such as knowledge, power, and benevolence, indeed lack intrinsic maxima.

I submit that the objection in question fails to undermine the maximal God approach because it is based on a mistaken analysis of great-making properties. Consider, first, knowledge. According to what I call the 'bottom-up analysis', one can acquire a body of knowledge of a given size by adding incremental units of knowledge one by one. Suppose that person *A* knows 500 true propositions and person *B* does not know anything. According to the bottom-up approach, *B* can acquire an overall body of knowledge of the same size as *A*'s by acquiring each unit of knowledge that *A* knows one by one until there are 500 units in *B*'s body of knowledge. This analysis is, however, untenable because people do not acquire knowledge in this way. In fact, ordinarily, people know infinitely many things. For example, if I know that *p*, then, according to the KK principle, I also know that I know that *p*, and I also know that I know that I know that *p*, and so on. If we adopt the bottom-up approach it seems that one can never reach the body of knowledge that I have, even though it is clearly possible to reach it and even surpass it.

What we learn from this example is that the fact that knowledge has infinite degrees does not entail that it lacks an intrinsic maximum. We can apply the same reasoning to power and benevolence. The proper definitions of power and benevolence are highly disputed but we can understand them roughly as follows: Power is a capacity to do things and benevolence is a disposition to act benevolently. Now I have infinitely many capacities to do things. For example, I have the capacity to lift 3 kg, 3.3 kg, 3.33 kg, and so on ad infinitum. Similarly, I have a disposition to act benevolently in infinitely many situations. For example, I have a disposition to act benevolently towards injured puppies who weigh 3 kg, 3.3 kg, 3.33 kg, and so on ad infinitum. These examples suggest that the fact that power and benevolence have infinite degrees does not entail that they lack intrinsic maxima. Hence, omniscience, omnipotence, and omnibenevolence should be understood from a top-down rather than bottom-up perspective. Maximal knowledge, power, and benevolence correspond to the intrinsic, unsurpassable maxima of knowledge, power, and benevolence, which subsume infinite degrees of knowledge, power, and benevolence.[7]

[7] Mann (1975) also discusses the objection in question.

4.3 Objections Concerning the Monotheistic Aspect of Perfect Being Theism

The objections in the second set raise worries about the implications of the maximal God approach for the monotheistic aspect of perfect being theism.

Objection 4: The Maximal God Approach Undermines the Uniqueness of God

One might claim that the maximal God approach undermines the uniqueness of God because it gives up God's omniscience, omnipotence, and omnibenevolence. Once the uniqueness of God is compromised, one might say, we cannot sustain perfect being theism as a version of monotheism.

As I explained in Chapter 3, we do not necessarily have to give up God's omniscience, omnipotence, and omnibenevolence to adopt the maximal God approach. The approach merely leaves open the option that God is not omniscient, omnipotent, and omnibenevolent while holding the more modest maximal God thesis that God is the being that has the maximal consistent set of knowledge, power, and benevolence. It might turn out that God is indeed omniscient, omnipotent, and omnibenevolent, which is compatible with the maximal God thesis. Furthermore, even if it turns out that God is *not* omniscient, omnipotent, and omnibenevolent, we can still maintain God's uniqueness because, according to the maximal God approach, God is the only being than which no greater is metaphysically possible. The maximal God approach, therefore, does not compromise the uniqueness of God.

Objection 5: The Existence of a Second Greatest Possible Being is Problematic

Given the assumption of the maximal God approach that a comparison can be made between God and other possible beings by referring to their degrees of knowledge, power, and benevolence, it follows that there is a second greatest possible being that is almost as great as God. Indeed, I compared God and such a possible being in Chapter 3. One might claim that the existence of such a being is problematic for perfect being theists.

I do not think that this objection is forceful enough to undermine the maximal God approach. While it is true that the approach entails that there is a second greatest possible being that is close to God in terms of knowledge, power, and benevolence, so does the omni God approach. The thesis that knowledge, power, and benevolence are degreed entails that there can be a ranking of beings in terms of these great-making properties. Since perfect being theists hold that only God occupies the top link in such a ranking they have to hold, whether they adopt the maximal God approach or the omni God approach, that there are one or more beings that occupy the second link. Hence, a second greatest possible being is an inevitable consequence. It is important to emphasize that this does not mean that the second greatest possible being is *actual*. Given that such a being does not reach the maximal greatness of God as the being than which no greater is metaphysically possible, perfect being theists do not need to think that the ontological argument entails the existence of such a being. And since there is no evidence for the existence of such a being, we can assume that it is a merely possible being.

Objection 6: The Maximal God Approach Entails Polytheism

One might argue that the maximal God approach is untenable because it entails polytheism. This is problematic because, again, perfect being theism is a form of monotheism.

On the face of it, this objection is not particularly interesting because it applies to any monotheistic concept of God, not uniquely to my maximal concept of God. No matter which concept of God monotheists introduce, critics can always ask why there cannot be another being that achieves the same level of greatness as that of God. One might insist, however, that this problem *is* unique to the maximal concept of God because the maximal concept seems to entail that more than one combination of knowledge, power, and benevolence can yield the highest degree of overall greatness. Suppose that knowledge, power, and benevolence are equally weighted based on the overall axiological value of their possessor and that omniscience, omnipotence, and omnibenevolence together represent 10 units each of axiological value. If God is omniscient, omnipotent, and omnibenevolent, He therefore possesses 10 units of each of these great-making properties and 30 units overall. Now the maximal God approach says that God might not possess omniscience, omnipotence, and omnibenevolence because the maximal consistent set of knowledge, power, and benevolence might not correspond to the set of omniscience, omnipotence, and omnibenevolence. This means that God might not possess 10 units each or, consequently, 30 units overall. Suppose now that God possesses only 29 units of overall greatness, consisting of knowledge (9 units), power (10 units), and benevolence (10 units). This initially appears problematic for perfect being theism as a version of monotheism because there seem to be other ways to possess 29 units of overall axiological value. It seems in particular that one can possess 29 units by having 10 units of knowledge, 9 units of power, and 10 units of benevolence, or by having 10 units of knowledge, 10 units of power, and 9 units of benevolence. It seems, therefore, that the maximal God approach entails polytheism because it allows there to be multiple beings that are as great as God.

This objection, however, is not as forceful as it might initially appear because it makes some assumptions that are disputable. First, it assumes that if maximal overall greatness corresponds to 29 units consisting of 9 units of knowledge, 10 units of power, and 10 units of benevolence, then the same overall greatness can be achieved by having 10 units of knowledge, 9 units of power, and 10 units of benevolence, or by having 10 units of knowledge, 10 units of power, and 9 units of benevolence. However, it might well be the case that while the maximum achievable size of knowledge is 9 units, the maximum achievable size of power and the maximum achievable size of benevolence are 10 units each. In such a case, the only combination that yields the highest overall greatness (29 units) consists of 9 units of knowledge, 10 units of power, and 10 units of benevolence. Second, the objection assumes that all three of the great-making properties, knowledge, power, and benevolence, are equally weighted towards the overall axiological value of the possessor. However, it might well be the case, for example, that power and benevolence are more heavily weighted than knowledge. Suppose, for instance, that power and benevolence are twice as valuable as knowledge. This means that if the smallest component of omniscience is worth 1 unit of axiological value, the smallest components of omnipotence and omnibenevolence are worth 2 units each. Suppose further that although 10 units of knowledge, 10 units of power, and 10 units of benevolence can be achieved independently, the maximum total value of overall greatness that is achievable is smaller than 30 units. In this case, again, even though God's overall value falls short of that of the combination of omniscience, omnipotence, and omnibenevolence, there is only one way to possess the maximal consistent set of knowledge, power, and benevolence, namely to have 9 units of knowledge, 10 units of power, and 10 units of benevolence. Neither having 10 units of knowledge, 9 units of power, and 10 units of benevolence nor having 10 units of knowledge, 10 units of power, and 9 units of benevolence is possible here. There are many other cases in which there still is only one way to possess the maximal consistent set even though the maximal consistent set does not comprise omniscience, omnipotence, and omnibenevolence. These examples undermine the objection in question. To pursue this objection further, critics have to show that none of these examples reflects reality.

Second, more importantly, the objection in question assumes the overall greatness view, which we discussed in detail in Chapter 2. According to this view, the intensity and extensity of one's great-making properties can be converted into one's overall greatness. However, as I argued in that chapter, that is not the only plausible account of great-making properties. According to the comprehensive greatness view, God occupies the top link in all local chains of being because, for every non-divine possible being *y*, God is either: (i) intensively superior to *y* or (ii) extensively superior to *y* and the great-making properties that God and *y* share are present in God at the same degree of intensity as in *y*. Cases satisfying (ii) are not relevant because our assumption here is that all possible beings in consideration are extensively equal, but cases satisfying (i) represent situations in which there is only one way to possess the maximal consistent set of knowledge, power, and benevolence, even if it does not coincide with the set of omniscience, omnipotence, and omnibenevolence. These cases suggest that even if we accept the possibility that God does not possess omniscience, omnipotence, and omnibenevolence, we do not have to commit ourselves to the possibility that another being reaches the same axiological value as God by having a different combination of knowledge, power, and benevolence. (See scenarios S_{2A} and S_{2B} in Chapter 3 for specific examples.)

Objection 7: The Maximal God Approach Entails the Existence of Two Possible Beings That are Jointly Greater Than God

One might argue that the maximal God approach is untenable because the possibility that God is not omniscient, omnipotent, and omnibenevolent entails that there are two possible beings that are jointly greater than God, which is a disturbing result for perfect being theists.

It is peculiar to compare the greatness of one possible being against the greatness of multiple possible beings combined. The perfect being thesis says that God is the being than which no greater is metaphysically possible, which suggests that God is greater than every single metaphysically possible being, but not that God is greater than every group of metaphysically possible beings. If a comparison between God and a group of metaphysically possible being were legitimate, even a version of perfect being theism based on the omni God thesis can be easily refuted by presenting the following argument: There are two metaphysically possible beings such that they are individually less great than God but jointly as great as God. If perfect being theism is true, no group of metaphysically possible beings is as great as God. Therefore, perfect being theism is false.

This argument does not succeed precisely because it is not legitimate to compare the greatness of one possible being with the greatness of two possible beings combined when our interest lies in making comparisons between individual possible beings. In a parallel manner, the objection in question fails.

4.4 Objections Concerning Evil

The argument from evil is often considered the strongest argument against perfect being theism. The objections in the third set insist that the maximal God approach cannot undermine the argument.

Objection 8: The Maximal God Approach is not Applicable to the Argument from Evil

One might claim that, contrary to what I say, the maximal God approach is not applicable to some Type-C arguments, particularly the argument from evil. The maximal God approach seems to work very well when it is applied to Type-A and Type-B arguments because they focus on purely logical matters concerning God's own nature. For example, if the paradox of the stone (a Type-A argument) is right in saying that it is logically impossible for any being to be omnipotent, then the maximal God approach can reasonably conclude that God, as the being than which no greater is metaphysically possible, does not have to be omnipotent. Similarly, if the argument from God's inability to sin (a Type-B argument) is right in saying that it is logically impossible for any being to be omnipotent and omnibenevolent simultaneously, then the maximal God approach can reasonably conclude that God does not have to be omnipotent and omnibenevolent simultaneously. The argument from evil, however, does not have the same structure because its focus is not on a purely logical matter concerning God's own nature. Its focus is rather on the apparent inconsistency between God's nature and an external, contingent fact about the existence of evil, a fact that is independent of God's nature. Hence, one might say, the maximal God approach is not applicable to the argument from evil.[8]

According to the maximal God approach, however, we do not have to worry about the argument from evil unless it shows that God is *far* from omniscient, omnipotent, and omnibenevolent, indeed so far that He cannot be the being than which no greater is metaphysically possible. In other words, the maximal God approach is in danger only if the argument from evil shows that the quantity and quality of evil in the actual world are so significant that we have to 'compromise' God's knowledge, power, or benevolence to the extent that He can no longer be the being than which no greater is metaphysically possible. However, showing that the quantity and quality of evil in the actual world are so significant that we have to 'compromise' God's knowledge, power, or benevolence to such an extent is more demanding than showing that they are so significant that that we have to 'compromise' God's omniscience, omnipotence, and omnibenevolence. Hence, the maximal God approach does make it more difficult for critics to defend the argument from evil. Therefore, even though the argument from evil is concerned with an external, contingent fact that is independent of God's own nature, the maximal God approach remains effective.

Having said that, I do not pretend that we can completely eliminate the argument from evil by appealing to the maximal God approach. It might be the case that, ultimately, the maximal God approach has to appeal to a theodicy or some other account to develop a comprehensive response to the argument from evil. Also, it seems necessary to adopt an independent theistic response to address, for example, what Marilyn Adams calls the argument from 'horrendous evil'. This argument is concerned with the existential, personal aspects of pain and suffering

[8] Thanks to Toby Betenson for raising this objection. A similar point is made by Todd (2015).

considered from an individual point of view, rather than the logical, objective aspects of pain and suffering considered from a global point of view (Adams 2000).[9]

Objection 9: The Maximal God Approach is not Applicable to the Modal Argument from Evil

One might argue that even if the maximal God approach is applicable to the argument from evil, it is not applicable to the *modal* argument from evil. Our modal intuition seems to suggest that there is a 'very bad possible world', a possible world that is full of evil. According to the modal argument from evil, the possibility of a very bad world entails that there is no omniscient, omnipotent, and omnibenevolent God existing necessarily; that is, existing in all possible worlds. This argument seems to apply to the maximal God thesis as well as the omni God thesis.[10]

The modal argument from evil can be considered a Type-C argument because it purports to show that God's properties as specified in the omni God thesis are mutually inconsistent with a certain fact about the actual world (as well as all other possible worlds). What is unique about the modal argument from evil is that it is concerned with a necessary fact rather than a contingent fact. The modal argument from evil can also be construed as an extreme form of the argument from God's inability to sin, which is a Type-B argument. The argument from God's inability to sin says that God does not exist because if God can sin, He is not omnibenevolent and if God cannot sin, He is not omnipotent. This argument can be presented as follows: 'If there is a possible world in which God sins or allows horrible things to happen, then God is not necessarily omnibenevolent. On the other hand, if there is no possible world in which God sins or allows horrible things to happen, then God is not necessarily omnipotent.' The modal argument from evil can be construed as the following modification of the first conditional: 'According to our modal intuition, there *is* a possible world in which God allows

[9] For further discussion of the maximal God thesis and the argument from evil, see Nagasawa (2013b).

[10] Thanks to an anonymous referee for raising this argument. For the debate over the modal argument from evil see, for example, Almeida (2011), Guleserian (1983), Kraay (2011), and Morris (1987a).

horrible things to happen, which suggests that God is not necessarily omnibenevolent.'

We can respond to the objection in question as follows by appealing first to the maximal God approach: If it is *necessarily* true that there is a very bad possible world, then God is the greatest possible being within that world given the constraint of the necessary truth. In such a world, while God is not omniscient, omnipotent, and omnibenevolent, He is still the being than which no greater is metaphysically possible, albeit in a very limited and possibly trivial sense. A worry concerning this response is that there might be an extremely bad possible world in which the 'being than which no greater is metaphysically possible' in that world does not deserve to be called God.[11] It seems to me that a better response is to adopt a more radical solution introduced by Thomas Morris (1987a), which holds that, given that God exists necessarily, very bad possible worlds are not in fact possible worlds. Morris writes:

> God is a delimiter of possibilities. If there is a being who exists necessarily, and is necessarily omnipotent, omniscient, and good, then many states of affairs which otherwise would represent genuine possibilities, and which by all non-theistic tests of logic and semantics do represent possibilities, are strictly impossible in the strongest sense. (Morris 1987a, p. 48)

Our modal intuition that there is a very bad possible world does not take into account the thesis that God exists necessarily. Given this thesis, however, there just cannot be such a possible world. The question at this point is whether it is reasonable to accept such a thesis. In Chapter 7, I argue for a version of the modal ontological argument which uses this thesis.

4.5 Objections Concerning Methodological Issues

The objections in the fourth set pertains to the overall methodology of the maximal God approach.

[11] Similar points are made by Lembke (2012a) and Oppy (2011).

Objection 10: The Maximal God Approach is Ad Hoc

One might claim that the maximal God approach is untenable because it changes the extent of God's knowledge, power, and benevolence in an ad hoc manner whenever it encounters a new Type-A, Type-B, or Type-C argument against perfect being theism. One might contend that there seems no refutation of the maximal God approach even in principle given that its proponents can change the degree of God's properties whenever they find it convenient to do so.

Contrary to what this objection says, the maximal God approach does not change the extent of God's knowledge, power, and benevolence. Proponents of the maximal God approach accept the perfect being thesis that God is the being than which no greater is metaphysically possible and the maximal God thesis that He is the being that has the maximal consistent set of knowledge, power, and benevolence. The contents of these theses remain the same, irrespective of arguments brought against perfect being theism. That is, the extents of God's properties remain constant. Therefore, there is no ad hoc reasoning behind the approach. The only thing that could change is our *understanding* of God's properties. We might learn, for example, through a Type-A argument that God is not an omnipotent being. But this does not mean that the extent of God's power suddenly diminishes as the Type-A argument is introduced. It is rather that our knowledge of the extent of God's power changes. In other words, the change in question is epistemic, rather than metaphysical.

Objection 11: The Maximal God Approach is not New

I have claimed that the maximal God approach is a novel way to respond to arguments against perfect being theism. One might maintain, however, that the same suggestion has already been made.[12] J. L. Mackie, for example, writes as follows:

> It is plain, therefore, that [the problem of evil] can be easily solved if one gives up at least one of the propositions that constitute it. Someone who holds that there is in some sense a god, but one who is not wholly good, or, though powerful, not quite omnipotent, will not be embarrassed by this difficulty.
>
> (Mackie 1982, p. 151)

[12] Thanks to an anonymous referee for raising this objection.

One might claim that Mackie has in mind the maximal God approach in this quote.

What Mackie really seems to have in mind in the above quote is the option of simply giving up God's omnipotence or omnibenevolence. As I argue throughout this book, however, the maximal God approach does not necessarily encourage perfect being theists to do so. It encourages them only to leave open the option that God is not omniscient, omnipotent, and omnibenevolent. God might or might not be omniscient, omnipotent, and omnibenevolent but that outcome, according to the maximal God approach, does not affect the maximal God thesis, according to which God is the being that has the maximal consistent set of knowledge, power, and benevolence, or the perfect being thesis, according to which God is the being than which no greater is metaphysically possible. This approach allows perfect being theists to shift the burden of proof to the critics; those who argue against perfect being theism must demonstrate not only that omni God does not exist but also that maximal God does not exist. The latter is significantly more difficult to establish than the former. In general, there is a fundamental difference between giving up *p*, on the one hand, and leaving open the possibility that *p* is false, on the other.

Mackie is an atheist but most theistic philosophers who express reservations about the omni God thesis also suggest simply giving up God's omni-properties. Consider the following examples. In response to various Type-A and Type-B arguments, Peter Geach encourages Christian theists to give up God's omnipotence:

> Lying and promise-breaking are logically possible feats that Christians cannot hold to be possible for God. And making a thing which its maker cannot destroy is a logically possible feat, a feat some creatures do perform; but whether we say that God cannot perform this feat or that he can, there turns out to be some logically possible feat which God cannot perform. (Geach 1977, p. vi)

Geach concludes that it is more appropriate to call God's power 'almightiness' rather than omnipotence. To take another example, in response to the argument from God's inability to sin, a Type-B argument, Wes Morriston considers the possibility that while God is omnibenevolent, He is not omnipotent. Morriston writes that perhaps what the argument teaches us is that God is '(a) necessarily morally perfect; and (b) as powerful as is logically consistent with (a)'. In this way,

Morriston says, God remains powerful enough to create the world and perform miracles without being omnipotent (Morriston 2001a, p. 158). In response to the argument from evil, a Type-C argument, John Bishop claims that it is reasonable for theists to think that the existence of evil entails that God is not omnipotent. He writes, '[on the basis of the argument from evil] theists should reject the concept of God as an agent outside the natural order who has an absolutely unlimited power of intervention within nature' (Bishop 1993, p. 13). There are also a smaller number of philosophers who give up God's omnibenevolence. For example, in response to the argument from evil, Brian Davies contends that it is 'wholly inappropriate to think of God as something able to be either moral (well behaved) or immoral (badly behaved)' (Davies 1998, p. 178). He writes:

> To be blunt, I suggest that many contemporary philosophers writing on the problem of evil (both theists and non-theists) have largely been wasting their time.... They are like people attacking or defending tennis players because they fail to run a mile in under four minutes. Tennis players are not in the business of running four-minute miles. Similarly, God is not something with respect to which moral evaluation (whether positive or negative) is appropriate.
>
> (Davies 1998, p. 178)

As Nick Trakakis notes, process philosophers and the so-called 'Boston personalists' are also known for rejecting God's omni-properties (Trakakis 2007, pp. 337–9). Yet none of the above adopts the maximal God approach, which offers more flexibility than the option of simply giving up God's omniscience, omnipotence, or omnibenevolence. The only exceptions are perhaps Brian Leftow and Jerome I. Gellman.[13] In considering Anselm's perfect being theology, Leftow writes that 'it is a live possibility that He [God] cannot have all perfections'. He suggests that if two perfections *F* and *G* are incompatible, we must decide if something having all the other perfections plus *F* would be greater than something having all the other perfections plus *G* (Leftow 2004, pp. 143–4). In considering human experiences of God and the rationality of theistic belief, Gellman considers two types of theistic arguments: the 'argument from self-inconsistency' and the 'argument from evil'. What he calls the argument from self-consistency subsumes Type-A and Type-B

[13] Thanks to Tyron Goldschmidt for bringing Gellman's work to my attention.

arguments. The argument from evil is, of course, one of many Type-C arguments. He then maintains that if these arguments are sound then 'we would not thereby come to know that "our" God, *the very being who is purportedly known by experience*, did not exist'. He continues, 'What would have been proven about God is only that "our" God was not an absolute perfect being' (Gellman 1997, p. 161, emphasis in the original). Although Leftow's and Gellman's approaches seem compatible with the maximal God approach, their uses of them are quite distinct from mine. Leftow uses his approach to clarify Anselm's concept of God and Gellman uses his approach to defend experiences of God. It seems safe to conclude, therefore, that the maximal God approach is a new, comprehensive way of defending perfect being theism.

4.6 Conclusion

We have discussed a number of objections to the maximal God approach. Some of the objections are directed against the maximal God approach per se, while others are directed against a broader view. In response to the objections in the first set, I have argued that perfect being theists can maintain the perfect being thesis and the maximal God thesis with no negative implications for God's great-making properties. In response to the objections in the second set, I have argued that the maximal God approach does not collapse perfect being theism into a view other than monotheism. In response to the objections in the third set, I have argued that the maximal God approach undermines the argument from of evil even though, ultimately, it might not be possible to refute all versions of the argument without appealing to a theodicy or some other account. In response to the objections in the fourth set, I have argued that the maximal God approach is a new way of defending perfect being theism and does not face any methodological difficulties. It would be overly ambitious to think that we can resolve every single problem concerning God's nature and existence merely by replacing the omni God thesis with the maximal God thesis. Yet it seems safe to conclude that the maximal God approach is the most effective and comprehensive response to arguments against perfect being theism.

PART III

The Maximal God Defence of the Ontological Argument for Perfect Being Theism

5

A Partial Defence of the Classical Ontological Argument I

5.1 Introduction

We saw in Chapters 3 and 4 that we can undermine nearly all existing arguments against perfect being theism by replacing the omni God thesis, according to which God is an omniscient, omnipotent, and omnibenevolent being, with the maximal God thesis, according to which God is the being that has the maximal consistent set of knowledge, power, and benevolence. This suggests that there is no obvious reason to think that perfect being theism is false. But is there any reason to think that perfect being theism is *true*? In the rest of this book, I consider the ontological argument for perfect being theism. As I explained in Chapter 1, there is a close conceptual link between perfect being theism and the ontological argument; the perfect being thesis, according to which God is the being than which no greater is metaphysically possible, serves as a basis of the ontological argument as well as perfect being theism. In fact, the ontological argument cannot be constructed without this (or a sufficiently similar) thesis. Moreover, the ontological argument is one of very few direct arguments for perfect being theism. As we saw in Chapter 1, most other theistic arguments, such as the cosmological argument, the design argument, the moral argument, and the argument from miracles, do not, even if successful, establish the existence of the being than which no greater is metaphysically possible. They establish at most that there is a being with some impressive great-making properties. Only the ontological argument establishes, if it is successful, the existence of the very being that the perfect being thesis specifies.

In this chapter and Chapter 6, I discuss a version of the ontological argument that is commonly attributed to chapter 2 of Anselm's *Proslogion*.

I call this version the 'classical ontological argument' to distinguish it from the 'modal ontological argument' which, in the mid-twentieth century, Charles Hartshorne (1941, 1961, 1965) and Norman Malcolm (1960) claimed to have discovered in Chapter 3 of the *Proslogion*. My main aim is to establish the following three theses: (i) Anselm is the one who invented the classical ontological argument; (ii) the classical ontological argument is powerful because it is designed in such a way that no matter how one approaches it, one cannot refute it without making a significant metaphysical or epistemic assumption, one that is likely to be contentious in its own right; and (iii) existing attempts to refute the argument by revealing its shallow, logical problems (without making any significant metaphysical or epistemic assumptions) fail.

My plan for the current part of this book is as follows: First, I argue for thesis (i) in Section 5.2 and for thesis (ii) in Section 5.3. I then concentrate on defending thesis (iii) for the rest of the chapter and Chapter 6. In particular, in Sections 5.4 through 5.8, I assess Peter Millican's recent attempt to reveal a shallow, logical problem in the classical ontological argument without disputing the argument's deep metaphysical or epistemic assumptions. I argue that his attempt does not succeed. In Chapter 6, I continue defending thesis (iii). I argue against another attempt to reveal a shallow, logical problem, which appeals to parodies of the classical ontological argument. The conclusion that I establish over the course of this chapter and Chapter 6 comprises a partial defence of the classical ontological argument: as far as this specific version of the ontological argument is concerned, perfect being theists and their critics end in a draw because although there are powerful objections to the argument, they cannot undermine it without raising issues that are controversial independently of their relationships to the argument. This conclusion might not sound entirely encouraging for perfect being theists. Yet in Chapter 7, I offer a full defence of the modal ontological argument, as opposed to the classical ontological argument.

5.2 Anselm Invented the Classical Ontological Argument

I explained in Chapter 1 that Anselm is not the inventor of perfect being theism. I agree with Leftow (2011) that we can trace the origin of perfect being theism to Greco-Roman philosophy and with Wierenga (2011) that all the ingredients of perfect being theism had already been presented by the time of Augustine (and possibly earlier). Perfect being theism is also intimated in many verses in the Bible. Yet I submit that Anselm remains an important figure in the history of perfect being theism because he is the inventor of the classical ontological argument. (Notice, again, that my focus here is on the *classical* ontological argument. Whether Anselm also invented the *modal* ontological argument or only hinted at it remains in dispute. But I can set the modal argument aside as it is clear that no one earlier than Anselm introduced it.)

The classical ontological argument is commonly attributed to chapter 2 of Anselm's *Proslogion*. The following is Anselm's presentation of the argument in the chapter:

> Now we believe that You are something than which nothing greater can be thought. Or can it be that a thing of such a nature does not exist, since 'the Fool has said in his heart, there is no God'? But surely, when this same Fool hears what I am speaking about, namely, 'something-than-which-nothing-greater-can-be-thought', he understands what he hears, and what he understands is in his mind, even if he does not understand that it actually exists. For it is one thing for an object to exist in the mind, and another thing to understand that an object actually exists.... Even the Fool, then, is forced to agree that something-than-which-nothing-greater-can-be-thought exists in the mind, since he understands this when he hears it, and whatever is understood is in the mind. And surely that-than-which-a-greater-cannot-be-thought cannot exist in the mind alone. For if it exists solely in the mind even, it can be thought to exist in reality also, which is greater. If then that-than-which-a-greater-cannot-be-thought exists in the mind alone, this same that-than-which-a-greater-*cannot*-be-thought is that-than-which-a-greater-*can*-be-thought. But this is obviously impossible. Therefore there is absolutely no doubt that something-than-which-a-greater-cannot-be-thought exists both in the mind and in reality.
>
> (Anselm 1965, originally 1077–8, p. 117, emphasis in the original)

Using our contemporary terminology, we can rephrase Anselm's argument as follows: God is the being than which no greater is metaphysically possible. This being exists at least in the mind because even the Fool, who denies that such a being exists in reality, understands what it is. Suppose, for the sake of *reductio ad absurdum*, that such a being exists only in the mind and not in reality. If so, another being can be thought that is greater, namely the same being that is thought to exist in reality as well as in the mind. This means that a being can be thought that is greater than the being than which no greater is metaphysically possible. This, however, is obviously impossible. Therefore, it is not the case that such a being exists only in the mind. It exists both in the mind and in reality. Therefore, God exists. (Note that this represents a formulation of Anselm's argument that is commonly discussed in the community of analytic philosophers of religion. I do not mean to suggest that this is the exegetically accurate summary of the Anselmian text presented above.)

It seems that there are at least three essential characteristics of the classical ontological argument and that any argument that fails to have them cannot be deemed a version of the argument:

Characteristic 1: It is based on the definition of God according to the perfect being thesis; namely, as the being than which no greater is metaphysically possible (or something very similar to it).

Characteristic 2: It is a purely a priori argument. It does not have any premise that requires an empirical observation of the world.[1]

Characteristic 3: It derives the existence of God by appealing to a *reductio ad absurdum* aiming to derive the contradiction that a being can be thought that is greater than the being than which no greater is metaphysically possible.

Let us review some arguments that predate the *Proslogion* but are comparable to the classical ontological argument and see if they satisfy all the three essential characteristics. As we saw in Chapter 1, according to Cicero, Chrysippus presents the following argument, which is similar in some respects to the classical ontological argument:

> If there is anything in nature which the human mind, which human intelligence, energy and power could not create, then the creator of such things must be a being superior to man. But the heavenly bodies in their eternal orbits could not be created by man. They must therefore be created by a being greater than man. But what is such a greater being but a god? For if no gods exist, then what is there in nature greater than man? He alone is endowed with the supreme gift of reason. Only an arrogant fool would imagine that there was nothing in the whole world greater than himself. Therefore there must be something greater than Man. And that something must be God. (Cicero 1972, originally 45 BC, p. 130, Book II, 16)

Chrysippus's argument is similar to the classical ontological argument in the sense that it tries to derive the existence of God by appealing to His

[1] The claim that even the Fool, who denies the existence of the being than which no greater is metaphysically possible, understands what the being is should not be interpreted as an a posteriori claim. It should be interpreted as an illustrative way of making the a priori claim that the being than which no greater is metaphysically possible is at least conceivable.

greatness. Chrysippus's talk of 'an arrogant fool' also reminds us of Anselm's quote above, which he derives from the Bible's 'the Fool has said in his heart, there is no God' (Psalm 53:1 and 14:1). Yet Chrysippus's argument is distinct from the classical ontological argument because it fails to have any of the three abovementioned characteristics. First, it is not based on the definition of God as the being than which no greater is metaphysically possible. It requires only that God be greater than man. Second, Chrysippus's argument is not purely a priori. It is based on the empirical premise that 'the heavenly bodies in their eternal orbits could not be created by man'. This claim seems to suggest that what Chrysippus has in mind is in fact a version of the cosmological argument rather than the classical ontological argument. Third, Chrysippus's argument does not appeal to a *reductio ad absurdum*; it rather appeals to a categorical derivation. I conclude, therefore, that Chrysippus's argument is not, despite certain similarities, a version of the classical ontological argument.

Sextus Empiricus discusses the following argument defended by the Stoics, which is also somewhat comparable to the classical ontological argument. Call it the 'Stoic argument':

> Next let us consider the nature of the absurd consequence of abolishing Divinity. If Gods do not exist, piety is not existent. For piety is 'the science of service to the Gods,' and there cannot be any service of things non-existent, nor consequently will any science thereof exist; and just as there cannot be any science of service to Hippocentaurs, they being non-existent, so there will not be any science of service to Gods if they are non-existent. But piety exists; so we must declare that Gods exists.—Again if Gods do not exist, holiness is non-existent, it being 'a kind of God-ward justice'; but according to the common notions and preconceptions of all men holiness exists, and because of this a holy thing also exists; and therefore the Divine exists.—If, however, Gods do not exist, wisdom is abolished, it being 'the science of things both divine and human'; and just as there is no science of things both human and Hippocentaurean owing to the fact that men exist but Hipppocentaurs do not exist, so too there will be no science of things divine and human if men exist but Gods subsist not. But it is absurd to assert that wisdom does not exist; therefore it is also absurd to maintain that the Gods are non-existent.
>
> (Sextus Empiricus 1936, originally second century, pp. 67–9, Book I, 123–5)

Sextus Empiricus also presents an argument introduced by Zeno of Citium, which is a variation of the above argument: 'One may reasonably honour the Gods; but those who are non-existent one may not reasonably honour; therefore Gods exist' (Sextus Empiricus 1936, originally second century, p. 73, Book I, 133). According to Sextus Empiricus, some criticize the argument by developing a parody argument: 'The wise one may reasonably honour; but one may not reasonably honour the non-existent; therefore wise men exist'. The critics claim that the conclusion of this parody argument is absurd because the 'wise one' has not been discovered. This seems to suggest that the original argument itself is absurd. Sextus Empiricus reports that Diogenes the Babylonian offers a response to this parody objection:

> [T]he second premiss in Zeno's argument is virtually this—'but those who are not of such a nature as to exist one may not reasonably honour'; for when this premiss is accepted it is evident that the Gods are of such a nature as to exist. But if so, they do actually exist. For if they had once existed at any time, they also exist now, just as, if atoms had existed, they also exist now; for according to the conception of such bodies, they are imperishable and uncreate[d]. Hence the argument will deduce a consequent conclusion. But it is not true of the wise that they actually exist because they are of such a nature as to exist.
>
> (Sextus Empiricus 1936, originally second century, p. 73, Book I, 134–6)

The appeal of the critics to a parody argument reminds us of the appeals to parody arguments by critics of the classical ontological argument such as Gaunilos, which I discuss in detail in Chapter 6. Diogenes's and Zeno's contention that Gods are of such a nature as to exist also reminds us of Descartes's version of the ontological argument, which he presents in the *Discourse on the Method* and the *Principles of Philosophy*. Also, the claim that if Gods had once existed at any time they also exist now reminds us of the thesis that God exists necessarily, which is a basis of the modal ontological argument (even though the above text says that the same claim applies to atoms, which are understood to exist only contingently).

Do the Stoic argument and Zeno's argument satisfy the three main characteristics of the classical ontological argument? As to characteristic 1, the arguments in question are not based explicitly on the definition of God as the being than which no greater is metaphysically possible. However, it might be charitable to think that when the Stoic argument suggests that Gods are required for the existence of holiness, it implicitly assumes a similar definition of God (or a god). As to characteristic 2, it is not obvious that the Stoic argument and Zeno's argument are purely a priori. The premise of the Stoic argument that piety exists and the premise of Zeno's argument that one may reasonably honour the gods appear to be a posteriori propositions. As to characteristic 3, these arguments do appeal to a *reductio ad absurdum*. They purport to derive contradictions from the assumption that gods do not exist. Yet the contradictions that these arguments derive are radically different from the contradiction that the classical ontological argument derives. The Stoic argument tries to derive the contradiction that piety is both existent and non-existent or that the science of service to the Gods is both existent and non-existent. Zeno's argument tries to derive the contradiction that it is both possible and impossible to reasonably honour gods. These are distinct from the contradiction that the classical ontological argument derives: a being can be thought that is greater than the being than which no greater is metaphysically possible.

Sextus Empiricus discusses further arguments that he considers to be versions of the Stoic argument and Zeno's argument (Sextus Empiricus 1936, originally second century, p. 71, Book I, 131–2). These arguments say that gods exist because, if they do not, justice does not exist and prophecy does not exist. Structurally speaking, these arguments are more comparable to the moral argument, which says that if God does not exist, objective morality does not exist, and the cosmological argument, which can be presented as saying that if God does not exist, then the universe does not exist.

Cleanthes's argument, which Sextus Empiricus also reports, seems to be more reminiscent of the classical ontological argument:

> If one nature is better than another, there will be some best nature; if one soul is better than another, there will be some best soul: if, then, one animal is better than another, there will be some best animal; for such things are not of a kind to proceed *ad infinitum*. So then, as nature is not capable of increasing to infinity in goodness, nor soul, neither is the animal capable. One animal, however, is better than another, as (say) the horse than the tortoise, and the bull than the ass, and the lion than the bull. And of all the terrestrial animals Man is the highest and best in respect of the disposition of both body and soul; therefore a certain best and most excellent animal will exist. Yet Man cannot be absolutely the best animal, because, for instance, he walks in wickedness all his life, or, if not, at least for the greater part of it (for if ever he attains virtue, he attains it late and at the setting of life's sun), and he is the victim of fate and feeble and in need of countless aids—such as food and coverings, and all the other requirements of the body, which stands over us like a rigorous tyrant and demands its daily tribute, and threatens us with disease and death unless we provide for its washing and anointing and clothing and feeding. So that Man is not a perfect animal,

but imperfect and far removed from the perfect. But that which is perfect and best will be better than Man and fulfilled with all the virtues and not receptive of any evil; and this animal will not differ from God. God, therefore, exists.

(Sextus Empiricus 1936, originally second century, pp. 49–51, Book I, 88–91)

This argument has characteristic 1 of the classical ontological argument. Cleanthes, like many perfect being theists, considers God's greatness in terms of a hierarchy and tries to derive the existence of God by appealing to the thesis that He is the being than which no greater is metaphysically possible, or, using Cleanthes's terminology, as the 'absolutely best animal' or a 'perfect animal'. However, Cleanthes's argument seems to lack characteristic 2 because it appeals to such a posteriori claims as that 'Man cannot be absolutely the best animal' because 'he walks in wickedness all his life' and 'he is the victim of fate and feeble and in need of countless aids'. The argument seems to lack characteristic 3 as well because it does not appeal to a *reductio ad absurdum*.

It seems appropriate to regard Cleanthes's argument as a version of the so-called 'argument from degree', the most well-known versions of which are one of Anselm's arguments in the *Monologion* and Aquinas's Fourth Way in *Summa Theologica*, rather than a version of the classical ontological argument. The argument from degree is an attempt to derive the existence of the perfect God by appealing to the idea that varying degrees of perfection found in the universe cannot exist without the most perfect being. As P. G. Walsh notes, Aristotle presents a similar argument in Fragment 16 of Book III of his lost work *On Philosophy*, which is preserved in Simplicius's commentary on *On the Heavens* (288.28–289.15): 'In things in which there is better, there is also a best; since therefore in things that exist one thing is better than another, there is a best, and this would be divine' (Boethius 1999, originally 523, p. 140). Boethius defends a version of this argument in the following passage:

Now it cannot be denied that the perfect good exists, and that it is, so to say, the source of all goods, for everything said to be imperfect is so described because it is less than perfect. The logical conclusion is that if in any class of objects something imperfect appears, that class must also contain something perfect; for if such perfection is removed, one cannot even imagine how that which is called imperfect has come into existence. (Boethius 1999, originally 523, p. 57, Book III, 10)

Like the classical ontological argument, the argument from degree relies on the definition of God as the being than which no greater is metaphysically possible (or on a very similar definition). In this sense, this is, along with the ontological argument, among a very few direct arguments for perfect being theism. Yet it lacks some essential characteristics of the classical ontological argument. Boethius's version, unlike Cleanthes's, seems to satisfy characteristic 2 because it does not rely on any a posteriori claim. Yet it lacks characteristic 3 because it is not a *reductio ad absurdum* aiming to derive the contradiction that a being can be thought that is greater than the being than which no greater is metaphysically possible.

Many further attempts have been made to locate the classical ontological argument in texts older than Anselm's *Proslogion*. For example, Hartshorne (1965) and Johnson (1963) try to find it in Plato's work and Slattery (1969) tries to find it in Parmenides's work. None of the arguments they address, however, seems to be more similar to the classical ontological argument than any of the abovementioned arguments and none exhibits all three characteristics of the classical ontological argument.[2] I conclude, therefore, that Anselm is the one who invented the classical ontological argument and, hence, he remains one of the most important proponents of perfect being theism.

5.3 Why the Classical Ontological Argument Persists

The ontological argument is an argument for perfect being theism, so atheists of course find it uncompelling. It is worth emphasizing that many of them find the argument particularly uncompelling compared with other philosophical arguments. Robert Nozick, for example, writes that the ontological argument is the 'most famous of all fishy philosophical arguments' (Nozick 2001, p. 130). Theodore M. Drange's assessment of the argument is even more critical:

> Most philosophers regard [the ontological argument] as either cognitively meaningless or as a kind of play on words, a semantic puzzle to sort out if one has some extra time. There is hardly anyone who is a theist on the basis of the ontological argument. I taught philosophy to thousands of students, and not a single one of them ever put any stock in it. (Drange 2006)

[2] For other attempts to locate the ontological argument in texts earlier than the *Proslogion*, see Oppy (1995, pp. 4–5).

Even among theists, the ontological argument is not popular today. There are very few contemporary philosophers who explicitly subscribe to the ontological argument, especially the classical ontological argument. Other theistic arguments such as the cosmological argument—particularly the Kalam version and the fine-tuning version—and the moral argument seem to attract more supporters. It is then puzzling that scholarly books and papers assessing the classical ontological argument continue to appear more than nine centuries after Anselm introduced it.

I submit that the classical ontological argument remains discussed because, despite its simplicity, it is structured in such a way that no matter how one approaches it, one cannot refute it without making a significant metaphysical or epistemic assumption, one that is often contentious in its own right. That is, there is no obvious or uncontroversial objection to the argument. This, I believe, is the beauty of the argument.

Consider, for example, the well-known (and powerful) Kantian objection to the ontological argument (Kant 1929, originally 1781, pp. 500–7). According to this objection, the argument fails because it is based on the false assumption that existence is a predicate. Predicates are words that refer to properties of things. The ontological argument appears to treat existence as a predicate by construing the statement 'God exists' as 'God has the property of being existent'. According to the objection in question, the phrase 'is existent' is not comparable to ordinary predicates such as 'is tall' and 'has blond hair'. The Kantian objection is probably the most widely supported objection to the ontological argument. Yet defending it is not entirely straightforward as it involves issues that are inherently contentious. The Kantian objection cannot succeed without meeting the following two conditions: (i) existence is not a predicate, and (ii) the ontological argument does presuppose that existence is a predicate. However, both (i) and (ii) are disputable.

Regarding (i), several philosophers dispute if existence is a predicate. Colin McGinn (2000) and Barry Miller (2002), for example, argue that existence *is* a predicate at least in certain contexts. It is important to note that they advocate for this view independently of the debate over the ontological argument. This suggests that to defend Kant's objection, critics need first to solve controversial issues concerning existence in the philosophy of language, and that is not an easy task. Suppose, however, that critics of the ontological argument manage to establish that existence is indeed not a predicate. Does that mean that Kant's objection succeeds in refuting the ontological argument? That is not obvious either because (ii), the claim that the ontological argument presupposes that existence is a predicate is also controversial. No version of the ontological argument has a premise saying explicitly that existence is a predicate. This means that if the ontological argument assumes that existence is a predicate, it assumes it only implicitly. One version of the ontological argument that Descartes defends in *Meditations on First Philosophy* is based on the explicit assumption that 'existence is a perfection' (Descartes 1970, originally 1641, pp. 104–5). One might infer from this that Descartes assumes that existence is comparable to other predicates such as tallness or baldness.[3] Yet it is far from clear that the classical ontological argument is based on the assumption that existence is a predicate. The argument says that the being than which no greater is metaphysically possible exists not only in the mind but also in reality because otherwise we can conceive of a being that is greater than that being, which is contradictory. Here the classical ontological argument seems to remain intact even if we assume that existence is not a predicate. Whether or not existence is a predicate, it still seems to make sense to say that the being in question, if it exists, is greater than if it does not. And we can and do commonly compare what exists and what does not (e.g., 'it is better for there to be beautiful flowers in the garden than not').

The dispute concerning whether existence is a predicate might even be irrelevant to the cogency of the ontological argument. This is because even if existence is not a predicate, *necessary* existence, which is commonly attributed to God by perfect being theists, does seem to be a predicate because it uniquely characterizes its possessor, namely God. It seems to be a predicate that God has but many other beings do not. According to Norman Malcolm (1960), that necessary existence, rather than existence *simpliciter*, is a predicate is in fact what Anselm assumes in the *Proslogion*. Anselm says, 'And certainly this being so truly exists that it cannot even be thought not to exist. For something can be thought to exist that cannot be thought not to exist, and this is greater than that

[3] Another version that Descartes defends, however, clearly does not assume that existence is a predicate. That version is based on the idea that the existence of God is a self-evident truth, which is analogous to mathematical axioms.

which can be thought not to exist' (Anselm 1965, originally 1077–8). Malcolm interprets this as saying that the logical impossibility of non-existence is a perfection, which is equivalent to saying that necessary existence is a perfection (Malcolm 1960, p. 46). (I discuss necessary existence in detail in Chapter 7, where I discuss the modal ontological argument.)

There are many other objections to the ontological argument. I do not have space to discuss them here but a close examination suggests that nearly all of them, whether or not they ultimately succeed, fail to settle the debate over the argument because they involve deep philosophical complexities that are often disputed independently of the debate.[4] In other words, the debate over the ontological argument endures because there is no objection that does not provoke a philosophically substantial debate. Peter Millican (2004), however, maintains that there are two types of objection that do not raise deep philosophical issues. They are Millican's own new objection and the so-called 'parody objection', which was originally introduced by Anselm's contemporary Gaunilo. I discuss Millican's new objection in the rest of this chapter and the parody objection in Chapter 6.

5.4 The Theory of Natures

Millican focuses on the classical ontological argument even though he says that his objection applies to all versions of the ontological argument. He tries to show that no possible interpretation of the classical ontological argument can yield the conclusion that God exists by examining the theory of natures on which the argument allegedly relies. Millican thinks that his objection is 'far more solid and persuasive' than any other because it does not dispute contentious, deep philosophical complexities that underlie the argument. For example, it does not dispute the Kantian concern regarding whether existence is a predicate. Instead, it tries to reveal a 'fatal flaw' in the argument by considering its 'shallow logical

[4] See Millican (2004) for other objections to the ontological argument. I agree with his contention that, with few exceptions, his new objection and the parody objection are the only ones that claim to avoid deep philosophical complications (Millican 2004, pp. 441–8).

details' (Millican 2004, pp. 437–8, 465). In what follows, however, I argue that Millican's objection does not succeed. I pay particular attention to Millican's assumption that Anselm relies on what I call the 'principle of the superiority of existence'. I argue that (a) the textual evidence that Millican cites does not provide a convincing case that Anselm relies on the principle and that, moreover, (b) Anselm does not even need the principle for the classical ontological argument. I introduce a plausible interpretation of the classical ontological argument that is not vulnerable to Millican's objection and conclude that *even if* the classical ontological argument ultimately fails, it does not fail in the way Millican thinks it does.

Millican claims that to provide an appropriate framework for Anselm's reasoning, we need to formulate a theory that enables 'reference to be made to an "entity" (such as God) without presupposing either its existence or its non-existence' (Millican 2004, p. 449). Millican uses the term 'nature' to denote an existence-independent entity and speaks of a nature as 'instantiated' if such an entity exists in reality. According to Millican's theory of natures, the nature of, for example, Laika, i.e. the Russian space dog, can be expressed as follows:

<*Laika*>: <first dog to be sent into space>

In general, the first set of angle brackets encloses the name of a nature and the second set encloses at least one of the most significant properties of that nature. Following this format, the natures of Lassie, i.e. the television dog, and Kings Alfred and Arthur, i.e. British heroes, can be expressed as follows:

<*Lassie*>: <dog, catches villains, rescues victims, star of film and television>
<*Alfred*>: <King of England, defeated the Danes, translated Boethius>
<*Arthur*>: <saintly and heroic king, kept a court of knights, sought the Holy Grail>

Millican maintains that Anselm subscribes implicitly to this theory of natures, which enables him to rank these figures based on their greatness. According to Millican's interpretation, Anselm thinks that 'among the various criteria for greatness (power, wisdom, goodness, *etc.*) real existence [or instantiation] "trumps" all others, so that any nature which has a real archetype, however lowly its characteristic properties may be, will on that account alone be greater than any nature, however impressively characterised, which does not' (Millican 2004, p. 451). This means that, according to Millican's interpretation, Anselm endorses the following principle:

The principle of the superiority of existence: Any nature that is instantiated is greater than any nature that is not instantiated (or any nature that is conceived only in the mind).[5]

Assume that the linear model and the overall greatness view that we considered in Chapter 2 are correct. That is, the intensity and extensity of a nature's great-making properties can be converted into its overall greatness, and based on that we can construct a linear ranking of all possible beings. Suppose then that Lassie is significantly more courageous and smarter than Laika. According to the principle of the superiority of existence, however, the nature <Lassie> is less great than the nature <Laika> because, unlike the nature <Laika>, the fictional nature <Lassie> is not instantiated. It is controversial whether King Arthur really existed; that is, whether the nature <Arthur> was instantiated. If the nature <Arthur> *was* instantiated, then it is the greatest among the above four natures, for its existence immediately defeats the nature <Lassie> and its other great-making properties defeat the natures <Laika> and <Alfred>. On the other hand, if the nature <Arthur> was not instantiated, then it is not as great as the nature <Alfred> or even the nature <Laika>. It is only greater than the nature <Lassie>.

Now the nature of God can be expressed as follows:

<God>: <omniperfect, creator of the universe>

'Omniperfection' is Millican's terminology, which represents a set of all divine properties, such as omniscience, omnipotence, and

[5] Two remarks are in order here. First, the proposition that *x* is conceived only in the mind entails that *x* is not instantiated, but not *vice versa*. For there are, given our cognitive limitations, uninstantiated natures that cannot be conceived in the mind. However, throughout this chapter, I use the phrases 'is conceived only in the mind' and 'is not instantiated' interchangeably because I am not concerned with uninstantiated natures that cannot be conceived in the mind. Second, it is slightly odd that Millican allows natures to have existence, or instantiation, as their property insofar as he stipulates that natures are 'existence-independent entities' (Millican 2004, p. 446). If natures can be regarded as being existence-independent while being either instantiated or uninstantiated, then, for example, ideas and concepts are also existence-independent. It is then unclear why Millican needs to introduce the new terminology here. However, for my purposes I can set this concern aside.

omnibenevolence (or moral perfection). If the nature <God> is instantiated, then it is greater than the above four natures, or indeed any natures at all. On the other hand, if the nature <God> is not instantiated, then it is not even as great as the nature <Laika>; it is only greater than all other *un*instantiated natures.[6]

Using the concept of natures, Millican presents his interpretation of the classical ontological argument as follows:

> (1m) The phrase 'a-nature-than-which-no-greater-nature-can-be-thought' is clearly understood by the Fool, and apparently makes sense.
>
> (2m) Hence we can take the phrase 'a-nature-than-which-no-greater-nature-can-be-thought' as successfully denoting some specific nature.
>
> (3m) A nature which is instantiated in reality is greater than one which is not.
>
> (4m) So if a-nature-than-which-no-greater-nature-can-be-thought were not instantiated in reality, then it would be possible to think of a nature that is greater (for example, any nature that is in fact instantiated in reality).
>
> (5m) But this would be a contradiction, since it is obviously impossible to think of a nature that is greater than a-nature-than-which-no-greater-nature-can-be-thought.
>
> (6m) Therefore a-nature-than-which-no-greater-nature-can-be-thought must indeed be instantiated in reality. (Millican 2004, pp. 457–8)

Notice that premise (3m) is equivalent to the principle of the superiority of existence. Based on the above interpretation and the theory of natures, Millican provides a unique objection to the classical ontological argument. Whether or not it is legitimate to reformulate the classical ontological argument in terms of natures, as Millican does, is a matter of further debate. Here, however, I assume, in favour of Millican, that it *is* legitimate.

[6] The claim that <God> is, if instantiated, greater than all other uninstantiated natures is based on the monotheistic assumption that there is no more than one greatest uninstantiated nature.

5.5 Millican's Objection to the Classical Ontological Argument

Millican's objection is concerned with the most crucial phrase in the classical ontological argument, namely 'a-nature-than-which-no-greater-nature-can-be-thought', which appears in premises (1m), (2m), (4m), and (5m). Millican maintains that there are four possible interpretations of this phrase:

(i) A nature that is so great that no nature is greater
(ii) A nature that can be thought so great that no nature can be thought greater
(iii) A nature that is so great that no nature can be thought greater
(iv) A nature that can be thought so great that no nature is greater

Now assume that the following is the greatest non-divine nature instantiated:

<*Aurelius*>: <absolute Emperor of the Roman Empire, wise, just, beneficent>

On this assumption, atheists would think that the nature <Aurelius> is the greatest instantiated nature *simpliciter*, and *a fortiori* the greatest nature *simpliciter*. Millican argues that none of the above four possible interpretations of the phrase enables Anselm to convince atheists to hold that the nature <God>, rather than the nature <Aurelius>, is the greatest nature.

Consider each of (i) through (iv). Given the principle of the superiority of existence, the following observations can be made:

Interpretation (i) denotes an instantiated nature that is so great that no instantiated nature is greater. Atheists would think that, on this interpretation, the phrase 'a-nature-than-which-no-greater-nature-can-be-thought' refers to the nature <Aurelius> rather than the nature <God>. Here, the classical ontological argument yields the trivial conclusion that the greatest nature is instantiated, i.e. that there exists the greatest existent being.

Interpretation (ii) denotes a nature such that *if* it exists, it is so great that no greater nature can possibly be thought. In this case, the phrase refers successfully to the nature <God> and the classical ontological argument goes smoothly up to premise (4m). However, it fails at premise (5m), according to which it is impossible to think of a nature that is greater than a-nature-than-which-no-greater-nature-can-be-thought. Given the principle of the superiority of existence, atheists would claim that it *is* possible to think of a nature that is greater than a-nature-than-which-no-greater-nature-can-be-thought; namely, any nature that is instantiated (e.g., the nature <Laika>, the nature <Alfred>, the nature <Aurelius>, *etc.*). From the atheistic point of view, they are greater simply because, unlike the nature <God>, they are instantiated.

Interpretation (iii) denotes an instantiated nature that is so great that no greater nature can possibly be thought. Atheists would not think of this phrase as denoting any nature at all, because there is no such nature unless the nature <God> is instantiated. On this interpretation, premise (2m), i.e. that we can take the phrase 'a-nature-than-which-no-greater nature-can-be-thought' as successfully denoting some specific nature, is unwarranted.

Interpretation (iv) denotes a nature such that *if* it is instantiated, it is so great that no instantiated nature is greater. In this case, the phrase could refer to the nature <God>. (The phrase *could* refer to the nature <God> but it does not have to. For example, it could also refer to the nature of a being that is just like Aurelius but slightly more powerful.) However, the classical ontological argument fails, again, at premise (5m) because, given the principle of the superiority of existence, it *is* possible for atheists to think of a nature that is greater than the nature <God>, namely instantiated natures, such as the nature <Laika>, the nature <Alfred>, and the nature <Aurelius>.

Millican concludes that, therefore, Anselm's ontological argument fails to establish the existence of God.

5.6 Initial Response to Millican's Objection

Again, Millican's objection to the classical ontological argument assumes that Anselm endorses the principle of the superiority of existence. This principle is based on the ideas that real existence is a property and that it is superior to all other properties that a nature can have. That is, even such great-making properties as omniscience, omnipotence, and omnibenevolence cannot be more useful than existence when it comes to making a nature greater. Since this principle is the core of the theory of natures that Millican formulates, it is important to examine carefully whether Anselm really endorses it.

Millican provides three reasons for his claim that Anselm endorses the principle of the superiority of existence. The first is that what Millican takes as a correct translation of Anselm's relevant sentence in the *Proslogion* seems to prove it. M. J. Charlesworth translates the sentence as follows:

> (Translation 1) [I]f [God] exists solely in the mind even, it can be thought to exist in reality also, which is greater. (Anselm 1965, originally 1077–8, p. 117)

Millican (2004) claims that this is a mistranslation. He says that it should instead be translated as follows:

> (Translation 2) [I]f [God] exists solely in the mind, something that is greater can be thought to exist in reality also. (Millican 2004, p. 439)

According to Millican, Translation 2 implies that Anselm endorses the principle of the superiority of existence.

The second reason Millican offers is that Anselm gives no indication of disagreement when Gaunilo attributes the principle of the superiority of existence to him (Millican 2004, pp. 439–40, 452). Gaunilo expresses his interpretation of Anselm's claim as follows: '[i]f this same being exists in the mind alone, anything that existed also in reality would be greater than this being' (Gaunilo 1965, originally 1078, p. 157).[7] As Millican correctly points out, while this interpretation is essentially identical to the principle of the superiority of existence, Anselm does not, in his reply to Gaunilo, accuse him of misinterpreting him.

The third reason is that Millican thinks that 'the logic of Anselm's argument could not possibly be strengthened (and might well be weakened)' if Anselm does not endorse the principle of the superiority of existence (Millican 2004, p. 452).

I submit that these three reasons do not warrant Millican's claim that Anselm endorses the principle of the superiority of existence. As to the first reason, the principle is neither equivalent to, nor entailed by, Translation 2. Translation 2 suggests merely that if the nature <God> is not instantiated, then *some* nature that is greater can be instantiated in reality. The principle of the superiority of existence is, however, the much stronger claim that *any* nature that is instantiated in reality is greater than *any* nature that is conceived only in the mind, including the nature <God> conceived only in the mind. Millican needs to show that Translation 2 entails the principle of the superiority of existence, but the entailment relationship here is the opposite; the principle of the superiority of existence entails Translation 2, but not *vice versa*. Moreover, while it is true that Translation 2 is consistent with the principle of the

[7] Gaunilo seems to adopt the same interpretation also when he presents his 'Lost Island' parody of the ontological argument: 'For if [the Lost Island] did not exist, *any other island existing in reality* would be more excellent than it' (Gaunilo 1965, originally 1078, p. 165, emphasis added).

superiority of existence, so is Translation 1. Furthermore, if Anselm really has the principle in mind when he asserts Translation 2, what he compares with God that exists solely in the mind is a being that exists in reality, e.g. Laika, Alfred, Aurelius, *etc.* It is then puzzling why Anselm has to formulate the consequent of Translation 2 as a modal statement, 'something that is greater *can be thought to exist* in reality also', rather than a more straightforward, non-modal statement such as, 'something that is greater *exists* in reality also'.

The second reason seems stronger than the first because Gaunilo's interpretation of Anselm's claim is, indeed, equivalent to the principle of the superiority of existence. However, it is still not strong enough to warrant the conclusion that Anselm endorses the principle of the superiority of existence, because there is another possible explanation for the fact that Anselm does not correct Gaunilo's interpretation. There is a consensus among Anselm scholars that Anselm's presentations in the relevant texts, namely chapters 2 through 5 and 15 of his *Proslogion* and his response to Gaunilo, are highly ambiguous. There have been multiple interpretations of the texts and many distinct forms of the argument have been derived from them. Some contend that Anselm provides three distinct versions of the ontological argument in the texts;[8] some contend that he provides two;[9] some contend that he provides only one;[10] and yet others contend that he does not even attempt to provide an argument for the existence of God.[11] From these facts, we may hypothesize that Anselm remains purposefully ambiguous about the dialectic of his

[8] Leftow (2002) maintains that in addition to the two versions of the ontological argument mentioned below, Anselm introduces a third version in his response to Gaunilo.

[9] Hartshorne (1961, 1965) and Malcolm (1960), as I mention in the main text above, claim that we can attribute the classical ontological argument to chapter 2 and the modal ontological argument to chapter 3 of the *Proslogion*, respectively.

[10] La Croix (1993b) argues that, contrary to what Hartshorne and Malcolm say, the version of the ontological argument attributed to chapter 3 of the *Proslogion* is not distinct from the one attributed to chapter 2.

[11] Barth (1960, originally 1931) argues that Anselm does not, in the *Proslogion*, attempt to provide a deductive argument for the existence of God; he rather provides an expression of faith, which *presupposes* the existence of God. I have to say that this interpretation is particularly implausible because in the preface to the *Proslogion* Anselm states explicitly that his goal is the following: 'to find one single argument that for its proof required no other save itself, and that by itself would suffice to prove that God really exists, that He is the supreme good needing no other and it is He whom all things have need of for their being and well-being, and also to prove whatever we believe about the Divine Being' (Anselm 1965, originally 1077–8, p. 103). Anselm makes this statement because he is not satisfied

argument in the texts. If this hypothesis is true, it could well be the case that Anselm does not correct Gaunilo's interpretation because he does not want to commit himself to a specific interpretation of the argument.

The third reason that Millican thinks that Anselm accepts the principle of the superiority of existence is that he has to accept it for his ontological argument to retain its force. In what follows, I argue that this claim is false because, ironically, by giving up the principle of the superiority of existence, we can undercut Millican's own objection, which he claims reveals a 'fatal flaw' in the argument.

5.7 Further Response to Millican's Objection

I have argued that the textual evidence Millican cites does not show convincingly that Anselm endorses the principle of the superiority of existence. Nonetheless, perhaps Millican does not need to provide any such evidence; perhaps Anselm *has to* accept the principle of the superiority of existence because otherwise he cannot construct the classical ontological argument in the first place. In what follows, however, I argue that Anselm does not need the principle of the superiority of existence for the argument.

To construct the classical ontological argument, Anselm needs to justify at least the following claim: If there were a nature <God> that is instantiated in reality and a nature <God> that is conceived only in the mind, then the former would be greater than the latter. According to Millican, Anselm would justify this claim by appealing to the principle of the superiority of existence, which entails the following:

> (A) A nature <God> that is instantiated is greater than a nature <God> that is conceived only in the mind because any nature that is instantiated is greater than a nature <God>, or any nature, that is conceived only in the mind.

However, (A) is not the only possible justification. An alternative justification is the following:

with his earlier *Monologion* in which he relies on multiple theistic arguments that only jointly entail the existence of God.

(B) A nature <God> that is instantiated in reality is greater than a nature <God> that is conceived only in the mind because existence is a great-making property.[12]

(B) is much more modest than (A) because it does not entail either that existence is superior to any other great-making property, such as knowledge, power, and benevolence, or that any instantiated nature is greater than any uninstantiated nature. Using the terminology of Chapter 2, we may hold the following: a nature <God> that is instantiated in reality as well as in the mind is greater than (or genuinely superior to) a nature <God> that is conceived only in the mind because the former is extensively superior to the latter, and the great-making properties they share are present in the former at the same degree of intensity as in the latter. (B) entails that, since existence is *a* great-making property, a nature <God> that is instantiated has a larger number of great-making properties than a nature <God> that is not instantiated. If we take this as Anselm's reasoning in his ontological argument, then Millican's objection does not succeed in refuting the argument.

With the above alternative justification in mind, Millican's interpretation of the classical ontological argument can be amended as follows:

(1m) The phrase 'a-nature-than-which-no-greater-nature-can-be-thought' is clearly understood by the Fool, and apparently makes sense.

(2m) Hence, we can take the phrase 'a-nature-than-which-no-greater-nature-can-be-thought' as successfully denoting some specific nature.

[12] There are at least three interpretations of (B). The first interpretation is that a nature <God> that is instantiated in reality is greater than a nature <God> that is conceived only in the mind because *with respect to the nature <God>* existence is a great-making property. (This interpretation is linked to the idea that existence, or instantiation, is not a great-making property if the nature in question is, for example, intrinsically malevolent.) The second interpretation is that a nature <God> that is instantiated in reality is greater than a nature <God> that is conceived only in the mind because *with respect to any nature* existence is a great-making property. The third interpretation is that a nature <God> that is instantiated in reality is greater than a nature <God> that is conceived only in the mind because *with respect to a certain category of beings including the nature <God>* existence is a great-making property. I set this aside here because the distinction above does not affect my response to Millican's objection. See Chapter 2 for discussion of related issues.

(3m′) A-nature-than-which-no-greater-nature-can-be-thought that is instantiated in reality is greater than a-nature-than-which-no-greater-nature-can-be-thought that is conceived only in the mind (because existence is a great-making property).

(4m′) So if a-nature-than-which-no-greater-nature-can-be-thought were not instantiated in reality, then it would be possible to think of a nature that is greater; namely, a-nature-than-which-no-greater-nature-can-be-thought that is instantiated in reality.

(5m) But this would be a contradiction, since it is obviously impossible to think of a nature that is greater than a-nature-than-which-no-greater-nature-can-be-thought.

(6m) Therefore a-nature-than-which-no-greater-nature-can-be-thought must indeed be instantiated in reality.

Here, only the third and fourth premises of Millican's interpretation have been amended and the rest remain the same.

As we saw in Section 5.5, the thrust of Millican's objection to the classical ontological argument is that Anselm's reasoning fails on any of interpretations (i) through (iv) of the phrase 'a-nature-than-which-no-greater-nature-can-be-thought'. I submit that the above interpretation of the classical ontological argument does not fail if we adopt interpretation (ii), according to which the phrase 'a-nature-than-which-no-greater-nature-can-be-thought' denotes a nature that can be thought so great that no greater nature can be thought. In the case of Millican's interpretation of the classical ontological argument, while the phrase successfully denotes God, the argument fails at premise (5m). This is because, given the principle of the superiority of existence, or equivalently (3m), it *is* possible for atheists to think of a nature that is greater than a-nature-than-which-no-greater-nature-can-be-thought: namely, any nature that is instantiated (e.g. the nature <Laika>, the nature <Alfred>, the nature <Aurelius>, *etc.*). However, the above interpretation of the argument does not fail at (5m) in this way because it abandons the principle of the superiority of existence and replaces (3m) with (3m′). According to this interpretation, it is indeed *im*possible for atheists to think of a nature that is greater than a-nature-than-which-no-greater-nature-can-be-thought. Therefore, the argument goes through and successfully yields the conclusion that a-nature-than-which-no-greater-nature-can-be-thought must be instantiated in reality. If, as Millican says, Translation 1 above is a mistranslation, then there is no textual evidence that this is the correct interpretation of Anselm's argument. Yet it is at least as consistent with relevant passages in Anselm's texts as Millican's interpretation.[13]

Millican might try to reject the above interpretation of the classical ontological argument by appealing to the Kantian objection that existence is not a predicate. However, such an option is not available to him, for several reasons. First, if he appeals to the Kantian objection, he will have to address philosophically deep issues concerning existence which he wishes to avoid. Second, it is dialectically problematic for Millican to adopt the Kantian objection because he bases his own objection on the theory of natures, which assumes, at least for the sake of argument, that existence *is* a predicate, or, more precisely, a great-making property for a nature. Third, if the Kantian objection is tenable, Millican's objection is redundant because he can simply reject the argument, both his own and my interpretations of it, by appealing to that thesis alone.[14]

Whether or not the classical ontological argument on the above interpretation ultimately succeeds is, of course, a matter for further debate. Nevertheless, it seems clear that the argument does not fail in the way Millican thinks it does; if it does fail, the failure is not due to the shallow logical problem that Millican identifies.

5.8 Response to Millican's Rejoinder

Since I published the above response to Millican (Nagasawa 2007), he has published a rejoinder (Millican 2007), which I wish to address here. Before examining his rejoinder, it is important to recall two distinctive features of his objection to the classical ontological argument. The first feature is that, unlike many other existing objections, his objection is meant to undermine the argument without questioning

[13] In particular, my interpretation is at least as consistent with Translations 1 and 2 of Section 5.6 as Millican's interpretation.

[14] Millican might also try to reject my interpretation of the ontological argument by claiming that while existence is a property, it is not a *great-making* property. However, such a claim would have the same unwelcome consequences: (i) it would involve philosophically deep issues that Millican wants to avoid, (ii) it would contradict Millican's assumption that existence *is* a great-making property for a nature, and (iii) it would render Millican's original objection redundant.

any philosophically substantial assumptions. The following are two examples of well-known existing objections that Millican contrasts with his own objection, to which we should pay attention:

> The comparison difficulty: There seems to be something logically odd about purporting to compare something that exists only 'in the mind' with something existing in reality. Therefore Anselm's premise... which crucially depends on the possibility of doing so, is dubious. (Millican 2004, p. 443)
>
> The Kantian dogma: As Kant famously argued (anticipated to a significant extent by Gassendi and Hume), it seems dubious to consider something's existence as a property that characterizes it, and hence as a factor that can contribute to the assessment of its greatness. Rather, its existence seems to be something presupposed if it is to have any properties at all. (Millican 2004, p. 443)

Millican thinks that such objections as the comparison difficulty and the Kantian dogma are at best ineffective because to defend them, one has to commit oneself to deep and controversial metaphysical assumptions, such as that the greatness of an existent entity and the greatness of a non-existent entity are not comparable and that existence is not a property that characterizes its possessor. He maintains that his objection is better because it sets aside any metaphysical assumptions and focuses on only shallow logical details of the classical ontological argument. He tries to construct an objection by appealing to 'a radically non-Kantian theory of existence-independent "natures" within which [Anselm's] argument can be framed so as to resist the standard objections' and 'identify a hitherto unremarked flaw in [Anselm's] reasoning which not only invalidates the argument in its original form, but which also, unlike those standard objections, operates at a level which makes it ineradicable by any plausible reformulation' (Millican 2004, p. 438).

The second unique feature of Millican's objection is that it purports to be neutral with respect to the interpretation of the relevant text, even though it might appear otherwise initially. Consider, again, a key sentence in chapter 2 of Anselm's *Proslogion*. M. J. Charlesworth translates the sentence as follows:

> (Translation 1) [I]f [God] exists solely in the mind even, it can be thought to exist in reality also, which is greater. (Anselm 1965, originally 1077–8, p. 117)

This translation suggests that Anselm compares two beings: God existing only in the mind and God existing in the mind as well as in reality.

Millican (2004) claims, however, that this is a mistranslation. He says that it should instead be translated as follows:

> (Translation 2) [I]f [God] exists solely in the mind, something that is greater can be thought to exist in reality also. (Millican 2004, p. 439)

Millican says that Translation 2, which can fairly be regarded as a non-standard interpretation, implies that, contrary to what Translation 1 says, Anselm compares God existing only in the mind and something else (i.e. something that isn't God) existing in the mind as well as in reality.[15] However, in his rejoinder to me, Millican emphasizes that he is 'undogmatic about the interpretative issue' and 'insist[s on his objection] on a philosophical point' (Millican 2007, p. 1041). In fact, he thinks that 'objections in a similar spirit could be made against *all* versions of the [o]ntological [a]rgument', not just the classical version that Millican formulates on the basis of his non-standard reading of Anselm's text (Millican 2007, p. 1043).

Consider now Millican's rejoinder (2007). He agrees with me that my formulation of the classical ontological argument does not fail in the exact same way as the original version does. Nevertheless, he maintains that it 'fails in a closely related way' (Millican 2007, p. 1041). He claims, in particular, that it fails not for a deep metaphysical reason but, again, for its shallow logical details. In what follows, however, I argue that Millican's claim is not cogent because, contrary to what he says, to apply his objection to my above formulation of the classical ontological argument, he does have to rely on a deep metaphysical assumption as well as a specific reading of Anselm's text.

Millican accepts premises (1m) and (2m) of the above formulation. He agrees that if we interpret the phrase 'a-nature-than-which-no-greater-nature-can-be-thought' as, as I assume, *a nature that can be thought so great that no greater nature can be thought*, then the phrase is understood even by atheists and successfully denotes the nature

[15] See, for example, Oppy's 2008 paper, which surveys five recent formulations of the ontological argument provided by Millican, Timothy Chambers, Jordan Howard Sobel, Nicholas Everitt, and Brian Leftow. Among these five interpreters, only Millican formulates the argument in terms of the comparison of greatness between God existing only in the mind and something else existing both in the mind and in reality, instead of the comparison of greatness between God existing only in the mind and God existing both in the mind and in reality (Oppy 2008, pp. 114–15).

<God>. Millican argues, however, that I fail to defend the rest of the argument:

> But in [defending the rest of the argument] Nagasawa—just like Anselm—is blurring the distinction between the level of greatness that some nature *actually* has, and the level of greatness that it *can be thought* to have. Consider, for example, his initial statement of the claim that 'if there were <God> that is instantiated in reality and <God> that is conceived only in the mind, then the former would be greater than the latter'. This conditional may sound plausible, but in fact it is deeply muddled because its antecedent does not describe any possible situation: the nature <God>—which Nagasawa takes to be the referent of Anselm's key phrase—is either instantiated in reality or it is not, and *it cannot be both*. (Millican 2007, p. 1051, emphasis in the original)

This passage seems to miss my point. Again, the nature <God> is defined by Millican himself as follows:

<God>: <omniperfect, creator of the universe> (Millican 2004, p. 453)

My point quoted in the above passage is that the nature described as <omniperfect, creator of the universe> would be greater if it were instantiated in reality than if it were not. Here existence is treated as a property (or a predicate), so there is nothing contradictory in comparing an omniperfect creator of the universe *with* the property of being existent and the same being *without* that property. It is true, as Millican says, that the same being cannot be both existent and non-existent simultaneously, but that is irrelevant to my point.

Millican's response to my argument is more clearly explained in the following passage:

> Now with this point in mind look at Nagasawa's step (4m′), which says that if <God> were not instantiated in reality, then it would be possible to think of a nature 'that *is* greater', namely, <God> 'that *is* instantiated in reality ([Millican's] emphasis). But if <God> is not, in fact, instantiated in reality, then it is not possible to think of any nature that *in fact* achieves this higher level of greatness: thinking of <God> *as instantiated* adds nothing to its *actual* level of greatness. (Millican 2007, p. 1052, emphasis in the original)

This passage suggests that Millican's theory of natures does not allow the comparison of greatness between uninstantiated <*x*> and instantiated <*x*>, even though it might allow the comparison of greatness between uninstantiated <*x*> *being thought of not existing in reality* and uninstantiated <*x*> *being thought of existing in reality*. Millican thinks that the comparison of greatness between uninstantiated <*x*> and instantiated <*x*> does not make sense because if <*x*> is not instantiated in reality, there is no such thing as <*x*> that *is* instantiated in reality. That is why he rejects premises (3m′) and (4m′) of my alternative formulation, where the argument makes the comparison of greatness between a-nature-than-which-no-greater-nature-can-be-thought that is instantiated in reality and the same nature that is not instantiated in reality. Yet this means that Millican commits himself, implicitly, to a version of the comparison difficulty, which says, as we saw above, that '[t]here seems to be something logically odd about purporting to compare something that exists only "in the mind" with something existing in reality' (Millican 2004, p. 443). Thus, Millican's objection to the alternative formulation is not as metaphysically neutral as he thinks it is. The comparison difficulty, to which Millican does not allow opponents of the classical ontological argument to commit themselves, is hidden in his own theory of natures. (The version of the comparison difficulty that Millican endorses might be slightly weaker than the standard version above, because while the standard version does not seem to allow for the comparison of greatness between any instantiated nature, on the one hand, and any uninstantiated nature, on the other, his version allows for the comparison of greatness between instantiated <*x*> and uninstantiated <*y*> provided that *x* is not identical to *y*. For example, Millican allows for the comparison of greatness between the instantiated nature <Aurelius> and the uninstantiated nature <God>. As I explain below, however, whether or not Millican's comparison difficulty is weaker than the standard version is not important in this context.)

There is yet another problem for Millican, which is that his response to the alternative formulation contradicts his own claim that he does not rely on a specific reading of Anselm's text. As I mentioned earlier, the standard reading of the relevant passage in the *Proslogion* suggests that Anselm compares two beings: God existing only in the mind and God existing both in the mind and in reality, rather than God existing only in the mind and something else existing both in the mind and in reality. If, as Millican says himself, he is 'undogmatic about the interpretative issue' (Millican 2007, p. 1041), he has to be open to the standard reading. Yet the way in which he responds to the alternative formulation of the classical ontological argument excludes such a reading; his response does not allow us to make the comparison of greatness between God existing only in the mind and God existing both in the mind and in reality (or the nature <God> that is not instantiated in reality and the nature <God> that is instantiated in reality), despite the fact that it allows for the comparison of greatness between God existing only in the mind and God existing in the mind and also being *thought of* existing in reality.

In sum: Millican's objection to the alternative formulation precludes us from comparing God existing only in the mind and God existing both in the mind and in reality. This entails that his objection fails because it contradicts its own two unique abovementioned features. With respect to the first feature, i.e. purporting to be free from any deep metaphysical assumption, it *does* make such a deep metaphysical assumption as a version of the comparison difficulty. Admittedly, the version that Millican holds could be weaker than the original version; one might judge that Millican's is not even a version of the comparison difficulty. That is, however, beside the point. The point is that, contrary to his disclaimer, Millican commits himself to a deep metaphysical assumption, to which, again, he does not allow other opponents of the classical ontological argument to commit themselves. With respect to the second unique feature, i.e. purporting not to rely on a specific reading of the relevant Anselmian text, Millican's response to the alternative formulation of the classical ontological argument does rely on a specific, non-standard reading of Anselm's text. Conversely, if Millican does not adopt the non-standard reading, he cannot defend his objection in the first place.

5.9 Conclusion

I have argued mainly for the following three theses over the course of this chapter. First, even though Anselm is not an inventor of perfect being theism, he *is* the inventor of the classical ontological argument. While some earlier arguments initially appear to be similar to the classical ontological argument, a close examination suggests that they are not in fact versions of the argument. Second, the classical ontological argument remains disputed because it is, intentionally or unintentionally, structured cleverly in such a way that no matter how one approaches it, one cannot refute it without making a deep metaphysical or epistemic assumption, one that is likely to be contentious in its own right. This seems to be the most striking fact about the argument. Third, Millican's recent attempt to develop a shallow, logical objection, which aims to be neutral with respect to deep philosophical assumptions and specific interpretations of Anselm's texts, is untenable.

In Chapter 6, I discuss the parody objection to the classical ontological argument, an objection that also tries to refute the argument without making deep philosophical assumptions.

6

A Partial Defence of the Classical Ontological Argument II

6.1 Introduction

I argued in Chapter 5 that the dispute over the classical ontological argument for perfect being theism endures even nine centuries after Anselm introduced it because the argument is structured in such a way that one cannot refute it without making a significant metaphysical or epistemic assumption that is likely to be contentious in its own right. That is, there is no uncontroversial, straightforward refutation of the argument that would convince a majority of its defenders to concede that it does not succeed.

I then discussed Peter Millican's recent attempt to refute the argument without making any deep metaphysical or epistemic assumption. I argued, however, that his attempt does not succeed. In this chapter, I critically discuss another attempt of this kind to refute the argument, an attempt I call the 'parody objection'. The parody objection says that there is something wrong in the shallow, logical details of the ontological argument because, if the argument were successful, it would be possible to construct parallel parodies that establish with equal success the existence (or non-existence) of various absurd entities, such as the 'Lost Island', 'AntiGod', and the 'devil'.

The parody objection is certainly one of the oldest, if not *the* oldest, responses to the ontological argument. It was introduced by Gaunilo in the eleventh century soon after Anselm introduced the classical ontological argument. Its longevity notwithstanding, however, it seems to me that the strengths and weaknesses of the parody objection are often misunderstood. Here I critically discuss Gaunilo's version of the parody objection and some more recent, and more sophisticated, versions of the objection. I pay particular attention to Peter Millican's and Timothy Chambers's versions of the objection. As I discuss these versions, I defend the following hypothesis: The parody objection always fails because any parody of the ontological argument is such that either (i) it is not structurally parallel to the ontological argument (typically because its scope is too narrow), or (ii) it is not dialectically parallel to the argument (typically because it makes extraneous assumptions to which proponents of the argument are not committed or assumptions that are clearly false or inconsistent with at least one of the argument's premises). I argue, moreover, that, once a parody is modified in such a way as to avoid (i) and (ii), it is, ironically, no longer a parody—it is the ontological argument itself. Of course, one can hardly undermine the ontological argument by appealing to the ontological argument itself.

This chapter has the following structure: In Sections 6.2 and 6.3, I introduce Gaunilo's version of the parody objection concerning the Lost Island and explain why it fails to refute the classical ontological argument. In Section 6.4, I argue that, even though Gaunilo's version does not succeed, the parody objection remains more attractive than other existing objections to the classical ontological argument in some important respects. In Sections 6.5 and 6.6, I address Millican's recent defence of the parody objection, which appeals to the notion of 'AntiGod', and argue that it fails to undermine the classical ontological argument. I also improve Millican's argument and introduce parody arguments concerning the existence of the 'devil'. Yet I argue that versions of the parody objection based on these arguments fail to undermine the classical ontological argument. In Sections 6.7 and 6.8, I address Chambers's elaborate recent attempt to create a further difficulty for proponents of the classical ontological argument, an attempt that uses a parody argument against the existence of the devil. I argue that it also fails to undermine the classical ontological argument. In Section 6.9, I develop, based on the failure of all versions of the parody objection that I discuss, the abovementioned hypothesis concerning the limits of the objection. I conclude in Section 6.10.

6.2 Gaunilo's Island Parody

As I mentioned in Chapter 5, Anselm's presentations of the ontological argument in the relevant texts—namely, chapters 2 through 5 and 15 of his *Proslogion* and the response to Gaunilo—are highly ambiguous. There have been many alternative interpretations of the texts and many alternative forms of the argument have been derived from them. In what follows, I set aside the exegetical debate and keep our focus again on the classical, non-modal ontological argument, which is normally identified as occurring in chapter 2 of the *Proslogion*. I discuss the modal ontological argument, which is normally identified as occurring in chapter 3 of the *Proslogion*, in detail in Chapter 7. Here, then, I call any parody of the classical ontological argument a 'parody argument' and any attempt to undermine the classical ontological argument by appealing to a parody argument a 'parody objection'.

The following is a summary of the classical ontological argument that I provided in Chapter 5: God is the being than which no greater is metaphysically possible. This being exists at least in the mind because even the Fool, who denies that such a being exists in reality, understands what it is. Suppose, for the sake of *reductio ad absurdum*, that such a being exists only in the mind and not in reality. If so, another being can be thought that is greater, namely the same being that is thought to exist in reality as well as in the mind. This means that a being can be thought that is greater than the being than which no greater is metaphysically possible. This, however, is obviously impossible. Therefore, it is not the case that such a being exists only in the mind. It exists both in the mind and in reality. Therefore, God exists.

The structure of the above argument can be presented as follows:

The Classical Ontological Argument

(1o) God is the being than which no greater being is metaphysically possible.

(2o) God exists in the mind because even the Fool understands what it is.

(3o) If God exists only in the mind but not in reality, another being can be thought that is greater, namely the same being that is thought to exist in reality as well as in the mind, which is contradictory.

(4o) Therefore, it is not the case that God exists only in the mind.

(5o) Therefore, God exists both in the mind and in reality.

(6o) Therefore, God exists.

As I mentioned above, the parody objection was introduced for the first time by Anselm's contemporary Gaunilo. Gaunilo formulates the objection by appealing to a parody argument that purports to prove the existence of the 'Lost Island', or the greatest possible island. He writes:

> For example: they say that there is in the ocean somewhere an island which, because of the difficulty (or rather the impossibility) of finding that which does not exist, some have called the 'Lost Island'. And the story goes that it is blessed with all manner of priceless riches and delights in abundance much more even than the Happy Isles, and, having no owner or inhabitant, it is superior everywhere in abundance of riches to all those other lands that men inhabit. Now, if anyone tell me that it is like this, I shall easily understand what is said, since, nothing is difficult about it. But if he should then go on to say, as though it were a logical consequence of this: You cannot any more doubt that this island that is more excellent than all other lands truly exists somewhere in reality than you can doubt that it is in your mind; and since it is more excellent to exist not only in the mind alone but also in reality, therefore it must needs be that it exists. For if it did not exist, any other land existing in reality would be more excellent than it, and so this island, already conceived by you to be more excellent than others, will not be more excellent. If, I say, someone wishes thus to persuade me that this island really exists beyond all doubt, I should either think that he was joking, or I should find it hard to decide which of us I ought to judge the bigger fool—I, if I agreed with him, or he, if he thought that he had proved the existence of this island with any certainty, unless he had first convinced me that its very excellence exists in my mind precisely as a thing existing truly and indubitably and not just as something unreal or doubtfully real. (Gaunilo 1965, originally 1078, p. 165)

The structure of this argument can be presented as follows:

Gaunilo's Lost Island Argument

(1g) The Lost Island is the island than which no greater island is metaphysically possible.

(2g) The Lost Island exists in the mind because even the Fool understands what it is.

(3g) If the Lost Island exists only in the mind but not in reality, another island can be thought that is greater, namely the same island that is thought to exist in reality as well as in the mind, which is contradictory.

(4g) Therefore, it is not the case that the Lost Island exists only in the mind.

(5g) Therefore, the Lost Island exists in reality.

(6g) Therefore, the Lost Island exists.

The Lost Island argument is structurally parallel to the classical ontological argument. It merely replaces all occurrences of the word 'God' in the classical ontological argument with the term 'the Lost Island' and all occurrences of the word 'being' with the term 'island'. Given that the Lost Island argument has the same logical structure as the classical ontological argument, Gaunilo seems to advance his parody objection as follows: If the classical ontological argument were successful in establishing the existence of God, then the Lost Island argument would be equally successful in establishing the existence of the greatest possible island. However, we all know that there is no such thing as the greatest possible island in reality. Therefore, by *modus tollens*, the classical ontological argument is not successful in establishing the existence of God.

As I explained in Chapter 5, the classical ontological argument is a *reductio ad absurdum*. It tries to establish the existence of God by assuming for the sake of argument that God exists only in the mind and then deriving from it the absurdity that a being can be thought that is greater than God. The island objection can be considered a second-order *reductio ad absurdum* because it tries to refute the classical ontological argument, which itself is a *reductio ad absurdum*, by assuming for the sake of argument that it is sound and then deriving from this assumption the absurdity that the Lost Island exists in reality.

6.3 Responses to Gaunilo's Island Parody

Gaunilo's version of the parody objection fails on at least two grounds. First, the Lost Island argument is not strictly parallel to the classical ontological argument because its scope is narrower than that of the classical ontological argument. The classical ontological argument is concerned with the set of all possible beings, which effectively means that its scope is unlimited. On the other hand, the Lost Island argument is concerned with a very small subset of it, namely the set of all possible *islands*. It is far from clear that if an argument with a significantly limited scope is absurd, an analogous argument with a significantly wider scope is also absurd. Consider a parallel example. Suppose that we construct an argument that is concerned with all people. We then construct its parallel parody that is concerned with all weightlifters, which, of course, constitute a very small subset of the set of all people. It is far from obvious that the observation that a parallel argument about all weightlifters entails an absurd conclusion tells us anything about the soundness of the original argument about all people.

Second, the Lost Island argument is based on an assumption to which proponents of the classical ontological argument are not committed. The classical ontological argument is based on the implicit assumption that there are intrinsic maxima of properties traditionally attributed to God. So, for example, it assumes that there is a maximum amount of knowledge, power, and benevolence that any being, in particular a being than which no greater can be thought, can have. Similarly, the Lost Island argument is based on the implicit assumption that there are intrinsic maxima of properties that an island can have. So, for example, it assumes that there is a maximum amount of beautiful palm trees or pleasant beaches that any island, in particular an island than which no greater can be thought, can have. However, proponents of the classical ontological argument, who are committed to the assumption that there are intrinsic maxima of God's properties, are not committed to the assumption that there are intrinsic maxima of an island's properties. Moreover, as Alvin Plantinga points out, there is an obvious reason to reject such an assumption about an island's properties: For any island *i* it is always possible to make *i* greater by adding, for example, one more beautiful palm tree or one more pleasant beach (Plantinga 1974a, p. 91). (One might argue that the perfect being concept of God as the being than which no greater is metaphysically possible is as untenable as the concept of an island than which no greater is metaphysically possible because if we apply the same reasoning, we can show that for any being *x*, it is always possible to make *x* greater by adding one more great-making property. I addressed this objection in Chapter 4.) Gaunilo's version of the parody objection fails, therefore, to undermine the classical ontological argument.

6.4 The Virtues of the Parody Objection

The failure of Gaunilo's version of the parody objection is unlikely to devastate critics of the classical ontological argument because this objection is often regarded as a second-class, supplementary objection to the argument or a mere curious consequence that one can derive from it.

Few critics consider it as something that could constitute a serious objection. Yet I believe that the parody objection is more important and possibly more compelling than other objections to the argument. In this section, I elaborate on this point by focusing on two of its main virtues.

The first virtue of the parody objection is that, unlike other objections, the parody objection does not dispute any controversial metaphysical or epistemic assumptions of the ontological argument (Millican 2004, pp. 460–3). This virtue is particularly important in our context. Again, most existing objections to the ontological argument fail to persuade a majority of defenders because they make deep philosophical assumptions that are controversial. Consider the Kantian objection to the ontological argument once more, because it helps us to highlight this point and advance the rest of our discussion here. Again, the objection says that the ontological argument is unsuccessful because it is based on the false assumption that existence is a predicate (Kant 1929, originally 1781, pp. 500–7). While existence often behaves grammatically like a predicate, according to the objection it is not a real predicate. Such sentences as '*x* exists' and '*x* is existent' are not comparable to '*x* is tall' or '*x* has blond hair', where the predicates denote properties of *x*. Although many critics believe that this is a knock-down objection to the ontological argument, defending it is far from easy. For, in order to defend it, one has to establish not only that the ontological argument presupposes that existence is a predicate, which itself is controversial, but also that existence is, indeed, not a predicate, which is even more controversial, independently of the debate over the ontological argument.[1] Thus, to refute the argument by appealing to the Kantian objection, one needs first to solve the difficult problem regarding the nature of existence.

The parody objection is attractive because it purports to avoid this sort of complication. To defend this objection, one need not dispute any contentious metaphysical or epistemic assumptions underlying the ontological argument. The parody objection accepts, at least for the sake of argument, all the ontological argument's premises and assumptions.

[1] For more on the controversy over existence as a predicate see, for example, McGinn (2000), Miller (2002), Moore (1936), and Nelson (2012).

So, for instance, if the ontological argument does indeed assume that existence is a predicate, the objection agrees with that assumption for the sake of argument. It then constructs a parallel argument that derives an absurd conclusion. In this sense, the parody objection is as metaphysically and epistemically sympathetic as possible to the ontological argument, until the last stage in which it purportedly reveals an absurdity entailed by a parallel parody.

The second virtue of the parody objection is that it applies to multiple versions of the ontological argument. Kant introduces his own objection to Descartes's version of the ontological argument because it appears manifest that Descartes assumes that existence is a predicate when he states, 'existence is a perfection'. It is, however, unclear that the same objection applies equally to other versions of the ontological argument. For example, as we can see in the above formulation, none of the premises of Anselm's classical ontological argument says that existence is a predicate. If any of the premises requires that existence be a predicate, it must do so in a very subtle and implicit way. Contrary to existing objections such as Kant's, the parody objection applies to all versions of the classical ontological argument because it can be constructed by merely rephrasing seemingly crucial terms in any version of the argument. As I mentioned above, Gaunilo uses the objection to undermine the classical ontological argument. Gassendi, Descartes's contemporary, uses it to undermine the Cartesian version of the argument (by appealing to a parody argument for the existence of a 'perfect Pegasus'), and Graham Oppy (1996) uses it to undermine Gödel's modal ontological argument.[2]

Of course, the parody objection is not almighty. One main drawback of the objection is that it does not pinpoint exactly what is wrong with the ontological argument. If the objection is successful, it shows only that

[2] Gassendi advances a parody objection to the ontological argument in his letter to Descartes: 'I might also . . . say that in the idea of a perfect Pegasus, there was contained not only the perfection of having wings, but also that of existing. For as God is thought to be perfect in every kind of perfection, so is Pegasus thought to be perfect in its own kind, and you can bring forward in criticism nothing which cannot, if the parallel between the two be duly observed, be taken to hold of both alike' (Plantinga 1965, pp. 47–8). Caterus, another contemporary of Descartes, also tries to undermine the ontological argument by providing a parallel argument for the existence of an 'existing lion' (Plantinga 1965, p. 39).

there is *something* wrong *somewhere* in the argument.[3] However, while it is important to know exactly where the flaw lies in the full set of premises, the parody objection alone is, in principle, sufficient to refute the ontological argument.

Given its virtues, it seems sensible for critics to try to develop an improved version of the parody objection that is not vulnerable to criticisms raised against Gaunilo's version. If they succeed in developing an effective parody objection, they can in principle refute multiple versions of the ontological argument simultaneously without raising deep philosophical complications. That would be a great accomplishment. In the rest of this chapter, I discuss Millican's and Chambers's attempts to do just that. They purport to develop new, strengthened versions of the parody objection, which appeal to arguments for or against the existence of beings other than the Lost Island, such as AntiGod and the devil.

6.5 Millican's AntiGod Parody

One might wonder at this point why I have devoted space in two chapters to discussing Millican's objections to the classical ontological argument. One might think that this is an unusually narrow focus because there is a vast literature involving a great deal of good critical work on the classical ontological argument.[4] I focus on Millican's objections and comparable objections raised by Gaunilo and Chambers because they are fundamentally different from other existing objections. I believe that proponents and opponents of the classical ontological argument end in a draw because, while there are powerful objections to the classical ontological argument, nearly all of them make metaphysical or epistemic assumptions that are controversial independently of their relationships to the argument. It is therefore important to examine the versions of the parody objection defended by Gaunilo, Millican, and Chambers because they are among the very few objections to the classical ontological argument that are intended to avoid making contentious metaphysical or epistemic assumptions.

Let us quickly recap Millican's theory of natures (Millican 2004; see Chapter 5). This is necessary as he uses it in formulating the classical

[3] See Millican (2004), p. 463.

[4] Thanks to an anonymous reader for raising this concern.

ontological argument and his parallel parody. Again, the theory of natures enables 'reference to be made to an "entity" (such as God) without presupposing either its existence or its non-existence' (Millican 2004, p. 449). Millican uses the term 'nature' to denote an existence-independent entity and speaks of a nature as 'instantiated' if such an entity exists in reality.

According to Millican's theory of natures, the nature of, for example, Lassie can be expressed as follows:

> <*Lassie*>: <dog, catches villains, rescues victims, star of film and television>

In general, the first set of angle brackets encloses the name of a nature and the second set encloses at least one of the most significant properties of that nature. Following this format, the natures of Kings Alfred and Arthur can be expressed as follows:

> <*Alfred*>: <King of England, defeated the Danes, translated Boethius>
> <*Arthur*>: <saintly and heroic king, kept a court of knights, sought the Holy Grail>

Millican maintains that in defending the classical ontological argument, Anselm subscribes implicitly to this theory of natures, which enables him to rank natures on the basis of their greatness. According to Millican's interpretation, Anselm thinks that 'among the various criteria for greatness (power, wisdom, goodness, *etc.*) real existence [or instantiation] "trumps" all others, so that any nature which has a real archetype, however lowly its characteristic properties may be, will on that account alone be greater than any nature, however impressively characterised, which does not' (Millican 2004, p. 451). This suggests that, according to Millican's interpretation, Anselm endorses the following principle:

Principle of the superiority of existence (PSE): Any nature that is instantiated is greater than any nature that is not instantiated (or any nature that is conceived only in the mind).

In Chapter 5, I questioned the legitimacy of Millican's attribution of the principle to Anselm. In this chapter, however, I accept it for the sake of argument.

It is controversial whether King Arthur really existed; that is, whether the nature <Arthur> was instantiated. If the nature <Arthur> *was* instantiated, then it is the greatest among the three natures, for its existence immediately defeats the nature <Lassie> and its other great-making properties defeat the nature <Alfred>. On the other hand, if the nature <Arthur> was not instantiated, then it is not as great as the nature <Alfred>; it is only greater than the nature <Lassie>.

Using the concept of natures, Millican formulates the classical ontological argument as follows:

Millican's Formulation of the Classical Ontological Argument

(1m) The phrase 'a-nature-than-which-no-greater-nature-can-be-thought' is clearly understood by the Fool, and apparently makes sense.

(2m) Hence we can take the phrase 'a-nature-than-which-no-greater-nature-can-be-thought' as successfully denoting some specific nature.

(3m) A nature which is instantiated in reality is greater than one which is not.

(4m) So if a-nature-than-which-no-greater-nature-can-be-thought were not instantiated in reality, then it would be possible to think of a nature that is greater (for example, any nature that is in fact instantiated in reality).

(5m) But this would be a contradiction, since it is obviously impossible to think of a nature that is greater than a-nature-than-which-no-greater-nature-can-be-thought.

(6m) Therefore a-nature-than-which-no-greater-nature-can-be-thought must indeed be instantiated in reality. (Millican 2004, pp. 457–8)

Notice that premise (3m) is equivalent to the PSE. Premise (4m) says that if a-nature-than-which-no-greater-nature-can-be-thought were not instantiated in reality, then, given (3m) or the PSE, it would be possible to think of a nature, for example the nature <Alfred>, that is greater than a-nature-than-which-no-greater-nature-can-be-thought. This is, of course, as (5m) says, contradictory. The argument concludes that a-nature-than-which-no-greater-nature-can-be-thought is therefore instantiated in reality; that is, God exists.

In developing his parody objection, Millican says that there must be something wrong with the classical ontological argument because we can construct from it a parallel parody that yields the absurd conclusion that AntiGod exists—call it the 'AntiGod argument'. According to Millican,

AntiGod is a being that has almost all the properties that God has. The only difference is that, instead of being morally perfect, AntiGod is 'most effectively evil'. Millican writes, 'The result, after appropriate substitutions, will be an argument beginning something like this':

> The AntiGod Argument
>
> (1a) The phrase 'a-nature-than-which-no-more-effectively-evil-nature-can-be-thought' is clearly understood by the Fool, and apparently makes sense.
>
> (2a) Hence we can take the phrase 'a-nature-than-which-no-more-effectively-evil-nature-can-be-thought' as successfully denoting some specific nature. (Millican 2004, p. 461)

Given that it has the same structure as the classical ontological argument, the AntiGod argument appears to establish the existence of AntiGod as certainly as the classical ontological argument establishes the existence of God. The conclusion of the above argument, i.e. that AntiGod exists, seems absurd and is unacceptable, particularly to perfect being theists. Millican concludes, therefore, that the classical ontological argument, which is parallel to the parody argument, fails.

In what follows, I argue that Millican's version of the parody objection is untenable because the AntiGod argument is not, in fact, parallel to the classical ontological argument.

6.6 Response to Millican's AntiGod Parody

As I explained above, Millican amends the first two premises of Anselm's classical ontological argument, (1m) and (2m). To render the AntiGod argument formally valid and also parallel to the classical ontological argument, however, he has to amend all the other premises as well. He needs, as he does in (1m) and (2m), to replace the term 'greater' in all the premises with 'more-effectively-evil'. Thus, (3m) should be amended as follows:

> (3a) A nature which is instantiated in reality is *more effectively evil* than one which is not.

However—and here is the first difficulty with the AntiGod parody—(3a) is, unlike (3m), subject to an obvious counterexample. Consider, for instance, the following nature:

> <Morally Perfect Being>: <morally perfect>

Suppose that the nature <Morally Perfect Being> is instantiated. According to (3a), the nature <Morally Perfect Being> is more effectively evil than any nature that is not instantiated. This is surely wrong; an existent *morally perfect* being cannot be more effectively evil than a non-existent being.

To resolve this difficulty, Millican needs to amend (3a) as follows:

(3a′) An *evil* nature which is instantiated in reality is *more effectively evil* than one which is not.

This modification renders the parody argument not truly structurally parallel to the classical ontological argument. I nevertheless set this point aside in favour of Millican.

Millican needs to amend (4m) and (5m) as follows:

(4a) So if a-nature-than-which-no-*more-effectively-evil*-nature-can-be-thought were not instantiated in reality, then it would be possible to think of a nature that is *more effectively evil* (for example, any *evil* nature that is in fact instantiated in reality).

(5a) But this would be a contradiction, since it is obviously impossible to think of a nature that is *more effectively evil* than a-nature-than-which-no-*more-effectively-evil*-nature-can-be-thought.

From these premises can be derived the following conclusion:

(6a) Therefore a-nature-than-which-no-*more-effectively-evil*-nature-can-be-thought must indeed be instantiated in reality.

This parody argument is formally valid. Millican cannot, however, appeal to it to reject the classical ontological argument because there is no reason for proponents of the argument to accept (3a′). Even if they were to accept the entirety of the theory of natures that Millican attributes to the classical ontological argument, they would not be obliged to accept such a claim about effective evilness as (3a′). The theory of natures is concerned with greatness and has nothing to do with effective evilness. For the parody argument to work, it has to be structured in such a way that proponents of the classical ontological argument cannot but accept its premises. Yet Millican's AntiGod parody is not structured in that way.

Millican's objection faces a further difficulty. The above parody argument is not only structurally but also dialectically not parallel to the classical original argument; it is explicitly question-begging in a way in which the classical ontological argument is not. Millican does not provide a definition of effective evilness but the assumption seems to be that, necessarily, if a nature is effectively evil, then that nature is instantiated. Or, more generally, if a nature is effective with respect to something, then, necessarily, that nature is instantiated. There is no such thing as an effective but uninstantiated nature. This is because the phrase 'effective' is used here to mean effective *in reality*. Millican formulates the parody argument in terms of effective evilness rather than evilness *simpliciter* precisely because, otherwise, the argument fails to yield the conclusion that AntiGod exists. However, this means that the parody argument begs the question. Sometimes the classical ontological argument is accused of being question-begging, but it is, at least, not question-begging in the way in which the AntiGod argument is. In particular, the classical ontological argument does not assume in its premises that God is *effectively* great.

Fortunately, however, it is possible to construct an improved parody argument that satisfies the following conditions: (a) it shares the spirit of the AntiGod argument; (b) it is structurally parallel to the classical ontological argument; (c) it is no more question-begging than the classical ontological argument.

This new parody argument, call it the 'devil argument', can be formulated as follows:[5]

The Devil Argument

(1d) The phrase 'a-nature-than-which-no-*worse*-nature-can-be-thought' is clearly understood by the Fool, and apparently makes sense.

(2d) Hence we can take the phrase 'a-nature-than-which-no-*worse*-nature-can-be-thought' as successfully denoting some specific nature.

(3d) A nature which is instantiated in reality is *worse* than one which is not.

(4d) So if a-nature-than-which-no-*worse*-nature-can-be-thought were not instantiated in reality, then it would be possible to think of a

[5] I use the term 'devil' because in the literature on the ontological argument it is commonly used to refer to the worst possible being. I am aware that this does not necessarily match the theological concept of the devil.

nature that is *worse* (for example, any nature that is in fact instantiated in reality).

(5d) But this would be a contradiction, since it is obviously impossible to think of a nature that is *worse* than a-nature-than-which-no-*worse*-nature-can-be-thought.

These premises entail the following conclusion:

(6d) Therefore a-nature-than-which-no-*worse*-nature-can-be-thought must indeed be instantiated in reality.

The devil argument is clearly structurally parallel to the classical ontological argument because it merely replaces the term 'greater' in the original argument with 'worse'. The thrust of this argument is that a-nature-than-which-no-*worse*-nature-can-be-thought, or the nature of the devil, must be instantiated because, if it were not, then it would be possible to think of a nature that is worse than the nature in question (for example, the nature of an evil dictator) that is instantiated in reality.

However, while this argument *is* structurally parallel to the classical ontological argument, Millican cannot use it for the purpose of undermining the latter. This is because premise (3d) is inconsistent with (3m), or equivalently with the principle of the superiority of existence, which is a crucial premise of the classical ontological argument. (3d) implies that the nature of the devil must be instantiated in reality because otherwise the devil cannot be the worst possible being. Yet (3m) implies that the nature of the devil must not be instantiated because the worst possible being does not have any great-making properties, including existence. Notice that what (3m) implies, but not what (3d) implies, is consistent with my understanding of great-making properties that I discussed in detail in Chapter 2. Great-making properties should be understood as *intrinsically* great properties that, all else being equal, contribute to the greatness of their possessors. They should not be understood as properties that are great in the sense that they are beneficial to their possessor, others, or the world. Again, for a parody objection to work, it has to be designed in such a way that proponents of the classical ontological argument cannot but accept its premises.

One might reject the claim that (3m) and (3d) are inconsistent by saying the following: Every instantiated nature has some value, while no uninstantiated nature has any value at all. Therefore, it is vacuously true that anything that is of some value is greater *and* worse than anything that is of no value. Therefore, every instantiated nature is greater and worse than any uninstantiated nature.[6] But this claim entails a contradiction. Suppose that <*X*> is an instantiated nature and <*Y*> is an uninstantiated nature. If the abovementioned claim is correct, the following two propositions are true:

(A) The nature <*X*> is greater than the nature <*Y*> (because any instantiated nature is greater than any uninstantiated nature).

(B) The nature <*X*> is worse than the nature <*Y*> (because any instantiated nature is worse than any uninstantiated nature).

(B) entails the following:

(C) The nature <*Y*> is greater than the nature <*X*>.

Given the transitivity of greatness, we can derive the following from (A) and (C):

(D) The nature <*X*> is greater than the nature <*X*>.

(D) is obviously self-contradictory. (Whether or not greatness is always transitive is a matter of dispute. However, it is only minimally controversial that greatness *simpliciter*, which concerns us here, is transitive.) Hence, critics cannot hold legitimately that, if the classical ontological argument were successful, then the devil argument would be successful, and *vice versa*.

One might claim at this point that (3m) and (3d) can be consistently held if (3m) is restricted to good beings and (3d) is restricted to bad beings.[7] In this way, one might say, there is just as much reason to believe (3d) as (3m). This response, however, is untenable. An assumption in perfect being theism is, again, that great-making properties are understood as *intrinsically* great properties rather than as properties that are great in relation to their possessors or in relation to others and the world. Hence, for example, power is considered a great-making property because it is intrinsically great, whether it is possessed by a criminal or a saint. Similarly, if instantiation is a great-making property, then it is

[6] Thanks to Joseph Jedwab for raising this objection.

[7] I am indebted to an anonymous reader on this point.

considered great in this context whether it is possessed by the nature of God or the nature of the devil. If the devil is the worst possible being, then his nature must lack all great-making properties including instantiation.

What happens, then, if we replace (3d) with (3m)? We can obtain the following; call it the 'no-devil argument':

The No-Devil Argument

(1d) The phrase 'a-nature-than-which-no-*worse*-nature-can-be-thought' is clearly understood by the Fool, and apparently makes sense.

(2d) Hence we can take the phrase 'a-nature-than-which-no-*worse*-nature-can-be-thought' as successfully denoting some specific nature.

(3m) A nature which is instantiated in reality is greater than one which is not.

(4d′) So if a-nature-than-which-no-*worse*-nature-can-be-thought *were* instantiated in reality, then it would be possible to think of a nature that is *worse* (for example, any nature that is *not* instantiated in reality).

(5d) But this would be a contradiction, since it is obviously impossible to think of a nature that is *worse* than a-nature-than-which-no-*worse*-nature-can-be-thought.

These premises entail the following conclusion:

(6d′) Therefore a-nature-than-which-no-*worse*-nature-can-be-thought must indeed *not* be instantiated in reality.[8]

There are a number of reasons that the no-devil argument is not a threat to proponents of the classical ontological argument. First, the conclusion of the no-devil argument is much more innocuous than that of the devil argument. The classical ontological argument is contentious because it

[8] The devil and no-devil arguments are not particularly new. The devil argument was introduced by Albert A. Cock in 1917–18, and rediscovered in the 1950s. As far as I know, the no-devil argument was formulated for the first time by C. K. Grant in 1957. For discussions of these arguments, see Cock (1917–18), Devine (1975), Gombocz (1973), Grant (1957), Grim (1979), Haight and Haight (1970), Millican (1989), Oppy (1995, 2006), Power (1992), Richman (1958, 1960, 1976), and Waldman (1959).

derives, through a priori reasoning alone, the existence of a being, namely God. However, the no-devil argument derives, thorough a priori reasoning alone, only the *non*-existence of a being, namely the devil. While it is disputed whether we can establish the existence of a being through a priori reasoning alone, it is undisputed that we can derive the non-existence of many beings through a priori reasoning alone (e.g. a square circle, a married bachelor, *etc.*). Second, the conclusion of the no-devil argument seems theologically unproblematic. Most perfect being theists would be willing to accept the conclusion that there is no such being as the devil, particularly as defined as the being than which no worse can be thought. Evidently, Anselm himself seems to think that a being than which no worse can be thought does not exist (Oppy 1995, p. 183). Finally, the no-devil argument does not constitute an effective parody objection because it is not structurally parallel to the classical ontological argument. The third premise is identical to its counterpart in the classical ontological argument but all other premises are not identical to theirs; rather, they are mirror images of the counterparts, with the term 'greater' replacing the term 'worse'.

Therefore, even the improved versions of the AntiGod argument cannot constitute a successful refutation of the classical ontological argument.

6.7 Chambers's Devil Parody

We have seen that none among the set consisting of the AntiGod argument, the devil argument, and the no-devil argument is forceful enough to constitute a successful parody objection to the classical ontological argument. Yet Timothy Chambers (2000) argues that the no-devil argument, in particular, might not be as innocuous as it seems at first sight because we can develop an effective parody objection by appealing to it. In this section and Sections 6.8–6.9, I critically discuss his argument.

Unlike Millican, Chambers formulates the classical ontological argument without relying on the theory of natures. His formulation is as follows:

Chambers's Formulation of the Classical Ontological Argument

(1c) There is, in the understanding at least, something than which nothing greater can be thought.

(2c) If it is even in the understanding alone, it can be thought to be in reality also,

(3c) Which would be greater.

(4c) There exists, therefore, both in the understanding and in reality, something than which a greater cannot be thought. (Chambers 2000, pp. 100–2)

I assume, for the sake of argument, that this is an accurate formulation of the classical ontological argument. Chambers then introduces what he calls the 'no-devil corollary':

The No-Devil Corollary

(1n) There is, in the understanding at least, something than which nothing lesser (worse) can be thought.

(2n) If it exists in the understanding and in reality, it can be thought to exist in the understanding alone,

(3n) Which would be still less (worse).

(4n) There does not exist in reality, therefore, something than which a lesser (worse) cannot be thought. (Chambers 2000, p. 110)

Notice that the no-devil corollary is essentially identical to the no-devil argument that I discussed in Section 6.6. The no-devil corollary derives, as does the no-devil argument, the non-existence of the devil by paralleling Anselm's reasoning. Moreover, the no-devil corollary appears to be no less innocuous than the no-devil argument. The fact that the non-existence of some beings is shown a priori is unsurprising, and the claim that the devil does not exist in reality does not seem problematic to most perfect being theists. Chambers claims, however, that the innocuousness of the no-devil corollary is only superficial. According to him, it can lead to a new, more effective parody objection which undermines the classical ontological argument.

To construct the new parody objection, Chambers introduces another parody argument, which is comparable to the no-devil corollary presented above. Chambers calls it the 'extreme no-devil corollary':

The Extreme No-Devil Corollary

(1e) Suppose there is, in the understanding at least, something than which nothing lesser (worse) can be thought.

(2e) If it exists in the understanding, then it is possible that it does not exist in the understanding,

(3e) Which would be still less (worse).

(4e) There does not exist in the understanding, therefore, something than which a lesser (worse) cannot be thought. (Chambers 2000, p. 111)

The extreme no-devil corollary derives the conclusion that the devil does not exist even in the understanding, apparently by endorsing the following principle: Any being that does not exist in the understanding is lesser (worse) than any being that exists in the understanding. Notice that this is analogous to Millican's principle of the superiority of existence, which we discussed in Section 6.5.

By appealing to the no-devil and the extreme no-devil corollaries, Chambers runs his parody objection to the classical ontological argument as follows:

Chambers's Version of the Parody Objection to the Classical Ontological Argument

(1p) If Anselm's argument is sound, then so is the no-devil corollary.

(2p) We understand the expression, 'something than which nothing lesser (worse) can be thought', if we understand the expression 'something than which nothing greater can be thought'.

(3p) The extreme no-devil corollary is sound if the no-devil corollary is.

(4p) If the extreme no-devil corollary is sound, then its conclusion is true, i.e., the conclusion that there does not exist in the understanding something than which a lesser (worse) cannot be thought.

(5p) If we understand the description, 'That than which a lesser (worse) cannot be thought', then the subject of that description exists in the understanding.

Therefore,

(6p) If Anselm's argument is sound, then we do *not* understand the description, 'That than which a greater cannot be thought'.

(7p) Anselm's argument is sound only if we understand the description, 'That than which a greater cannot be thought'.

Therefore,

(8p) Anselm's argument is not sound. (Chambers 2000, pp. 110–12)

Chambers's presentation above is not very straightforward but the upshot of his parody objection is fairly simple: If the classical ontological argument were sound, then the no-devil corollary would also be sound. If the no-devil corollary were sound, then the extreme no-devil corollary would also be sound. However, the extreme no-devil corollary implies a claim that makes the classical ontological argument a failure: One cannot even understand the description of God as 'that than which no greater cannot be thought'. Therefore, the classical ontological argument, which relies on this description of God, is unsuccessful.

6.8 Objection to Chambers's Devil Parody

Chambers's version of the parody objection to the classical ontological argument is certainly intriguing, but it faces a number of difficulties.

First, premises (1p) and (3p) of Chambers's version of the parody objection jointly entail that if the classical ontological argument is sound, then the extreme no-devil corollary is sound. This, however, is false because the extreme no-devil corollary entails a thesis to which proponents of the classical ontological argument are not committed. The thesis in question is that not being existent in the understanding is worse than being existent in the understanding, which corresponds to premise (3e) of the extreme no-devil corollary. The classical ontological argument holds the thesis that existing in reality as well as in the understanding is better than existing in the understanding alone, which corresponds to premise (3c) of Chambers's formulation of the classical ontological argument above. But (3c) (or any other premise of the classical ontological argument) does not entail (3e). Proponents of the classical ontological argument who hold (3c) are not committed to the idea that the property of being existent in the understanding is a great-making property which the devil must lack.

Second, premise (3p) of Chambers's version of the parody objection, i.e. that the extreme no-devil corollary is sound if the no-devil corollary is, is clearly false. For the no-devil corollary and the extreme no-devil corollary are inconsistent. Consider the no-devil corollary. This argument shows, if it is sound, that a being than which no lesser (worse) can be thought exists in the understanding but not in reality. Meanwhile, the extreme no-devil corollary shows, if it is sound, that a being than which no lesser (worse) can be thought exists neither in the understanding nor in reality. From these two arguments, therefore, we can derive the claim that a being than which no lesser (worse) can be thought both exists and does not exist simultaneously in the understanding, which is, of course, logically impossible. So, contrary to what (3p) says, it is false that the extreme no-devil corollary is sound if the no-devil corollary is.

Third, Chambers's version of the parody objection seems to be based on an incorrect assumption about transitivity in the case of parody arguments. The point of the parody objection in general is to refute the classical ontological argument by showing that there is a parallel parody argument that seems to reveal the absurdity of the classical ontological argument. Yet what Chambers shows is not that there is a parallel argument that seems to reveal the absurdity of the classical ontological argument, but rather that there is *a parallel argument of the parallel argument* that seems to reveal the absurdity of the classical ontological argument. This strategy works if the following transitivity relationship holds: if argument *A1* and argument *A2* are parallel and argument *A2* and argument *A3* are parallel, then argument *A1* and argument *A3* are parallel. This relationship does not, however, seem to hold, particularly not among the set of arguments consisting of the classical ontological argument, the no-devil corollary, and the extreme no-devil corollary. Chambers essentially says the following: The classical ontological argument is parallel to the no-devil corollary and the no-devil corollary is parallel to the extreme no-devil corollary; however, we can derive a contradiction if we assume that the extreme no-devil corollary and the classical ontological argument are parallel. Chambers thinks that the reason we can derive a contradiction is that the classical ontological argument is unsound. However, contrary to what Chambers says, the classical ontological argument is not parallel to the extreme no-devil corollary. If the extreme no-devil corollary is really parallel to the classical ontological argument, we should be able to obtain the corollary by substituting relevant terms in the argument without changing its structure. However, as we have seen, we cannot obtain the corollary in this way. In fact, it makes more sense to think that we can derive a contradiction because, as Graham Oppy correctly points out, the conclusion of the extreme no-devil corollary—i.e. (4e), according to which there does not exist in the understanding, therefore, something than which a lesser (worse) cannot be thought—is the *negation* of the first premise of the no-devil corollary—i.e. (1n), according to which there is, in the understanding at least, something than which nothing lesser (worse) can be thought (Oppy 2006, p. 81).

Chambers's parody argument is one of the most elaborate applications of the devil argument. However, it fails to refute the classical ontological argument.

6.9 A Hypothesis Concerning the Parody Objection

We have seen that, while the parody objection is more powerful than many other existing objections in various respects, even the most sophisticated contemporary versions of it, such as Millican's and Chambers's, do not succeed in defeating the classical ontological argument. In this section, by comparing the parody argument concerning Lost Island on the one hand, and the parody arguments concerning AntiGod and the devil on the other, I contemplate why the parody objection always fails.

As we saw in Section 6.2, Gaunilo's version of the parody objection appeals to the Lost Island argument, which purports to derive that the greatest possible island exists. As I explained in Section 6.3, proponents of the classical ontological argument commonly reject Gaunilo's objection on two grounds. First, the scope of the Lost Island argument is narrower than that of the classical ontological argument. The Lost Island argument is concerned with all possible *islands*, while the classical ontological argument is concerned with all possible *beings*. The set of all possible islands is a very small subset of the set of all possible beings. Second, the Lost Island argument is based on an assumption about intrinsic maxima to which proponents of the classical ontological argument are not committed. Proponents of the classical ontological argument are committed to the assumption that there are intrinsic maxima of God's properties, such as knowledge and power, but they are not committed to the assumption that there are intrinsic maxima of an island's properties, such as the number of beautiful palm trees and pleasant beaches.

Resorting to the parody arguments concerning AntiGod and the devil is in effect an attempt to overcome these two difficulties that the Lost Island argument faces. In response to the first difficulty, the parody arguments concerning AntiGod and the devil maintain the same scope as that of the classical ontological argument. It covers all possible beings (except for a version of the AntiGod argument whose scope is all possible *evil* natures rather than all possible natures *simpliciter*). In response to the second difficulty, the parody arguments concerning AntiGod and the devil assume nothing more about intrinsic maxima than does the classical ontological argument. This is because, unlike the Lost Island argument, they are not concerned with the upper limit of any property.

Unfortunately, however, the no-devil argument and the no-devil corollary face a difficulty of their own. They include premises that make assumptions to which proponents of the classical ontological argument are not committed. Millican's AntiGod argument includes premise (3a), which says that a nature that is instantiated in reality is *more effectively evil* than one that is not. A modified version of the AntiGod argument includes premise (3a′), which says that an *evil* nature which is instantiated in reality is *more effectively evil* than one which is not. The devil argument includes premise (3d), which says that a nature which is instantiated in reality is *worse* than one which is not. The extreme no-devil corollary includes premise (3e), which says that not being existent in the understanding is worse than being existent in the understanding. These parody arguments are all problematic because proponents of the classical ontological argument are not committed to any of (3a), (3a′), (3d), or (3e). None of them is entailed or implied by any of the premises of the classical ontological argument. (Moreover, as we have seen above, (3a) is clearly false, (3a′) is not structurally parallel to a corresponding premise of the classical ontological argument, and (3d) is inconsistent with a corresponding premise of the classical ontological argument.)

Of these parody arguments, the one that is most structurally similar to the classical ontological argument is the no-devil argument (which is essentially the same as the no-devil corollary). Yet we have seen that the no-devil argument is not exactly parallel to the classical ontological argument because premise (3m), unlike the other premises of the no-devil argument, is not a mirror image of a corresponding premise of the classical ontological argument. Moreover, ironically, as I explained above, the conclusion of the no-devil argument is so innocuous that, even if we assume that it is a perfect parallel to the classical ontological argument, it does not raise a threat for proponents of the classical ontological argument. An effective parody argument has to derive an absurd conclusion which proponents of the classical ontological argument would not be able to accept.

One might claim at this point that a parody argument does not have to parallel the classical ontological argument exactly or rely on premises to which proponents of the classical ontological argument are committed because, after all, it is only a parody. The purpose of the parody objection is, one might say, to illustrate that there is something wrong with the classical ontological argument by presenting an absurd parody which is comparable, but not necessarily strictly parallel, to the classical ontological argument.

If this claim is correct, however, the parody objection is too weak. In Section 6.4, I contended that while the parody objection does not pinpoint exactly what is wrong with the classical ontological argument, it is, in principle, sufficient to refute the argument. However, if the above interpretation is correct, the parody objection is far from sufficient. Its being true merely that the classical ontological argument and a parody argument are superficially similar and that the parody argument is unsound does not entail that the classical ontological argument is also unsound. This point can be emphasized by interpreting the parody objection as an example of an argument by analogy.[9] An argument by analogy infers that two things have a common property by appealing to their similarity in a certain respect. The following is a general scheme of an argument by analogy: *A* and *B* are similar; *A* has property *x*; therefore, *B* has property *x* too. For example: kangaroos are similar to wallabies; kangaroos are marsupials; therefore, wallabies are marsupials too. The parody objection can be presented with the same structure: The parody arguments are similar to the classical ontological argument; the parody arguments are unsound; therefore, the classical ontological argument is unsound too. For an argument by analogy to be effective, two things that are analogized have to be *relevantly and sufficiently similar*. What we have observed shows, however, that none of the parody arguments succeeds because they are not relevantly or sufficiently similar to the classical ontological argument.

In defence of the parody objection, one might claim as follows: The purpose of the parody objection is not to show that proponents of the classical ontological argument are committed to an absurd parody argument. The purpose is to show rather that between the classical

[9] Thanks to an anonymous reader on this point.

ontological argument and a parody argument, there is no reason to choose one over the other, because one is a mirror image of the other.[10]

We cannot apply this interpretation to the version of the parody argument that appeals to the no-devil argument (which is, again, essentially the same as the no-devil corollary) because, again, the no-devil argument is not a mirror image of the classical ontological argument. As we have seen, we cannot obtain it merely by replacing the term 'greater' in the classical ontological argument with the term 'worse' in the non-devil argument. Moreover, it is incorrect to say that one cannot choose one over the other between the classical ontological argument and the no-devil argument. As I noted above, most proponents of the classical ontological argument would accept, if necessary, the no-devil argument because its conclusion is both philosophically and theologically innocuous. Apply the interpretation in question, then, to the version of the parody argument that appeals to the devil argument. Unlike the no-devil argument and the no-devil corollary, the devil argument *is* a mirror image of the classical ontological argument; one can obtain the devil argument merely by replacing the term 'greater' in the classical ontological argument with the term 'worse'. It is, however, incorrect to say that one cannot choose between the classical ontological argument and the devil argument. Consider, for example, the third premise of the classical ontological argument:

(3m) A nature which is instantiated in reality is greater than one which is not.

The counterpart of this premise in the devil argument is the following:

(3d) A nature which is instantiated in reality is *worse* than one which is not.

If the interpretation in question is to succeed, proponents of the classical ontological argument need to be attracted to (3d) as much as they are to (3m). However, perfect being theists would reject (3d) straight away because, as I explained in Section 6.6 and Chapter 2, perfect being theists understand great-making properties, such as existence, as intrinsically great properties rather than as properties that are great in relation to

[10] I am indebted to Joseph Jedwab on this point.

their possessors or in relation to the world or others. So even if it is attributed to the nature of the devil, existence remains a great-making property.

An effective parody argument would derive an absurd conclusion while being structurally and dialectically parallel to the classical ontological argument. Starting with the Lost Island argument, proponents of the parody argument have improved their case to the extent that they have developed the parody arguments concerning AntiGod and the devil. I have argued, however, that these arguments are also inadequate as parody objections to the classical ontological argument. These observations lead us to the following hypothesis. The parody objection always fails because any parody argument is such that either (i) it is not structurally parallel to the classical ontological argument (typically because its scope is too narrow), or (ii) it is not dialectically parallel to the classical ontological argument (typically because it makes assumptions to which proponents of the classical ontological argument are not committed or assumptions that are clearly false or inconsistent with premises of the classical ontological argument).

To circumvent (i) and (ii), proponents of the parody objection have to try to develop a better parody argument by eliminating problematic assumptions while keeping its structure parallel to that of the classical ontological argument. However, ironically, once a parody argument is modified in this way, it is no longer a parody; it is the classical ontological argument itself. Of course, one cannot undermine the classical ontological argument by appealing to the classical ontological argument itself.

6.10 Conclusion

There are powerful objections to the classical ontological argument, such as the Kantian objection, but they cannot be definitive refutations of the argument because, again, they raise deep metaphysical or epistemic issues that are contentious independently of their relationships to the argument. In Chapter 5, I discussed Millican's shallow, logical objection through which he tries to overcome this difficulty, but I argued that it does not succeed. In this chapter, I have considered another kind of shallow, logical objection, which appeals to parodies. I have argued, however, that not only Gaunilo's classical version of the parody objection but even the most sophisticated contemporary versions fail. It seems therefore appropriate to conclude this chapter by reiterating my partial defence of the classical ontological argument: proponents of the classical ontological argument and their critics end in a draw; there might be a successful refutation of the argument, but it is inevitable that it raises a substantial philosophical dispute that cannot be easily settled. In Chapter 7, I provide a full defence of the ontological argument. My defence there is, however, a defence of the *modal* ontological argument rather than the classical ontological argument.

7

Maximal God and the Modal Ontological Argument

7.1 Introduction

My aim in this part of the book has been to find an argument *for* perfect being theism, as we saw in Part II that, by appealing to the maximal concept of God, we can refute nearly all existing arguments *against* perfect being theism. I argued in Chapters 5 and 6 that the dispute between proponents and opponents of the classical ontological argument ends in a draw because while there are some strong objections to the argument, none of them can be defended without making a significant metaphysical or epistemic assumption, one that is likely to be contentious in its own right. This means, in other words, that although there is no knock-down objection to the classical ontological argument, we cannot rely on the argument without reservation. In this final chapter, therefore, I develop a new, full defence of the *modal* ontological argument, an alternative argument for perfect being theism. I focus mainly on the so-called 'possibility premise' of the argument, the premise according to which it is possible that God exists. Many attempts have been made to establish this premise because once the premise is shown to be true, the modal ontological argument seems to entail the existence of God straight away as a matter of logic. I closely examine existing attempts but argue that, unfortunately, none of them is compelling. I then introduce a new way of establishing the possibility premise by appealing, again, to the maximal God thesis. That is, I hope to show that the maximal concept of God allows us not only to refute arguments against perfect being theism but also to establish a successful argument *for* perfect being theism.

This chapter has the following structure. In Section 7.2, I introduce the modal ontological argument and explain its structure and significance.

In Section 7.3, I focus on the possibility premise and reject five existing arguments for it. In Section 7.4, I develop a new way of establishing the possibility premise, which uses the maximal God thesis. I conclude in Section 7.5.

7.2 The Modal Ontological Argument

For centuries it had been assumed that Anselm defends only one version of the ontological argument, i.e. the classical ontological argument, in the *Proslogion*. However, this assumption was challenged in the middle of the twentieth century. In *Philosophers Speak of God*, which Charles Hartshorne published with his student William L. Reese in 1953, he claimed that, in addition to the classical ontological argument presented in Chapter 2 of the *Proslogion*, Anselm proposes a hitherto unknown version of the argument, i.e. the modal ontological argument, in chapter 3.[1] Norman Malcolm made the same point in 1960 in his paper, 'Anselm's Ontological Argument', and Hartshorne discussed the modal ontological argument in detail in 1961 in his paper, 'The Logic of the Ontological Argument'.

The following is Anselm's text from the *Proslogion* in which Hartshorne and Malcolm find the modal ontological argument:

> And certainly this being so truly exists that it cannot be even thought not to exist. For something can be thought to exist that cannot be thought not to exist, and this is greater than that which can be thought not to exist. Hence, if that-than-which-a-greater-cannot-be-thought can be thought not to exist, then that-than-which-a-greater-cannot-be-thought is not the same as that-than-which-a-greater-cannot-be-thought, which is absurd. Something-than-which-a-greater-cannot-be-thought exists so truly then, that it cannot be even thought not to exist. (Anselm 1965, originally 1077–8, p. 119).

Malcolm summarizes the modal ontological argument as follows:

> If God, a being a greater than which cannot be conceived, does not exist then He cannot *come* into existence. For if He did He would either have been *caused* to come into existence or have *happened* to come into existence, and in either case He would be a limited being, which by our conception of Him He is not. Since

[1] Hartshorne had already introduced the modal ontological argument in 1941 in his book *Man's Vision of God*, but he was not explicit about the fact that it is found in chapter 3 of the *Proslogion*. See chapter 9 of Hartshorne (1941).

> He cannot come into existence, if He does not exist His existence is impossible. If He does exist He cannot have come into existence (for the reasons given), nor can He cease to exist, for nothing could cause Him to cease to exist nor could it just happen that he ceased to exist. So if God exists His existence is necessary. Thus God's existence is either impossible or necessary. It can be the former only if the concept of such a being is self-contradictory or in some way logically absurd. Assuming that this is not so, it follows that He necessarily exists.[2]
>
> (Malcolm 1960, pp. 49–50)

The core of the above argument is the thesis that if God exists, His existence is necessary. If God's existence is a matter of necessity rather than contingency, it has to be the case that either it is necessary that God exists or it is necessary that He does not exist. In other words, the existence of God is either necessary or impossible. Yet it seems obvious that God's existence is not impossible; it does not appear to involve any contradiction or logical absurdity. This seems to entail that God's existence is necessary rather than impossible. Therefore, the argument concludes, God exists.

Anselm's presentations of the ontological argument in the *Proslogion* and in his response to Gaunilo are highly intractable, so some dispute whether Anselm really presents two versions of the ontological argument in it. Richard R. La Croix (1993b), for example, claims that, contrary to what Hartshorne and Malcolm contend, the modal ontological argument attributed to chapter 3 of the *Proslogion* is identical to the classical ontological argument attributed to chapter 2. Even Malcolm himself writes, 'There is no evidence that [Anselm] thought of himself as offering two different proofs' (Malcolm 1960, p. 45). But these exegetical issues are not important for our philosophical discussion here. What impresses many philosophers is not Hartshorne's and Malcolm's 'discovery' that Anselm defends more than one version of the ontological argument in the *Proslogion*, but the strength of the modal ontological argument when it is compared with the classical ontological argument. By focusing on God's *necessary* existence rather than His mere existence, the modal ontological argument seems to undercut existing objections to the classical ontological argument. For example, as I explained in previous chapters, the classical ontological argument faces the powerful Kantian

[2] Malcolm's use of the phrases 'come into existence' and 'cease to exist' seems problematic as it implies that he understands God's necessary existence in terms of temporality or causation rather than modality. I set this point aside in our discussion here.

objection, according to which the argument fails because it is based on the false assumption that existence is a predicate. Malcolm claims that the modal ontological argument does not rely on such an assumption. Instead, it relies on the weaker assumption that the logical impossibility of non-existence—that is, necessary existence—is a predicate (Malcolm 1960, p. 46). Necessary existence does seem to be a predicate because it uniquely characterizes its possessor. Many contingent beings, such as people, tables, and planets, do not have that property while some other beings, such as God and numbers, do seem to have it. On the other hand, mere existence does not seem to be a predicate because, while predicates are meant to uniquely characterize their possessors, everything that exists is, of course, existent.

Not only Malcolm and Hartshorne but also many other philosophers have introduced subtly distinct formulations of the modal ontological argument.[3] I base my discussion below on Plantinga's formulation, which is arguably the most elegant and compelling formulation in the literature (Plantinga 1974a, 1974b). This formulation is based on two key notions. The first is the following:

Maximal excellence: Necessarily, a being is maximally excellent in a given possible world only if it is omnipotent, omniscient and omnibenevolent in that world.[4]

If there is a maximally excellent being in a given possible world, that being is omnipotent, omniscient, and omnibenevolent in that world. Plantinga's use of the term 'maximal' is slightly confusing in our context because the above definition suggests that if God is maximally excellent, He is an omni being rather than a maximal being. Nevertheless, I set this point aside and adhere to Plantinga's terminology. Note that being omnipotent, omniscient, and omnibenevolent is only a necessary, and not sufficient, condition for maximal excellence. The following is the second key notion:

Maximal greatness: Necessarily, a being is maximally great only if it is maximally excellent in every possible world.

[3] For the taxonomy of distinct formulations of the modal ontological argument, see chapter 4 of Oppy (1995).

[4] Plantinga uses the term 'wholly good' instead of 'omnibenevolent', but I use the latter to be consistent with our terminology throughout this book.

In other words, necessarily, a being is maximally great only if it is necessarily maximally excellent. That is, necessarily, a being is maximally great only if it is necessarily omniscient, omnipotent, and omnibenevolent. Note, again, that maximal excellence in every possible world is only a necessary, and not sufficient, condition for maximal greatness. Unlike maximal excellence, maximal greatness is not indexed to a specific possible world. If there is a being that is maximally great, that being is omnipotent, omniscient, and omnibenevolent not only in a specific possible world but in all possible worlds.

Plantinga's version of the modal ontological argument, which appeals to the notions of maximal excellence and maximal greatness, can be presented as follows:

(1x) It is possible that a maximally great being exists.

(2x) Therefore, it is possible that necessarily a maximally excellent being exists.

(3x) Therefore, it is possible that necessarily an omniscient, omnipotent, and omnibenevolent being exists.

(4x) Therefore, necessarily an omniscient, omnipotent and omnibenevolent being exists.

(5x) Therefore, an omniscient, omnipotent and omnibenevolent being exists in the actual world. (Plantinga 1974a, 1974b)

Premise (1x) is often referred to as the 'possibility premise'. I discuss this premise in detail below. The derivation of intermediate conclusion (2x) is uncontentious as it follows a priori from premise (1x) and Plantinga's formulation of maximal greatness. The thesis that it is possible that a maximally great being exists entails that it is possible that necessarily a maximally excellent being exists because maximal greatness is a necessary version of maximal excellence. The derivation of intermediate conclusion (3x) is also uncontentious as it follows a priori from premise (2x) and Plantinga's formulation of maximal excellence. The thesis that it is possible that necessarily a maximally excellent being exists entails that it is possible that necessarily an omniscient, omnipotent, and omnibenevolent being exists because maximal excellence entails omniscience, omnipotence, and omnibenevolence. Intermediate conclusion (4x) is derived from (3x) on the following assumption: if it is possible that p is necessary, then, simply, p is necessary. That is, if you have 'possibly, necessarily *p*' then you can drop 'possibly' and obtain 'necessarily *p*' because 'possibly, necessarily *p*' is logically equivalent to 'necessarily *p*'. This assumption is based on the axioms of a system of modal logic called 'S5'. It is safe to say that the derivation of intermediate conclusion (4x) is also uncontentious because S5 is regarded as the most standard system of modal logic. Conversely, proponents of the modal ontological argument should be pleased if the only way to refute the argument is to reject S5, which is widely accepted. The derivation of conclusion (5x) is also uncontentious because it follows logically from intermediate conclusion (4x). The thesis that it is necessarily true that an omniscient, omnipotent, and omnibenevolent being exists means that such a being exists in all possible worlds, including the actual world.

The most interesting fact about the modal ontological argument is that it shows that *if* the existence of God, or a maximally great being, is *possible*, then it is *necessary*, which entails that it is also *actual*. That is, if atheists allow the mere possibility of the existence of God, then, according to the argument, they cannot but accept the necessity and actuality of the existence of God. In other words, if the argument is sound, then the only way to show that God does not exist is to show that the existence of God is impossible. This means that, according to the argument, the existence of God is either 0 per cent or 100 per cent probable. This is remarkable.

Here is another way to look at the significance of the modal ontological argument: The modal ontological argument reduces the burden on theists dramatically. They no longer need to appeal to such theistic arguments as the cosmological argument, the design argument, the moral argument, or the argument from miracles to demonstrate that God's existence is actual. All they need to do is to show somehow that the existence of God is *possible*. The mere possibility of God's existence entails its actuality. Hence, the modal ontological argument places us only a half-step away from a definitive proof of the existence of God. If we can show that the existence of God is at least possible, we can simply plug that into the modal ontological argument and derive the conclusion that the existence of God is necessary and, hence, actual.

The crucial question then is whether premise (1x), the possibility premise, is indeed true. Given that the modal ontological argument is formally valid and no other step in the argument seems dubious, we can dispute only that premise. Perfect being theists have therefore spent a lot of time and effort arguing for the possibility premise. In Section 7.3, I discuss many existing arguments for the premise. I claim, however, that none of them is compelling. In Section 7.4, I introduce a novel argument for the premise by appealing to the maximal concept of God.

7.3 Existing Arguments for the Possibility Premise

Again, the possibility premise of the modal ontological argument says that it is possible that there is God, or, using Plantinga's terminology, a being that is maximally great. The importance of establishing the possibility of God's existence was acknowledged long before Hartshorne and Malcolm published their work on the modal ontological argument. For instance, Descartes's contemporary Marin Mersenne writes:

> The conclusion [of Descartes's ontological argument] should have been: 'Hence, once we have made a sufficiently careful investigation of what God is, we can with truth affirm that existence belongs to the nature of God'. Now it does not follow from this that God in fact exists, but merely that he would have to exist if his nature is possible, or non-contradictory. In other worlds, the nature or essence of God cannot be conceived apart from existence; hence, granted the essence, God really exists. This comes down to an argument which others have stated as follows: 'If there is no contradiction in God's existing, it is certain that he exists; but there is no contradiction in his existing'. The difficulty here is with the minor premiss 'but there is no contradiction in his existing': those who attack the argument either claim to doubt the truth of this premiss, or deny it outright.
> (Cottingham, Stoothoff, and Murdoch 1984, p. 91)

Leibniz similarly remarks as follows:

> [The ontological argument] is not fallacious, but it is an incomplete demonstration, which assumes something which should also be proved in order to make the argument mathematically evident. The point is that it is tacitly assumed that this idea of a wholly great or wholly perfect being is possible and does not imply a contradiction. (Leibniz 1996, originally 1704, p. 438)

Mersenne merely points out the importance of establishing the possibility of God's existence and does not try to provide any argument for this possibility. However, many other philosophers, including Leibniz, have tried to construct elaborate arguments for it. Let us critically examine these arguments.[5]

[5] For historical discussion of the possibility premise, see Harrelson (2009), pp. 56–60, 143–50.

Argument 1: Conceivability Entails Possibility

The most obvious way to argue for the possibility premise is to appeal to the conceivability of the existence of God. This argument—call it the 'argument from conceivability'—can be presented as follows:

(1v) The existence of God is conceivable.
(2v) Conceivability entails possibility.
(3v) Therefore, the existence of God is possible.

As far as I know, this argument is not explicitly endorsed by any proponent of the modal ontological argument. The argument is widely known, however, because deriving possibility from conceivability is a common strategy in philosophy. Premise (1v) says that it is conceivable that God exists. It might be questioned whether the existence of God is possible, let alone actual, but it seems at least conceivable because, as Anselm says, even the 'Fool' understands what theists express when they claim that God exists. That is, even the Fool can conceive of the existence of God. Premise (2v) represents the so-called 'conceivability principle', which has been disputed in the philosophy of mind for some time. Philosophers distinguish many types of conceivability. For example, van Cleve (1983) distinguishes between 'strong conceivability' and 'weak conceivability'. David J. Chalmers (2002), to take another example, distinguishes between '*prima facie* conceivability' and 'ideal conceivability'; 'positive conceivability' and 'negative conceivability'; and 'primary conceivability' and 'secondary conceivability'. There is no space here to discuss all these distinctions but Chalmers's distinction between *prima facie* conceivability and ideal conceivability is useful here:

Prima facie conceivability: *S* is *prima facie* conceivable for a subject when *S* is conceivable for that subject on first appearance.

Ideal conceivability: *S* is ideally conceivable when *S* is conceivable on ideal rational reflection. (Chalmers 2002, p. 147)

I submit that the argument from conceivability for the possibility premise is not tight enough for the following reason: Obviously, proponents of the argument appeal to the conceivability of the existence of God instead of appealing directly to its possibility because they think that the conceivability is easier to establish. This means that there is a certain gap between conceivability and possibility. Conversely, if there is no gap between conceivability and possibility, then they should simply appeal to the possibility instead of the conceivability. Now the question is: how wide is the gap between the conceivability and the possibility of God's existence? There is no gap if we are ideal, rational agents in this context. For example, if we are omniscient with respect to relevant facts about God and worlds, then there is no gap between the conceivability of the existence of God and its possibility. That is, the gap is non-existent (or at least minimal) if the existence of God is ideally conceivable, as opposed to *prima facie* conceivable. Yet it is difficult to show that God is ideally conceivable.

Atheists often claim that the *non*-existence of God is conceivable. If that is conceivable, then it follows with premise 2 above that the non-existence of God is possible. That is, there is a possible world in which God does not exist. If we plug this into the modal ontological argument, we can then derive that it is necessary that God does not exist, which is diametrically opposite to the conclusion that perfect being theists wish to derive. To block this response, perfect being theists might argue that the non-existence of God is only *prima facie* conceivable and not ideally conceivable. Yet atheists can make a parallel move, saying that the existence of God is only *prima facie* conceivable and not ideally conceivable. So it looks as though the dispute between proponents and opponents of this argument for the possibility premise ends in a stalemate.

The difficulty of defending the argument from conceivability can be highlighted by comparing it with the so-called 'zombie argument' discussed in the philosophy of mind:

(1z) The existence of zombies is conceivable.
(2z) Conceivability entails possibility.
(3z) Therefore, the existence of zombies is possible.

Zombies are duplicates of humans in all physical respects but without phenomenal consciousness. The zombie argument has attracted a lot of attention because if it is sound, it undermines physicalism, which is the dominant view in the philosophy of mind. The second premise of the zombie argument is identical with the second premise of the argument from conceivability for the possibility premise and, again, this premise is disputed.[6] So, with respect to this premise, the argument from

[6] See, for example, Chalmers (1996), Gendler and Hawthorne (2002), and Kirk (2005).

conceivability is as contentious as the zombie argument. The first premise of the zombie argument seems to be exactly parallel to the first premise of the argument from conceivability, i.e. that the existence of God is conceivable. One might therefore think that, with respect to this premise too, the argument from conceivability is as contentious as the zombie argument. Yet I claim that the argument from conceivability is more contentious than the zombie argument in this respect because God's existence is more ontologically demanding than zombies' existence. Zombies are not necessary beings, so proponents of the zombie argument can allow that zombies do not exist in some possible worlds. On the other hand, proponents of the argument from conceivability do not allow that God does not exist in some possible worlds. As we have seen, once we allow that the non-existence of God is conceivable and possible, then God's necessary existence is undermined and the argument from conceivability cannot support the modal ontological argument. In this sense, the existence of God is more ontologically demanding than that of zombies and, hence, the argument from conceivability is more difficult to defend than the zombie argument. It seems safe to conclude, therefore, that the argument from conceivability is at least as contentious as, and possibly more contentious than, the zombie argument, which has been vigorously disputed among philosophers. Defending the argument is therefore not an easy task.

Argument 2: Experientiability Entails Possibility

One might try to derive the possibility of the existence of God from its imaginability instead of its conceivability by putting forward the following argument:

(1i) The existence of God is imaginable.
(2i) Imaginability entails possibility.
(3i) Therefore, the existence of God is possible.

Alexander Pruss says that in many cases imaginability can be construed as a mental simulation of an experience (Pruss 2001, p. 114). The fact that we think we can imagine a certain state of affairs gives us some reason to think that we can in principle experience that state of affairs. And if we can experience a state of affairs, then that state of affairs is possible. However, imaginability is not a very good guide to possibility because we might miss relevant details of an object of the imagination or misidentify such an object. This observation suggests that we should try to derive the possibility of the existence of God directly from the fact that it has been experienced instead of deriving it indirectly through the imaginability of its being experienced. Pruss indeed pursues this line of reasoning in attempting to establish the possibility premise of the modal ontological argument.[7] Pruss (2001) constructs his argument by appealing to the following passage in a text of the eighth-century Hindu philosopher Adi Śaṃkara:

> If a thing outside awareness is as impossible as a barren woman's son how can we even feel *as if* something is outside? Nothing even *appears* to be like an impossibility. (Pruss 2001, p. 111)

Pruss contends that the above passage hints at the following principle: if x is impossible, x does not even appear in experiences, including mystical experiences; conversely, if x appears in experiences, x is possible. If we apply this principle to God, we can derive that if God appears in experiences, then God is possible.[8] And, according to Pruss, it is indeed true that God appears in experiences. Many high mystics claim that they have had experiences *as of* God. It might well be the case that such experiences are not veridical. Perhaps the high mystics just hallucinate; yet if the existence of God is impossible in the same way the existence of a square circle or a married bachelor is impossible, then God does not even appear in hallucinations.

Let us present Pruss's response from another angle. The traditional argument from religious experience for the existence of God says that theists are justified in believing that God exists because they have had veridical religious experiences. This argument is not easy to defend because it is difficult to demonstrate that these subjective, inner sensory experiences *are* veridical. Yet if Pruss is right, it is unnecessary to prove that these experiences are veridical. Even if these experiences are not veridical, given Śaṃkara's principle above, they are sufficient to show that the existence of God is at least possible. And, again, the mere

[7] Clement Dore (1975) develops a similar strategy but I focus on Pruss's argument here because his is more clearly presented. For critical discussions of Dore's argument, see Baker (1983) and Dore (1984).

[8] Pruss uses the term 'a maximally great being' but I use the term 'God' to keep consistency throughout this chapter.

possibility of the existence of God is all we need for the possibility premise of the modal ontological argument.

Pruss acknowledges that mystics can mislabel or misidentify what is presented in their mystical experiences. He illustrates this point with the following parallel example: Suppose that it is an essential property of living elephants to have heads, but that it appears to me that I am faced with a living headless elephant. If we apply Śaṃkara's principle, it follows that headless living elephants are possible, which is false. To set aside such complications, Pruss adds that Śaṃkara's principle applies only to things that 'really seem': '"An *x* really seems to s" is true if and only if *s* would be correctly identifying the content of a single phenomenal experience of hers if she were identifying it to be an *x*' (Pruss 2001, p. 116). So the above example does not entail that living headless elephants are possible because in the example I fail to correctly identify the content of my phenomenal experience.

Pruss's approach is ingenious but I am not convinced that it succeeds in establishing the possibility premise. In the context of the modal ontological argument, what is referred to as 'God' is a being with such very specific properties as necessary existence, omniscience, omnipotence, and omnibenevolence. Pruss claims that high mystics have had experiences *as of* such a being but that seems far from clear. Regarding necessary existence, Pruss says that what high mystics have experienced and identified as a maximally great being must exist necessarily because otherwise the greatness of such a being would be 'too fragile' to be maximal (Pruss 2001, p. 117). Yet it seems far from obvious that there would be any phenomenal differences that humans could detect between, for example, experiences *as of* God, as a maximally excellent being existing in all possible worlds, and experiences *as of* a maximally excellent being existing in all but one remote possible world. Similarly, it seems far from obvious that there would be any phenomenal differences that humans could detect between experiences *as of* God, as a being that is omnipotent, and experiences *as of* a being that is nearly omnipotent except for its inability to perform one trivial task. To establish the possibility premise by appealing to religious experiences, the contents of the phenomenal experiences do have to match perfectly with the concept of God that is required for the modal ontological argument. There is no question that high mystics have had experiences that are in principle *compatible* with the concept of God that is required for the modal ontological argument. Yet it is not clear whether they match perfectly with such a concept.

An appeal to religious experiences would clearly establish the possibility of the existence of God if we could show that the experiences of high mystics actually do involve God Himself, rather than some other comparable being. But if we could show that God Himself is indeed involved, then, ironically, the modal ontological argument turns out to be redundant. The involvement of God itself entails that God exists.

Argument 3: Flourishing Life

Pruss (2010) proposes another ingenious, refreshingly new argument for the possibility premise. His argument is based on a principle according to which a propositional belief that is at the motivational centre of a flourishing and intellectually sophisticated life is probably possibly true.[9] Suppose that many individuals and communities have led a flourishing and intellectually sophisticated life for a long time while holding a motivationally central belief that *p*. According to Pruss, this entails that *p* is probably possibly true. One can hold a central but *false* belief. To quote Pruss's example, a doctor can lead a flourishing and intellectually sophisticated life bringing a cancer treatment to patients even if his belief in the effectiveness of the treatment is false. Yet it seems difficult to think that such a belief can be the motivational centre of a flourishing and intellectually sophisticated life for a long time unless it is at least *possibly* true. Pruss argues that given these observations, and given the fact that there have been many flourishing lives in history at whose motivational centres lies the proposition that God exists, we can conclude that God's existence is probably possible. Hence, according to Pruss, the possibility premise of the modal ontological argument is probably true.

The most obvious response to Pruss's argument seems to be to point out that there have been many flourishing lives in history whose motivational centres are propositions based on atheism or other alternatives to monotheism, such as pantheism and polytheism. If we apply Pruss's

[9] Buras and Cantrell (2009) defend a somewhat similar argument for the possibility premise. They try to show that God's existence is possible by appealing to the notion of natural desire. They claim that, since natural desires are a guide to possibility and human beings naturally desire at least one state of affairs for which the existence of God is a necessary condition, it is possible that God exists.

reasoning to beliefs relevant to these positions, we seem to be able to show that the *non*-existence of God and the existence of pantheistic or polytheistic gods are probably possibly true, too. This is not good news for perfect being theists because the thesis that the non-existence of God or the existence of pantheistic or polytheistic gods are probably possibly true seems to undermine the possibility of God's necessary existence. Pruss offers a careful examination of this objection. I do not have space to discuss it in detail here, but the thrust of his response is that such beliefs concerning atheism, pantheism, and polytheism are either: (i) harmless because they are compossible or co-conceivable with the existence of God according to perfect being theism; (ii) irrelevant because, on close examination, the beliefs in question do not centrally or rationally contribute to life as much as theistic belief does; or (iii) false because we can undercut such beliefs by providing decisive arguments against them.

It seems to me that a more promising objection to Pruss's approach is concerned with the role of necessary existence in a belief at the motivational centre of a life. The possibility premise of the modal ontological argument says that it is possible that there is God (or, using Platinga's terminology, it is possible that there is a maximally great being). Again, for a possibility claim to be usable in the modal ontological argument, it has to state that the existence of God, understood *as a necessarily existent being*, is possible. On the other hand, if the claim is that the existence of God, understood merely as, say, an omniscient, omnipotent, and omnibenevolent being, without any mention of necessary existence, is possible, then it does not support the modal ontological argument. Yet it seems that the motivationally central belief held by the majority of theists that God exists does not seem to assume, even implicitly, the idea that God exists necessarily. Ordinary religious believers who have never studied the philosophy of religion do not normally entertain the idea that God is a being that exists in all possible worlds, let alone holding it at their motivational centre.

Pruss is aware of this objection and tries to respond to it. He says that whether the belief that God is maximally excellent in all possible worlds is motivationally central to anyone is irrelevant. All we need, according to Pruss, is the centrality of the belief that God exists, where God is understood as a being with maximal greatness, which, unbeknownst to many, entails necessary existence. He writes, 'One can believe that there is a maximally great being... without believing that there is a being that has maximal excellence in every world, just as one can believe that Frank has inherited all of Susan's property without believing that Frank has inherited Susan's horse' (Pruss 2010, p. 247). However, this response does not seem to succeed. As Pruss says, the success of his argument for the possibility of the existence of God depends on many factors, such as how motivationally central the belief is, how flourishing the individual or community *x* is, how much of *x*'s humanly excellent activity flows from that belief, how rational is the motivational connection between the belief and the humanly excellent activity, how intellectually sophisticated *x* is, how long the involved time span is, how large community *x* is, and so on (p. 236). It seems implausible to think that the probability of the possibility of the necessary existence of God itself increases as positive values are assigned to these factors because most believers are not even aware that necessary existence is entailed by God's maximal greatness. That is, it seems implausible to think that the probability of the possibility of God's necessary existence specifically increases as the probability of the existence of God conceived more generally increases. We can make the following analogous claim: the belief that Frank has inherited all of Susan's property might play an important role in Frank's flourishing. Yet the more specific fact that Frank has inherited Susan's horse as part of her property does not seem to be able to play any role in his flourishing unless he is aware of it.

The success or otherwise of my above objection to Pruss is not ultimately very crucial because even if Pruss's argument is indeed sound, it does not establish precisely the possibility premise anyway. The conclusion of Pruss's argument is that the existence of God is *probably* possibly true. If we plug this into the modal ontological argument, the conclusion of the modal argument has to be weakened accordingly: *probably*, an omniscient, omnipotent, and omnibenevolent being exists in the actual world. This is much weaker than the original conclusion that an omniscient, omnipotent, and omnibenevolent being does exist in the actual world. While the weaker conclusion is still significant, it compromises the virtue of the modal ontological argument as an a priori derivation of the existence of God. It is also likely to generate further disputes about how to assign a value to the probability claim. Given that, as I mentioned above, the probability in question depends on numerous factors, it is not easy to determine the probability of the possibility of the existence of God by appealing to Pruss's criteria.

Argument 4: The Deontic Argument

Carl R. Kordig (1981) introduces a deontic argument for the possibility premise. Despite its originality, this argument has attracted little attention in the literature:

> Define God as a most perfect being. What is most perfect is, in particular, deontically perfect.... What is deontically perfect, ought to exist. Thus, God ought to exist. Atheists maintain that God *does not* exist. Even they should grant that a most perfect being (God) *ought* to exist. But what ought to exist can exist. Hence, God can exist. (Kordig 1981, p. 207, emphasis in the original)

This argument relies on the 'ought implies can' principle, which is attributed to Kant. Kordig does not specify exactly what he means by deontic perfection but Oppy suggests the following interpretation: A deontically perfect being is such that: (i) it has all the properties that it ought to have and (ii) it has no property that it ought not to have (Oppy 1995, p. 73, ft. 7). Oppy also suggests an alternative interpretation which retains thesis (i) but replaces thesis (ii) with the following thesis: (ii′) the being has no property for which it is not the case that the being ought to have it. Some might find thesis (ii′) too strong. Thesis (ii′) entails thesis (ii), but not *vice versa*. I assume here that one or the other of Oppy's two interpretations of deontic perfection is correct.

Grim and Oppy claim that Kordig's argument fails because a deontically perfect being does not have to have necessary existence, which the modal ontological argument requires God to have (Grim 1982; Oppy 1995, pp. 73–4). Kordig's argument purports to show that it is possible that a deontically perfect being exists, which is equivalent to saying merely that such a being exists in at least one possible world. But this cannot be plugged into the modal ontological argument, which is concerned with God's existing in *all possible worlds*. Kordig might respond to Grim and Oppy by maintaining that a truly deontically perfect being does exist necessarily. It seems that a being that is deontically great in all possible worlds is deontically superior to a being that is deontically great in only a limited number of possible worlds. Hence, Kordig may conclude, necessary existence *is* entailed by true deontic perfection. And, as the being than which no greater is metaphysically possible, God must be a truly deontically perfect being.

Unfortunately, even if we assume that a deontically perfect being is a necessary being, Kordig still seems to fail to derive the possibility of the existence of God Himself. Kordig seems right in saying that, given the assumption that God is the being than which no greater is metaphysically possible, He must be a deontically perfect being. But that does not mean that any argument for the possibility of the existence of a deontically perfect being is a direct argument for the possibility of the existence of God. This is because it is far from clear that a deontically perfect being has other properties commonly ascribed to God, such as significant knowledge, power, and benevolence. Here is a parallel example: Suppose that God is a timeless being. That does not mean that any argument for the possibility of a timeless being is a direct argument for the possibility of the existence of God. If it is possible that God exists, then it is possible that a timeless being exists, but if it is possible that a timeless being exists, it does not immediately follow that it is possible that God exists. Therefore, even if Kordig's argument for the possibility premise establishes that it is possible that a deontically perfect being exists, it does not establish the possibility premise of the modal ontological argument, the premise that it is possible that God exists. Hence, even if Kordig's argument is sound, we cannot plug it into the modal ontological argument.

Another related point that should be raised here is that Kordig's claim that God ought to exist can be challenged by proponents of so-called 'anti-theism'. Virtually all theists (and many atheists) hold so-called 'pro-theism', according which it would be good for God to exist. Anti-theism, on the other hand, says that it would not be good for God to exist. Thomas Nagel, for example, says that he not only does not want God to exist but he wants God not to exist (Nagel 1997, p. 130). To evaluate anti-theism, it is necessary to give a careful axiological comparison of possible scenarios in which God does and does not exist. I do not mean to suggest that anti-theism is correct but it is worth pointing out that not everyone agrees with Kordig that God ought to exist.[10]

Finally, Kordig's application of the 'ought implies can' principle seems dubious. The thesis that 'God ought to exist' seems irrelevant to the principle because the principle is concerned with 'ought' in relation to an agent's action, such as 'Peter ought to rescue a drowning child' and 'Susan ought to donate to a charity'. When we say 'God ought to exist',

[10] For pro-theism and anti-theism see, for instance, Kahane (2011), Kraay and Dragos (2013), Mawson (2012), and Nagel (1997).

we are not making any comparable claim about God's action. We are rather making a claim that it is *desired* that God exists. The 'ought implies can' principle applies to 'can' understood as an agent's capability of performing a certain action rather than as a metaphysical possibility of a certain state of affairs being realized.[11] Therefore, Kordig's argument for the possibility premise fails.

Argument 5: Positive Properties

The last argument for the possibility premise that I discuss here before introducing my own is one originally introduced by Leibniz in the seventeenth century and revived by Kurt Gödel in the twentieth century. Leibniz presents his formulation of the ontological argument as follows:

> [W]hatever follows from the idea or definition of anything can be predicated of that thing. Since the most perfect being includes all perfections, among which is existence, existence follows from the idea of God (or the idea of the most perfect being, or the idea of that than which nothing greater can be thought). Therefore existence can be predicated of God. But one must realize that from this argument we can conclude only that, if God is possible, then it follows that he exists. For we cannot safely use definitions for drawing conclusions unless we know first that they are real definitions, that is, that they include no contradictions, because we can draw contradictory conclusions from notions that include contradictions, which is absurd. To clarify this I usually use the example of the fastest motion. Everyone can see that any spoke of the wheel extended beyond the edge would move faster than a nail on the rim of the wheel. Therefore the nail's motion is not the fastest, contrary to the hypothesis. However, at first glance we might seem to have the idea of a fastest motion, for we certainly understand what we say; but yet we certainly have no idea of impossible things. And so, in the same way, the fact that we think about a most perfect being is not sufficient for us to assert that we have an idea of it. And so, in the demonstration given a bit earlier, either we must show or we must assume the possibility of a most perfect being in order properly to draw the conclusion. However, nothing is truer than that we have an idea of God and that a most perfect being is possible, indeed, necessary; yet the argument

[11] I benefited from discussion with Michael Ridge, Martin Smith, and Patrick Todd on this point. One of the very few views that oppose the point is axiarchism. According to this view, roughly speaking, there is x because it ought to be the case that there is x. In other words, axiarchism advocates that value is a foundation of ontology. Axiarchism is an extreme view because it tries to explain why there is x (not even why it is *possible* that there is x) based on the thesis that it *ought to be the case* that there is x. Axiarchists who endorse theism might not need the modal ontological argument because it seems that they can directly derive the existence of God from the thesis that God ought to exist. For axiarchism see Leslie (1979, 2001), Leslie and Kuhn (2013), and Parfit (1998).

is not sufficient for drawing the conclusion and was long ago rejected by Aquinas.[12] (Leibniz 1989b, originally 1684, pp. 25–6, emphasis in the original)

I mentioned in Section 7.2 that Hartshorne and Malcolm are the ones who in the middle of the twentieth century 'discovered' the modal ontological argument in Anselm's *Proslogion*. However, the core of the modal ontological argument is already present in the above quote. That is why we can consider Leibniz a philosopher who proposes an argument for the possibility premise of the modal ontological argument. In the above quote, Leibniz says that God, as the 'most perfect being' or 'that than which nothing greater can be thought', is necessarily existent and, hence, that the existence of God follows from the idea of God. However, he contends, the possibility of God must be established first. If the existence of God is not possible, then the concept of God is contradictory. This makes the modal ontological argument a failure insofar as any conclusion can be trivially derived from a contradiction. Hence, Leibniz contends, the modal ontological argument is incomplete until it is shown that the existence of God is possible.

Now a crucial question for us here is how Leibniz argues for the possibility premise. Leibniz's strategy is to derive the possibility of God from what we may call 'positive properties'.

By a *perfection* I mean every simple quality which is positive and absolute or which expresses whatever it expresses without any limits.

But because a quality of this kind is simple, it is unanalyzable or undefinable, for otherwise either it will not be one simple quality but an aggregate of many or, if it is one, it will be contained within limits and hence will be understood through negation of what is beyond these limits; which is contrary to hypothesis, since it is assumed to be purely positive.

From this it is not difficult to show that *all perfections are compatible with each other* or can be in the same subject. (Leibniz 1989a, originally 1676, p. 167, emphasis in the original)

In the above quote, Leibniz claims that perfections, or positive properties, are simple properties which cannot be analysed further and are free

[12] It is interesting to note that Leibniz claims in this quote that there cannot be such a thing as the fastest motion. Physicists have proved that nothing can travel faster than light (at least in this world), which undermines Leibniz's claim.

from any limits. He maintains that positive properties are mutually consistent because of their positivity. He implies that positive properties can be mutually inconsistent only with non-positive properties, even though he does not explicitly say so in the above quote.

Leibniz also writes:

> [The possibility of a most perfect Being] will be clear if I show that all (positive) attributes are compatible with each other. But attributes are either analyzable or unanalyzable. If they are analyzable, they will be the aggregate of those into which they are analyzed. Therefore it would be enough to have shown the compatibility of all the first, or unanalyzable, attributes, that is, those which are conceived through themselves. For if individual [attributes] are thus compatible, pluralities will be too, and therefore also composites.
>
> (Leibniz 1923, originally seventeenth century, p. 572)[13]

In the above passage, Leibniz seems to claim that aggregates of positive properties are mutually consistent because their unanalysable, fundamental constituents are positive properties, which are also mutually consistent. As long as the aggregates do not contain non-positive properties, no inconsistency can arise from them.

Furthermore, Leibniz writes in *Monadology* 45:

> Therefore God alone (or the Necessary Being) has this prerogative that if he be possible he must necessarily exist, and, as nothing is able to prevent the possibility of that which involves no bounds, no negation, and consequently, no contradiction, this alone is sufficient to establish *a priori* his existence.
>
> (Leibniz 2005, originally 1714, p. 54)

In the above passage, Leibniz applies his view of positive properties to the possibility premise of the modal ontological argument. He contends that it is possible that God exists because his properties are all boundless and positive and do not involve any contradiction.

The thrust of Leibniz's argument for the possibility premise seems to be the following: Perfections are positive properties that are simple, absolute, and limitless. Even if some of the perfections are composite rather than simple, they are still positive because they are composed of simple positive properties. Since simple positive properties are mutually consistent, their composites are also mutually consistent. The idea of God contains no contradiction because God has only positive properties

[13] This is Adams's translation as quoted on p. 146 of his 1994 book.

or composites of positive properties.[14] Therefore, it is possible that God exists.

Leibniz's argument for the possibility premise was revived in the twentieth century by the mathematician Kurt Gödel. As a secret private project, towards the end of his life Gödel developed a version of the modal ontological argument, which he believed to be a successful proof of the existence of God. Oppy provides the following clear summary of Gödel's version of the modal ontological argument, which was left only in handwritten notes. The argument consists of the following three definitions, six axioms, and three theorems (Oppy 2006, p. 70):[15]

Definition 1: x is God-like if and only if x has as essential properties those and only those properties which are positive.

Definition 2: A is an essence of x if and only if for every property B, x has B necessarily if and only if A entails B.

Definition 3: x exists necessarily if and only if every essence of x is necessarily exemplified.

Axiom 1: If a property is positive, then its negation is not positive.

Axiom 2: Any property entailed by—that is, strictly implied by—a positive property is positive.

Axiom 3: The property of being God-like is positive.

Axiom 4: If a property is positive, then it is necessarily positive.

Axiom 5: Necessary existence is positive.

Axiom 6: For any property P, if P is positive, then being necessarily P is positive.

Theorem 1: If a property is positive, then it is consistent, that is, possibly exemplified.

Theorem 2: If something is God-like, then the property of being God-like is an essence of that being.

Theorem 3: Necessarily, the property of being God-like is exemplified.

[14] It is not entirely clear whether Leibniz allows God to have neutral properties but that is irrelevant to our discussion here. For the sake of simplicity, I assume that he does not allow it. Gödel contends that God's essential properties are all positive.

[15] For further discussions of Gödel's modal ontological argument see, for example, Anderson (1990) and Sobel (2004).

We can clearly see that Leibniz's argument for the possibility premise is incorporated into Gödel's version of the modal ontological argument. Like Leibniz, Gödel appeals to the notion of a positive property to show that a set of properties ascribed to God is consistent. Through the consistency of the set Gödel argues for the possibility premise that it is possible that God exists (or, using Gödel's terminology, that the property of being God-like is possibly exemplified), from which he derives that it is necessary that God exists (or, using Gödel's terminology, that the property of being God-like is necessarily exemplified) and, hence, that it is actual that God exists (or, using Gödel's terminology, that the property of being God-like is actually exemplified).

I think that while Leibniz and Gödel are on the right track, their arguments for the possibility premise are not convincing enough. To show this, we have first to identify exactly what are the positive properties that Leibniz and Gödel ascribe to God. Unfortunately, they give us very little information to guide us. In the above quotes, Leibniz says only that positive properties are simple and absolute and without any limits. Gödel, on the other hand, merely writes, in his handwritten notes, 'Positive means positive in the moral aesthetic sense (independently of the accidental structure of the world)' (Sobel 2004, p. 145). By positive properties 'in the moral aesthetic sense' Gödel probably means positive axiological values. This is consistent with what perfect being theists have in mind when they say that God is the being than which no greater is metaphysically possible. And Gödel presumably adds the clause 'independently of the accidental structure of the world' to signify that positive properties are intrinsically positive, rather than positive in relation to other things. However, he provides no further details.

It is reasonable to assume that both Leibniz and Gödel ascribe such great-making properties as omniscience, omnipotence, and omnibenevolence to God. In his answer to a sociologist's questionnaire that he filled in but never returned, Gödel describes his religious position as follows: 'Baptist Lutheran (but not member of any rel. cong.) My belief is *theistic*, not pantheistic, following Leibniz rather than Spinoza' (Wang 1987, p. 18). And Leibniz indeed explicitly ascribes omniscience, omnipotence, and omnibenevolence (or goodness) to God in his work.[16] If Leibniz and

[16] See, for example, his *Discourse on Metaphysics* (2012, originally 1686).

Gödel ascribe omniscience, omnipotence, and omnibenevolence to God, they must think of them as positive properties or composites of positive properties because otherwise they cannot use the possibility premise to derive the existence of God as the omniscient, omnipotent, and omnibenevolent being through the modal ontological argument. Yet their ascription of omniscience, omnipotence, and omnibenevolence to God is problematic because Type-B arguments, which we addressed in Chapters 1 through 4, seem to undermine it. According to Type-B arguments, God cannot consistently have properties such as those that Leibniz and Gödel ascribe to God (omniscience, omnipotence, and omnibenevolence) because they are mutually inconsistent. This means that, according to Type-B arguments, Leibniz and Gödel are wrong in thinking either: (i) that omniscience, omnipotence, and omnibenevolence are positive properties or composites of positive properties, or (ii) that positive properties and composites of positive properties are always mutually consistent.

Hence, if Leibniz and Gödel wish to establish the possibility of God, it is not sufficient for them to claim that omniscience, omnipotence, and omnibenevolence are positive properties or composites of positive properties. They have to show further that *all* Type-B arguments fail. This is a very difficult task. I conclude, therefore, that their attempts to establish the possibility premise are not compelling.

7.4 The Maximal God Argument for the Possibility Premise

I have criticized five existing arguments for the possibility premise of the modal ontological argument. I discussed Leibniz's and Gödel's argument, which is the oldest argument for the premise, last because it is distinct in important ways from the four other arguments. Notice that the four other arguments are *indirect* in the sense that they try to derive the possibility of the existence of God from other things. The first argument tries to derive it from the conceivability of the existence of God, the second argument from the experientiability of the existence of God, the third argument from the motivational centrality of the existence of God for a flourishing life, and the fourth argument from the deontic perfection of the existence of God. This means that these arguments take the following two steps to establish the possibility premise:

Step 1: Show that the existence of God is conceivable/experientiable/motivationally central/deontically perfect.
Step 2: Show that conceivability/experientiability/motivational centrality/deontically perfection entails possibility.

Both steps invite objections. Critics can question whether the existence of God is really conceivable/experientiable/motivationally central/deontically perfect and also whether conceivability/experientiability/motivational centrality/deontic perfection really entails possibility.[17] Leibniz's and Gödel's argument is more efficient than the other four arguments because it aims to derive the possibility of the existence of God *directly* in one step by focusing on the consistency between positive properties that God has. I have nevertheless shown that their arguments are not convincing enough because they face Type-B arguments. Yet I still think that Leibniz and Gödel are correct in thinking that the best way to establish the possibility premise is to show that God's great-making properties are mutually consistent (and also internally coherent).

In Chapter 4, I argued that we should not understand God's knowledge, power, and benevolence from a bottom-up perspective. That is, we should not understand them as large bodies of knowledge, power, and benevolence that can be built by adding incremental units of knowledge, power, and benevolence one by one. It is more appropriate to have a top-down perspective that begins with omniscience, omnipotence, and omnibenevolence and consider them as subsuming infinite degrees of knowledge, power, and benevolence. It seems that Leibniz and Gödel adopt a bottom-up perspective in considering God's greatness in relation to omniscience, omnipotence, and omnibenevolence. Leibniz and Gödel start with these properties or components of these properties and consider them 'building blocks' of God's greatness (or, using Gödel's terminology, the property of being God-like). They then argue that since these properties or their components are all positive, they are mutually consistent. This entails, according to them, that it is possible that God exists. However, as we have seen, Type-B arguments say that at least some of what they consider to be positive properties are *not* mutually consistent. (Moreover, Type-A arguments say that they are not internally incoherent either.)

[17] This corresponds to the fact that the zombie argument against physicalism in the philosophy of mind requires two steps, both of which invite objection: Step 1: Show that zombies are conceivable. Step 2: Show that conceivability entails possibility.

To develop a new argument for the possibility premise, I suggest that we adopt a top-down instead of a bottom-up perspective. That is, instead of starting with such 'building blocks' of God's greatness as incremental units of knowledge, power, and benevolence or even omniscience, omnipotence, and omnibenevolence, we should start with God's greatness itself. What Leibniz and Gödel try to show is that God's greatness is possibly exemplified because all units of knowledge, power, and benevolence, and *a fortiori* omniscience, omnipotence, and omnibenevolence, are positive and, hence, they are all mutually consistent. But it is better to start with God's overall greatness and unpack it in such a way that its components—that is, God's knowledge, power, and benevolence—are mutually consistent (and internally coherent). And we can indeed pursue such a strategy by appealing to the maximal God thesis.

Again, the maximal God thesis explicates the perfect being thesis by saying that God is the being that has the maximal consistent set of knowledge, power, and benevolence. According to the maximal God approach, this is what the perfect being thesis means when it says that God is the being than which no greater is metaphysically possible. This suggests that once we accept the maximal God thesis and the perfect being thesis, we can automatically derive that it is possible that God exists because here God is understood as the being that has the maximal *consistent* set of knowledge, power, and benevolence. In other words, the maximal concept of God is *by definition* internally coherent because its components are mutually consistent (and internally coherent). This guarantees the possibility of the existence of God. That is, the possibility of God's existence comes with perfect being theism for free given the maximal God thesis. It is important to remind ourselves that, as I discussed in Chapter 1, necessary existence is included in the notion of the being than which no greater is metaphysically possible. For God to be greater than all other metaphysically possible beings, He has to be ontologically superior to all other metaphysically possible beings. No being can be ontologically superior to all other metaphysically possible beings if it is a merely contingent being.

Recall that Plantinga's formulation of the modal ontological argument appeals to the following two theses:

Maximal excellence: Necessarily, a being is maximally excellent in a given possible world only if it is omnipotent, omniscient and omnibenevolent in that world.

> Maximal greatness: Necessarily, a being is maximally great only if it is maximally excellent in every possible world.

What I have argued above suggests that these theses should be replaced with the following theses; call them 'real maximal excellence' and 'real maximal greatness', respectively:

> Real maximal excellence: Necessarily, a being is really maximally excellent in a given possible world only if it has the maximal consistent set of knowledge, power, and benevolence in that world.
>
> Real maximal greatness: Necessarily, a being is really maximally great only if it is really maximally excellent in every possible world.[18]

Once we accept that the real maximal excellence thesis and the real maximal greatness thesis apply to God, then the consistency between God's knowledge, power, and benevolence is given and there is no need to provide an additional argument for the possibility premise. In other words, the possibility of the existence of God is automatically given once we accept the maximal God thesis and the perfect being thesis. So, somewhat ironically, the sixth (and my own) argument for the possibility premise is that we do not need any argument for it. In this way, the possibility premise, arguably the only controversial premise of the modal ontological argument, is established and the argument successfully derives the existence of God.

7.5 Conclusion

We saw in Chapters 3 and 4 that the maximal God thesis undermines most arguments against perfect being theism. In this chapter, we have seen, moreover, that the maximal God thesis allows us to establish a strong argument for perfect being theism. In particular, the thesis provides a way to complete the modal ontological argument by offering a new way of establishing the long-disputed possibility premise. Again, as far as the classical ontological argument is concerned, perfect being theists and their critics seem to end in a draw. I hope to have shown

[18] The four theses here, maximal excellence, maximal greatness, real maximal excellence, and real maximal greatness, specify only necessary conditions. To represent complete specifications of God, they need to specify sufficient conditions as well.

over the course of this chapter, however, that as far as the modal ontological argument is concerned, perfect being theists win.

I am a counterexample to the common perception that no one subscribes to perfect theism because of the ontological argument. I do not think that the modal ontological argument is a definitive *proof* of the existence of God, but I do think that it is a good argument. The argument is formally valid, so the conclusion cannot be false if all the premises are true.[19] And all the premises do seem true; I cannot think of any successful objections to them. Hence, it seems to me that the argument is no less compelling than many other philosophical arguments that are widely considered persuasive.

Plantinga writes that while he personally thinks that the modal ontological argument is sound, he does not think that the argument is powerful enough to persuade atheists who are not willing to accept the possibility premise (Plantinga 1974a). I believe that the modal ontological argument is more powerful than he thinks it is, particularly in light of the maximal God approach, which offers a new argument for the premise. The ontological argument is often considered question-begging because its conclusion appears to be smuggled in through one of the premises. In the case of the modal ontological argument, the conclusion can be seen to be smuggled in through the possibility premise because it is effectively the only premise of the argument and if, as the premise says, it is possible for God to exist, then it follows logically that God exists. That is why, as Plantinga says, atheists tend to reject the possibility premise. However, showing that a deductive argument like the modal ontological argument is question-begging is not easy because the conclusion of any valid deductive argument is entailed necessarily by the set of its premises. So it is not so obvious that whether atheists feel that the conclusion is smuggled in through the possibility premise is relevant to the plausibility of the argument. What *is* relevant is whether the possibility premise is plausible enough for open-minded atheists. If they initially agree with the possibility premise but reject it after realizing that it entails that God exists, then that would be an ad hoc move. I hope to have shown that the modal ontological argument is compelling enough, at least for those who are willing to avoid such an ad hoc move.

[19] Actually, Plantinga's formulation of the modal ontological argument consists of only one premise: It is possible that there is a being that is maximally great.

Conclusion

I conclude this book by summarizing the two most crucial points for which I have argued.

First, most perfect being theists take it for granted that the perfect being thesis, i.e. that God is the being than which no greater is metaphysically possible, entails the omni God thesis, i.e. that God is the omniscient, omnipotent, and omnibenevolent being. They should not. Perfect being theists should hold instead that the perfect being thesis entails the maximal God thesis, i.e. that God is the being that has the maximal consistent set of knowledge, power, and benevolence. By doing so, they can undercut nearly all existing arguments against perfect being theism at once.

Second, the modal ontological argument for perfect being theism successfully establishes that *if* it is possible that God exists, then God exists. This is a significant achievement. The crucial question then is whether it is indeed possible that God exists. Once we hold that the perfect being thesis entails the maximal God thesis, we can show that it is possible that God exists because God as understood in the maximal God thesis is the being that has the maximal *consistent* sent of knowledge, power, and benevolence.

I conclude therefore that, given the maximal concept of God, we have good reason to think that perfect being theism is true and no good reason to think that perfect being theism is false.

References

Abbruzzese, John E. (1997), 'The Coherence of Omniscience: A Defence', *International Journal for Philosophy of Religion* 41, pp. 25–34.

Adams, Marilyn McCord (2000), *Horrendous Evils and the Goodness of God*, Ithaca, NY: Cornell University Press.

Adams, Marilyn McCord and Robert Merrihew Adams (eds.) (1990), *The Problem of Evil*, Oxford: Oxford University Press.

Adams, Robert Merrihew (1972), 'Must God Create the Best?', *Philosophical Review* 81, pp. 317–32.

Adams, Robert Merrihew (1994), *Leibniz: Determinist, Theist, Idealist*, New York: Oxford University Press.

Adams, Robert Merrihew (1999), *Finite and Infinite Goods*, Oxford: Oxford University Press.

Almeida, Michael (2011), 'Theistic Modal Realism', *Oxford Studies in Philosophy of Religion* 3, pp. 1–15.

Almeida, Michael (2012), 'The Logical Problem of Evil Regained', *Midwest Studies in Philosophy* 36, pp. 163–76.

Alter, Torin (2002), 'On Two Alleged Conflicts Between Divine Attributes', *Faith and Philosophy* 19, pp. 47–57.

Anderson, C. A. (1990), 'Some Emendations of Gödel's Ontological Proof', *Faith and Philosophy* 7, pp. 291–303.

Anscombe Elizabeth and Peter Thomas Geach (eds. and trans.) (1970), *Descartes: Philosophical Writings*, Nashville, TN: Thomas Nelson and Sons.

Anselm (1965, originally 1077–8), 'Proslogion', in Charlesworth, M. J. (ed. and trans.), *St Anselm's Proslogion*, Oxford: Clarendon Press, pp. 101–55.

Anselm (1998, originally 1076), 'Monologion', in Davies, B. and Evans, G. R. (eds. and trans.), *Anselm of Canterbury: The Major Works*, Oxford: Oxford University Press, pp. 5–81.

Aquinas, Thomas (1967, originally 1485), *Summa Theologiae*, trans. by Thomas Gilby, London: Eyre and Spottiswoode.

Ariew, Roger and Daniel Garber (eds. and trans.) (1989), *G. W. Leibniz Philosophical Essays*, Indianapolis: Hackett.

Aristotle (1883, originally fourth century BC), *History of Animals*, trans. by Richard Cresswell, London: George Bell and Sons.

Aristotle (2004, originally 350 BC), *The Metaphysics*, trans. by Hugh Lawson-Tancred, London: Penguin Books.

Augustine (1961, originally 398), *Confessions*, trans. by R. S. Pine-Coffin, London: Penguin Books.

Augustine (1974, originally 390), 'Letter 18 to Coelestinus', in Vernon J. Bourke (ed. and trans.), *The Essential Augustine*, Second Edition, Indianapolis: Hackett, pp. 45–6.

Augustine (1993, originally 387–9), *On Free Choice of the Will*, trans. by Thomas Williams, Indianapolis: Hackett.

Augustine (2009, originally 397), *On Christian Doctrine*, trans. by J. F. Shaw, Mineola, NY: Dover Publications.

Baker, John Robert (1983), 'Religious Experience and the Possibility of Divine Existence', *International Journal for Philosophy of Religion* 14, pp. 225–32.

Barnes, Jonathan (1972), *The Ontological Argument*, London and Basingstoke: Macmillan.

Barrett, J. L. (2004), *Why Would Anyone Believe in God?*, Lanham, MD: Altamira Press.

Barrow, John D. and Frank J. Tipler (1986), *The Anthropic Cosmological Principle*, Oxford: Oxford University Press.

Barth, Karl (1960, originally 1931), *Anselm: Fide Quaerens Intellectum*, trans. by Ian W. Robertson, Richmond, VA: John Knox Press.

Bayne, Tim and Yujin Nagasawa (2006), 'The Grounds of Worship', *Religious Studies* 42, pp. 299–313.

Bayne, Tim and Yujin Nagasawa (2007), 'Grounds of Worship Again: A Response to Crowe', *Religious Studies* 43, pp. 475–80.

Beall, J. C. (2000), 'A Neglected Response to the Grim Result', *Analysis* 60, pp. 38–41.

Beaty, Michael and Charles Taliaferro (1990), 'God and Concept Empiricism', *Southwest Philosophy Review* 6, pp. 97–105.

Bishop, John (1993), 'Evil and the Concept of God', *Philosophical Papers* 22, pp. 1–15.

Bliss, Ricki and Kelly Trogdon (2014), 'Metaphysical Grounding', in Edward N. Zalta (ed.), *The Stanford Encyclopedia of Philosophy* (Winter 2014 Edition), URL = <http://plato.stanford.edu/archives/win2014/entries/grounding/> (accessed 22 July 2016).

Blumenfeld, David (1978), 'On the Compossibility of the Divine Attributes', *Philosophical Studies* 34, pp. 91–103.

Boethius (1999, originally 523), *The Consolation of Philosophy*, trans. by P. G. Walsh, Oxford: Oxford University Press.

Bohn, Einar Duenger (2012), 'Anselmian Theism and Indefinitely Extensible Perfection', *Philosophical Quarterly* 62, pp. 671–83.

Bourke, Vernon J. (ed. and trans.) (1974), *The Essential Augustine*, Second Edition, Indianapolis: Hackett.

Bringsjord, Selmer (1989), 'Grim on Logic and Omniscience', *Analysis* 49, pp. 186–9.

Broad, C. D. (1939), 'Arguments for the Existence of God', *Journal of Theological Studies* 40, pp. 16–30, 156–67; reprinted in Broad, C. D. (1953) *Religion, Philosophy and Psychical Research: Selected Essays*, London: Routledge, pp. 175–201 (page numbers refer to reprinting).

Broad, C. D. (1953), *Religion, Philosophy and Psychical Research: Selected Essays*, London: Routledge.

Buckareff, Andrei and Yujin Nagasawa (eds.) (2016), *Alternative Concepts of God: Essays on the Metaphysics of the Divine*, Oxford: Oxford University Press.

Buras, Todd and Mike Cantrell (2009), 'Natural Desire and the Existence of God', unpublished manuscript.

Carr, Bernard (ed.) (2009), *Universe or Multiverse?*, Cambridge: Cambridge University Press.

Cartwright, Richard (1994), 'Speaking of Everything', *Noûs* 28, pp. 1–20.

Chalmers, David J. (1996), *The Conscious Mind*, Oxford: Oxford University Press.

Chalmers, David J. (2002), 'Does Conceivability Entail Possibility?', in Gendler, T. S. and Hawthorne, J. (eds.), *Conceivability and Possibility*, Oxford: Clarendon Press, pp. 145–200.

Chambers, Timothy (2000), 'On Behalf of the Devil: A Parody of Anselm Revisited', *Proceedings of the Aristotelian Society* 100, pp. 93–113.

Chang, Ruth (ed.) (1997), *Incommensurability, Incomparability, and Practical Reason*, Cambridge: Harvard University Press.

Charlesworth, M. J. (ed. and trans.) (1965), *St Anselm's Proslogion*, Oxford: Clarendon Press.

Cicero, Marcus Tullius (1972, originally 45 BC), *The Nature of the Gods*, trans. by C. P. McGregor, London: Penguin Books.

Cock, Albert A. (1917–18), 'The Ontological Argument for the Existence of God', *Proceedings of the Aristotelian Society* 18, pp. 363–84.

Copan, Paul and Chad Meister (eds.) (2008), *Philosophy of Religion: Classic and Contemporary Issues*, Oxford: Blackwell.

Cottingham, John, Robert Stoothoff, and Dugald Murdoch (eds. and trans.) (1984), *The Philosophical Writings of Descartes*, Volume II, Cambridge: Cambridge University Press.

Cray, Wesley D. (2011), 'Omniscience and Worthiness of Worship', *International Journal for Philosophy of Religion* 70, pp. 147–53.

Crowe, Benjamin (2007), 'Reasons for Worship: A Response to Bayne and Nagasawa', *Religious Studies* 43, pp. 465–74.

Danaher, John (2012), 'Stumbling on the Threshold: A Reply to Gwiazda on Threshold Obligations', *Religious Studies* 48, pp. 469–78.

Davies, Brian (1998), *Philosophy of Religion: A Guide to the Subject*, London: Cassell.

Davies, Brian (2004), 'Anselm and the Ontological Argument', in Davies, B. and Leftow, B. (eds.), *The Cambridge Companion to Anselm*, Cambridge: Cambridge University Press, pp. 157–78.

Davies, Brian and G. R. Evans (eds. and trans.) (1998), *Anselm of Canterbury: The Major Works*, Oxford: Oxford University Press.

Davies, Brian and Brian Leftow (eds.) (2004), *The Cambridge Companion to Anselm*, Cambridge: Cambridge University Press.

Davis, Stephen T. (1983), *Logic and the Nature of God*, Grand Rapids, MI: Eerdmans.

De Cruz, Helen and Johan De Smedt (2014), *A Natural History of Natural Theology: The Cognitive Science of Theology and Philosophy of Religion*, Cambridge, MA: MIT Press.

Descartes, René (1970, originally 1641), 'Meditations on First Philosophy', in Anscombe, E. and Geach, P. T. (eds. and trans.), *Descartes: Philosophical Writings*, Nashville, TN: Thomas Nelson and Sons, pp. 59–124.

Descartes, René (1982, originally 1644), *Principles of Philosophy*, trans. by Valentine Rodger Miller and Reese P. Miller, Dordrecht: Kluwer.

Descartes, René (1998, originally 1637), *Discourse on Methods*, Third Edition, trans. by Donald A. Cress, Indianapolis: Hackett.

Devine, P. E. (1975), 'The Perfect Island, the Devil, and Existent Unicorns', *American Philosophical Quarterly* 12, pp. 255–60.

Diller, Jeanine and Asa Kasher (eds.) (2013), *Models of God and Other Ultimate Realities*, New York: Springer.

Dore, Clement (1975), 'Examination of an Ontological Argument', *Philosophical Studies* 28, pp. 345–56.

Dore, Clement (1984), 'Reply to Professor Baker', *International Journal for Philosophy of Religion* 16, pp. 251–5.

Drange, Theodore M. (2006), 'Review of Jordan Howard Sobel's *Logic and Theism*', *The Secular Web*, URL= <http://www.infidels.org/library/modern/theodore_drange/sobel.html> (accessed 22 July 2016).

Eadmer (1962, originally 1124), *The Life of St Anselm: Archbishop of Canterbury*, Oxford: Clarendon Press.

Flint, Thomas P. and Alfred J. Freddoso (1983), 'Maximal Power', in Freddoso, A. J. (ed.), *The Existence and Nature of God*, Notre Dame, IN: University of Notre Dame Press, pp. 81–113.

Frankfurt, Harry (1964), 'The Logic of Omnipotence', *Philosophical Review* 73, pp. 262–3.

Freddoso, Alfred J. (ed.) (1983), *The Existence and Nature of God*, Notre Dame, IN: University of Notre Dame Press.

Gaunilo (1965, originally 1078), 'A Reply to the Foregoing by a Certain Writer on Behalf of the Fool', trans. by M. J. Charlesworth, in Charlesworth, M. J. (ed. and trans.), *St Anselm's Proslogion*. Oxford: Clarendon Press, pp. 156–67.

Geach, Peter (1977), *Providence and Evil*, Cambridge: Cambridge University Press.

Gellman, Jerome I. (1997), *Experience of God and the Rationality of Theistic Belief*, Ithaca, NY: Cornell University Press.

Gendler, Tamar Szabó and John Hawthorne (2002), *Conceivability and Possibility*, Oxford: Clarendon Press.

Goldschmidt, Tyron (ed.) (2013), *The Puzzle of Existence: Why is There Something Rather Than Nothing?*, London: Routledge.

Gombocz, Wolfgang (1973), 'St. Anselm's Disproof of the Devil's Existence in the *Proslogion*: A Counter Argument against Haight and Richman', *Ratio* 15, pp. 334–7.

Grant, C. K. (1957), 'The Ontological Disproof of the Devil', *Analysis* 17, pp. 71–2.

Green, Adam and Eleonore Stump (2016), *Hidden Divinity and Religious Belief: New Perspectives*, Cambridge: Cambridge University Press.

Grim, Patrick (1979), 'Plantinga's God and Other Monstrosities', *Religious Studies* 15, pp. 91–7.

Grim, Patrick (1982), 'Against a Deontic Argument for God's Existence', *Analysis* 42, pp. 171–4.

Grim, Patrick (1984), 'There Is No Set of All Truths', *Analysis* 44, pp. 206–8.

Grim, Patrick (1986), 'On Sets and Scenarios: A Reply to Menzel', *Analysis* 46, pp. 186–91.

Grim, Patrick (1990), 'On Omniscience and a "Set of All Truths": A Reply to Bringsjord', *Analysis* 50, pp. 271–6.

Grim, Patrick (1991), *The Incomplete Universe: Totality, Knowledge and Truth*, Cambridge, MA: MIT Press.

Grim, Patrick (2000), 'The Being That Knew Too Much', *International Journal for Philosophy of Religion* 47, pp. 141–54.

Grim, Patrick (2007), 'Impossibility Arguments', in Martin, M. (ed.), *The Cambridge Companion to Atheism*, Cambridge: Cambridge University Press, pp. 25–34.

Guleserian, Theodore (1983), 'God and Possible Worlds: The Modal Problem of Evil', *Noûs* 17, pp. 221–38.

Guleserian, Theodore (1985), 'Can Moral Perfection Be an Essential Attribute?', *Philosophical and Phenomenological Research* 46, pp. 219–41.

Gwiazda, Jeremy (2011), 'Worship and Threshold Obligations', *Religious Studies* 47, pp. 521–5.

Haight, David and Marjorie Haight (1970), 'An Ontological Proof of the Devil', *The Monist* 54, pp. 218–20.

Harrelson, Kevin J. (2009), *The Ontological Argument From Descartes to Hegel*, Amherst, NY: Humanity Books.

Hartshorne, Charles (1941), *Man's Vision of God*, New York: Harper and Row.

Hartshorne, Charles (1961), 'The Logic of the Ontological Argument', *Journal of Philosophy* 58, pp. 471–3.

Hartshorne, Charles (1965), *Anselm's Discovery: A Re-Examination of the Ontological Proof for God's Existence*, La Salle, IL: Open Court.

Hartshorne, Charles and William L. Reese (1953), *Philosophers Speak of God*, Chicago: University of Chicago Press.

Harwood, Robin (1999), 'Polytheism, Pantheism, and the Ontological Argument', *Religious Studies* 35, pp. 477–91.

Hick, John (1966), *Evil and the God of Love*, New York: Harper and Row.

Hick, John and Arthur C. McGill (ed.) (1968), *The Many-Faced Argument: Recent Studies on the Ontological Argument for the Existence of God*, London: Macmillan.

Hill, Daniel J. (1998), 'What's New in Philosophy of Religion?' *Philosophy Now* 21, pp. 30–3.

Hill, Daniel J. (2005), *Divinity and Maximal Greatness*, London: Routledge.

Hoffman, Joshua and Gary S. Rosenkrantz (2002), *The Divine Attributes*, Oxford: Blackwell.

Holmstrom-Hintikka, Ghita (ed.) (2000), *Medieval Philosophy and Modern Times*, Dordrecht: Kluwer.

Howard-Snyder, Daniel and Paul K. Moser (eds.) (2002), *Divine Hiddenness: New Essays*, Cambridge: Cambridge University Press.

Johnson, J. P. (1963), 'The Ontological Argument in Plato', *The Personalist* 44, pp. 23–34.

Kahane, Guy (2011), 'Should We Want God to Exist?', *Philosophy and Phenomenological Research* 82, pp. 674–96.

Kant, Immanuel (1929, originally 1781), *Critique of Pure Reason*, trans. by N. K. Smith, London: Macmillan.

Kenny, Anthony (1979), *The God of the Philosophers*, Oxford: Clarendon Press.

Kirk, Robert (2005), *Zombies and Consciousness*, Oxford: Oxford University Press.

Kordig, Carl R. (1981), 'A Deontic Argument for God's Existence', *Noûs* 15, pp. 207–8.

Kraay, Klaas (2008), 'Creation, World-Actualization, and God's Choice Among Possible Worlds', *Philosophy Compass* 3, pp. 854–72.

Kraay, Klaas J. (2010), 'Theism, Possible Worlds, and the Multiverse', *Philosophical Studies* 147, pp. 355–68.

Kraay, Klaas J. (2011), 'Theism and Modal Collapse', *American Philosophical Quarterly* 48, pp. 361–72.

Kraay, Klaas J. and Chris Dragos (2013), 'On Preferring God's Non-Existence', *Canadian Journal of Philosophy* 43, pp. 157–78.

Krauss, Lawrence M. (2012), *A Universe from Nothing: Why There is Something Rather than Nothing*, London: Simon and Schuster.

Kuhn, Robert Lawrence (2007), 'Why this Universe?: Toward a Taxonomy of Possible Explanations', *The Skeptic* 13, pp. 28–39.

Lachs, John (1963a), 'Omniscience', *Dialogue* 1, pp. 400–2.

Lachs, John (1963b), 'Professor Prior on Omniscience', *Philosophy* 37, pp. 361–4.

La Croix, Richard R. (1993a), *What is God?: The Selected Essays of Richard R. La Croix*, Buffalo, NY: Prometheus Books.

La Croix, Richard R. (1993b), 'Malcolm's *Proslogion* III Argument', in La Croix, R. (ed.), *What is God?: The Selected Essays of Richard R. La Croix*, Buffalo, NY: Prometheus Books, pp. 17–25.

Langtry, Bruce (2008), *God, the Best, and Evil*, Oxford: Oxford University Press.

Leech, David and Aku Visala (2011a), 'The Cognitive Science of Religion: A Modified Theist Response', *Religious Studies* 47, pp. 301–16.

Leech, David and Aku Visala (2011b), 'The Cognitive Science of Religion: Implications for Theism?', *Zygon* 46, pp. 47–64.

Leech, David and Aku Visala (2012), 'How Relevant is the Cognitive Science of Religion to Philosophy of Religion?', in Nagasawa, Y. (ed.), *Scientific Approaches to Philosophy of Religion*, Basingstoke: Palgrave Macmillan, pp. 165–83.

Leftow, Brian (2002), 'Anselm's Neglected Argument', *Philosophy* 77, pp. 331–47.

Leftow, Brian (2004), 'Anselm's Perfect-Being Theology', in Davies, B. and Leftow, B. (eds.), *The Cambridge Companion to Anselm*, Cambridge: Cambridge University Press, pp. 132–56.

Leftow, Brian (2011), 'Why Perfect Being Theology?', *International Journal for Philosophy of Religion* 69, pp. 103–18.

Leibniz, G. W. (1923, originally seventeenth century), *Sämtliche Schriften und Briefe*, Volume VI, Darmstadt and Berlin: Berlin Academy.

Leibniz, G. W. (1985, originally 1710), *Theodicy: Essays on the Goodness of God, the Freedom of Man and the Origin of Evil*, trans. by Austin Farrer, Chicago and La Salle, IL: Open Court.

Leibniz, G. W. (1989a, originally 1676), 'That a Most Perfect Being Exists', in Loemker, L. E. (ed.), *Gottfried Wilhelm Leibniz Philosophical Papers and Letters*, Dordrecht: Kluwer, pp. 167–8.

Leibniz, G. W. (1989b, originally 1684), 'Meditation on Knowledge, Truth, and Ideas', in Ariew, R. and Garber, D. (ed. and trans.), *G. W. Leibniz Philosophical Essays*, Indianapolis: Hackett, pp. 23–7.

Leibniz, G. W. (1996, originally 1704), *New Essays on Human Understanding*, trans. by Peter Remnant and Jonathan Bennett, Cambridge: Cambridge University Press.

Leibniz, G. W. (2005, originally 1714), 'The Monadology', in Montgomery, G. R. (ed. and trans.), *Discourse on Metaphysics and The Monadology*, Mineola, NY: Dover, pp. 47–63.

Leibniz, G. W. (2012, originally 1686), 'Discourse on Metaphysics', in Loptson, P., *Discourse on Metaphysics and Other Writings*, Peterborough, Ontario: Broadview Press, pp. 57–102.

Lembke, Martin (2012a), 'Omnipotence and Other Possibilities', *Religious Studies* 48, pp. 425–43.

Lembke, Martin (2012b), 'Grim, Omniscience, and Cantor's Theorem', *Forum Philosophicum* 17, pp. 211–23.

Leslie, John (1979), *Value and Existence*, Oxford: Blackwell.

Leslie, John (2001), *Infinite Minds: A Philosophical Cosmology*, Oxford: Oxford University Press.

Leslie, John and Robert Lawrence Kuhn (eds.) (2013), *The Mystery of Existence: Why is There Anything at All?*, Oxford: Wiley-Blackwell.

Lewis, David (1986), *On the Plurality of Worlds*, Oxford: Blackwell.

Loemker, Leroy E. (ed. and trans.) (1989), *Gottfried Wilhelm Leibniz Philosophical Papers and Letters*, Dordrecht: Kluwer.

Logan, Ian (2009), *Reading Anselm's Proslogion: The History of Anselm's Argument and its Significance Today*, Aldershot: Ashgate.

Loptson, P. (ed.) (2012), *Discourse on Metaphysics and Other Writings*, trans. by Robert Latta and George R. Montgomery, Peterborough, Ontario: Broadview Press.

Lovejoy, Arthur O. (1936), *The Great Chain of Being: A Study of the History of an Idea*, Cambridge, MA: Harvard University Press.

Mackie, J. L. (1955), 'Evil and Omnipotence', *Mind* 64, pp. 200–12.

Mackie, J. L. (1982), *The Miracle of Theism: Arguments For and Against the Existence of God*, Oxford: Clarendon Press.

Maitzen, Stephen (2005), 'Anselmian Atheism', *Philosophy and Phenomenological Research* 70, pp. 225–39.

Malcolm, Norman (1960), 'Anselm's Ontological Argument', *Philosophical Review* 69, 41–62.

Mann, William E. (1975), 'The Divine Attributes', *American Philosophical Quarterly* 12, pp. 151–9.

Manson, Neil A. (ed.) (2003), *God and Design: The Teleological Argument and Modern Science*, London: Routledge.

Mar, Gary (1993), 'Why "Cantorian" Arguments Against the Existence of God Do Not Work', *International Philosophical Quarterly* 33, pp. 429–42.

Martin, Michael (1974), 'A Disproof of the God of the Common Man', *Question* 7, pp. 115–24, reprinted in Martin, M. and Monnier, R. (eds.), *The Impossibility of God*, Amherst, NY: Prometheus Books, pp. 232–41.

Martin, Michael (1990), *Atheism: A Philosophical Justification*, Philadelphia: Temple University Press.

Martin, Michael (2000), 'Omniscience and Incoherency' in Holmstrom-Hintikka, G. (ed.), *Medieval Philosophy and Modern Times*, Dordrecht: Kluwer, pp. 17–34.

Martin, Michael (ed.) (2007), *The Cambridge Companion to Atheism*, Cambridge: Cambridge University Press.

Martin, Michael and Ricki Monnier (eds.) (2003), *The Impossibility of God*, Amherst, NY: Prometheus Books.

Mavrodes, George I. (1963), 'Some Puzzles Concerning Omnipotence', *Philosophical Review* 72, pp. 221–3.

Mawson, T. J. (2002), 'Omnipotence and Necessary Moral Perfection are Compatible: A Reply to Morriston', *Religious Studies* 38, pp. 215–23.

Mawson, T. J. (2008), 'Why is There Anything at All?', in Nagasawa, Y. and Wielenberg, E. (eds.), *New Waves in Philosophy of Religion*, Basingstoke: Palgrave Macmillan, pp. 36–54.

Mawson, Tim (2012), 'On Determining How Important it is Whether or Not There is a God', *European Journal for Philosophy of Religion* 4, pp. 95–105.

McGinn, Colin (2000), *Logical Properties*, Oxford: Oxford University Press.

Meister, Chad and James K. Dew (eds.) (2013), *God and Evil: The Case for God in a World Filled with Pain*, Downers Grove, IL: InterVarsity Press.

Mele, Alfred R. and M. P. Smith (1988), 'The New Paradox of Stone', *Faith and Philosophy* 5, pp. 283–90.

Miller, Barry (2002), *The Fullness of Being: A New Paradigm for Existence*, Notre Dame, IN: University of Notre Dame Press.

Millican, Peter (1989), 'The Devil's Advocate', *Cogito* 3, pp. 193–207.

Millican, Peter (2004), 'The One Fatal Flaw in Anselm's Argument', *Mind* 113, pp. 437–76.

Millican, Peter (2007), 'Ontological Arguments and the Superiority of Existence: Reply to Nagasawa', *Mind* 116, pp. 1041–53.

Montgomery, George R. (ed. and trans.) (2005), *Discourse on Metaphysics and The Monadology*, Mineola, NY: Dover.

Moore, G. E. (1936), 'Is Existence a Predicate?', *Proceedings of the Aristotelian Society*, Supplementary 15, pp. 154–88.

Morris, Thomas V. (1984), 'The God of Abraham, Isaac, and Anselm', *Faith and Philosophy* 1, pp. 177–87, reprinted in Morris, T. V. (ed.), *Anselmian Explorations*, Notre Dame, IN: University of Notre Dame Press, pp. 10–25 (page numbers refer to reprinting).

Morris, Thomas V. (1986), *The Logic of God Incarnate*, Ithaca, NY: Cornell University Press.

Morris, Thomas V. (1987a), *Anselmian Explorations*, Notre Dame, IN: University of Notre Dame Press.

Morris, Thomas V. (1987b), 'Perfect Being Theology', *Noûs* 21, pp. 19–30.

Morriston, Wes (2001a), 'Omnipotence and Necessary Moral Perfection: Are They Compatible?', *Religious Studies* 37, pp. 143–60.

Morriston, Wes (2001b), 'Omnipotence and the Anselmian God', *Philo* 4, pp. 7–20.

Morriston, Wes (2002), 'Omnipotence and the Power to Choose: A Reply to Wielenberg', *Faith and Philosophy* 19, pp. 358–67.

Morriston, Wes (2003), 'Are Omnipotence and Necessary Moral Perfection Compatible?: Reply to Mawson', *Religious Studies* 39, pp. 441–9.

Moser, Paul (2002), 'Cognitive Idolatry and Divine Hiding', in Howard-Snyder, D. and Moser, P. K. (eds.), *Divine Hiddenness: New Essays*, Cambridge: Cambridge University Press, pp. 120–48.

Nagasawa, Yujin (2007), 'Millican on the Ontological Argument', *Mind* 116, pp. 1027–40.

Nagasawa, Yujin (2008a), *God and Phenomenal Consciousness: A Novel Approach to the Knowledge Arguments*, Cambridge: Cambridge University Press.

Nagasawa, Yujin (2008b), 'A New Defence of Perfect Being Theism', *Philosophical Quarterly* 58, pp. 577–96.

Nagasawa, Yujin (2011), 'Anselmian Theism', *Philosophy Compass* 6, pp. 564–71.

Nagasawa, Yujin (ed.) (2012), *Scientific Approaches to Philosophy of Religion*, Basingstoke: Palgrave Macmillan.

Nagasawa, Yujin (2013a), 'Models of Anselmian Theism', *Faith and Philosophy* 30, pp. 3–25.

Nagasawa, Yujin (2013b), 'Maximal God and the Problem of Evil', in Diller, J. and Kasher, A., *Models of God and Other Ultimate Realities*, New York: Springer, pp. 233–43.

Nagasawa, Yujin (2016a), 'Modal Panentheism', in Buckareff, A. and Nagasawa, Y. (eds.), *Alternative Concepts of God: Essays on the Metaphysics of the Divine*, Oxford: Oxford University Press, pp. 91–105.

Nagasawa, Yujin (2016b), 'Hiddenness, Silence and Shusaku Endo', in Green, A. and Stump, E. (eds.), *Hidden Divinity and Religious Belief: New Perspectives*, Cambridge: Cambridge University Press, pp. 246–59.

Nagasawa, Yujin and Erik Wielenberg (eds.) (2008), *New Waves in Philosophy of Religion*, Basingstoke: Palgrave Macmillan.

Nagel, Thomas (1997), *The Last Word*, Oxford: Oxford University Press.

Nelson, Michael (2012), 'Existence', *The Stanford Encyclopedia of Philosophy* (Winter 2012 Edition), Edward N. Zalta (ed.), URL = <http://plato.stanford.edu/archives/win2012/entries/existence/> (accessed 22 July 2016).

Nozick, Robert (2001), *Invariances: The Structure of the Objective World*, Cambridge, MA: Belknap Press.

Oppy, Graham (1995), *Ontological Argument and Belief in God*, Cambridge: Cambridge University Press.

Oppy, Graham (1996), 'Gödelian Ontological Argument', *Analysis* 56, pp. 226–30.

Oppy, Graham (1997), 'Pantheism, Quantification and Mereology', *The Monist* 80, pp. 320–36.

Oppy, Graham (2006), *Arguing About Gods*, Cambridge: Cambridge University Press.

Oppy, Graham (2008), 'The Ontological Argument', in Copan, P. and Meister, C. (eds.), *Philosophy of Religion: Classic and Contemporary Issues*, Oxford: Blackwell, pp. 112–26.

Oppy, Graham (2011), 'Perfection, Near-Perfection, Maximality, and Perfect Being Theism', *International Journal for Philosophy of Religion* 69, pp. 119–38.

Parfit, Derek (1998), 'Why Anything? Why This?', *London Review of Books* 20, no. 2, pp. 24–7 and no. 3, pp. 22–5.

Peterson, Michael L. (ed.) (1992), *The Problem of Evil: Selected Readings*, Notre Dame, IN: University of Notre Dame Press.

Pike, Nelson (1969), 'Omnipotence and God's Ability to Sin', *American Philosophical Quarterly* 6, pp. 208–16.

Plantinga, Alvin (ed.) (1965), *The Ontological Argument from St. Anselm to Contemporary Philosophers*, New York: Anchor Book.

Plantinga, Alvin (1974a), *God, Freedom and Evil*, London: George Allen and Unwin.

Plantinga, Alvin (1974b), *The Nature of Necessity*, Oxford: Clarendon Press.

Plantinga, Alvin and Patrick Grim (1993), 'Truth, Omniscience, and Cantorian Arguments: An Exchange', *Philosophical Studies* 71, pp. 267–306.

Plato (1992, originally 380 BC), *Republic*, trans. by G. M. A. Grube and rev. by C. D. C. Reeve, Indianapolis: Hackett.

Pope, Alexander (1994, 1733–4), *Essay on Man and Other Poems*, New York: Dover Publications.

Power, William L. (1992), 'Ontological Arguments for Satan and Other Evil Beings', *Dialogue* 31, pp. 667–76.

Prior, A. N. (1963), 'Rejoinder to Professor Lachs on Omniscience', *Philosophy* 37, pp. 365–6.

Proclus (1992, originally fifth century), *Proclus' Commentary on Plato's* Parmenides, trans. by Glenn R. Morrow and John M. Dillion, Princeton, NJ: Princeton University Press.

Pruss, Alexander R. (2001), 'Śaṃkara's Principle and Two Ontomystical Arguments', *International Journal for Philosophy of Religion* 49, pp. 111–20.

Pruss, Alexander R. (2010), 'The Ontological Argument and the Motivational Centers of Lives', *Religious Studies* 46, pp. 233–49.

Rea, Michael (2015), *Evil and the Hiddenness of God*, Stamford, CT: Cengage Learning.

Richman, Robert J. (1958), 'The Ontological Proof of the Devil', *Philosophical Studies* 9, pp. 63–4.

Richman, Robert J. (1960), 'The Devil and Dr. Waldman', *Philosophical Studies* 11, pp. 78–80.

Richman, Robert J. (1976), 'A Serious Look at the Ontological Argument', *Ratio* 18, pp. 85–9.

Rogers, Katherin A. (1993), 'The Medieval Approach to Aardvarks, Escalators, and God', *Journal of Value Inquiry* 27, pp. 63–8.

Rowe, William L. (2004), *Can God Be Free?*, Oxford: Oxford University Press.

Rundle, Bede (2004), *Why is There Something Rather than Nothing?*, Oxford: Oxford University Press.

Savage, C. Wade (1967), 'The Paradox of the Stone', *Philosophical Quarterly* 76, pp. 74–9.

Schellenberg, J. L. (1993), *Divine Hiddenness and Human Reason*, Ithaca, NY: Cornell University Press.

Schellenberg, J. L. (2009), *The Wisdom to Doubt: A Justification of Religious*, Ithaca, NY: Cornell University Press.

Schellenberg, J. L. (2010), 'The Hiddenness Problem and the Problem of Evil', *Faith and Philosophy* 27, pp. 45–60.

Schellenberg, J. L. (2015), *The Hiddenness Argument: Philosophy's New Challenge to Belief in God*, Oxford: Oxford University Press.

Schloss, Jeffrey and Michael Murray (2009), *The Believing Primate: Scientific, Philosophical, and Theological Reflections on the Origin of Religion*, New York: Oxford University Press.

Seneca, Lucius Annaeus (2010, originally 62–4), *Natural Questions*, trans. by Harry M. Hine, Chicago: University of Chicago Press.

Sextus Empiricus (1936, originally second century), *Against Physicists* and *Against the Ethicists*, trans. by R. G. Bury, Cambridge, MA: Harvard University Press.

Simmons, Keith (1990), 'On an Argument Against Omniscience', presented at the American Philosophical Association Central Division.

Slattery, Michael P. (1969), 'The Negative Ontological Argument', *The New Scholasticism* 43, pp. 614–17.

Smith, A. D. (2014), *Anselm's Other Argument*, Cambridge, MA: Harvard University Press.

Smuts, Aaron (2012), 'The Power to Make Others Worship', *Religious Studies* 48, pp. 221–37.

Sobel, Jordan Howard (2004), *Logic and Theism: Arguments For and Against Beliefs in God*, Cambridge: Cambridge University Press.

Steinhart, Eric (2004), 'Pantheism and Current Ontology', *Religious Studies* 40, pp. 63–80.

Szatkowski, Miroslaw (ed.) (2013), *Ontological Proofs Today*, Berlin: De Gruyter.

Tillyard, E. M. W. (1972, originally 1942), *The Elizabethan World Picture*, New York: Vintage Books.

Todd, Patrick (2015), 'The Greatest Possible Being Needn't Be Anything Impossible', *Religious Studies* 51, pp. 531–42.

Trakakis, Nick (2007), *The God Beyond Belief: In Defence of William Rowe's Evidential Argument from Evil*, Dordrecht: Springer.

van Cleve, James (1983), 'Conceivability and the Cartesian Argument for Dualism', *Pacific Philosophical Quarterly* 64, pp. 35–45.

van Inwagen, Peter (2002), 'What is the Problem of the Hiddenness of God?', in Howard-Snyder, D. and Moser, P. K. (eds.), *Divine Hiddenness: New Essays*, Cambridge: Cambridge University Press, pp. 24–32.

Waldman, Theodore (1959), 'A Comment Upon the Ontological Proof of the Devil', *Philosophical Studies* 10, pp. 49–50.

Wang, Hao (1987), *Reflections on Kurt Gödel*, Cambridge, MA: MIT Press.

Wielenberg, Erik J. (2001), 'The New Paradox of the Stone Revisited', *Faith and Philosophy* 18, pp. 261–8.

Wierenga, Edward (2011), 'Augustinian Perfect Being Theology and the God of Abraham, Isaac, and Jacob', *International Journal for Philosophy of Religion* 69, pp. 139–51.

Witham, Larry (2008), *The Proof of God: The Debate that Shaped Modern Belief*, New York: Atlas & Co.

Wood, Graham (2011), 'Cognitive Science and Religious Belief', *Philosophy Compass* 6, pp. 734–45.

Wykstra, Stephen J. (1984), 'The Humean Obstacle to Evidential Arguments from Suffering: On Avoiding the Evils of "Appearance"', *International Journal of Philosophy of Religion* 16, pp. 73–93.

Zagzebski, Linda (2013), *Omnisubjectivity: A Defense of a Divine Attribute*, Milwaukee, WI: Marquette University Press.

Index

abstract objects 48
Adams, Marilyn 114
Adams, Robert 104
Anselm of Canterbury 1–3, 7, 10, 15, 20–4, 28–32, 36, 38, 40, 41, 48, 54, 55, 80, 81, 88, 92, 119, 120, 123–7, 130–52, 154, 155, 159, 161, 163, 169–71, 181, 182, 187, 198
Antigod parody objection 152, 153, 158, 160–6, 174, 175
Aquinas, Thomas 130, 198
argument from degree 130
argument from divine hiddenness, *see* type-C arguments
argument from evil, *see* type-C arguments
argument from experience, *see* type-B arguments
argument from God's inability to sin, *see* type-B arguments
argument from horrendous evil, *see* Adams, Marilyn
argument from moral admiration, *see* type-A arguments
argument from the imperfection of the actual world, *see* type-C arguments
Aristotle 17, 18, 42, 43, 46, 130, 131
atheism 3, 10–12, 14, 38, 192, 193
Augustine of Hippo 12, 21–4, 30, 31, 44, 45, 49, 125

Boethius 130, 131, 135, 161
Bohn, Einar 107
Broad, C. D. 51, 72–5

Calvin, John 27
Cantorian argument, *see* type-A arguments
Chalmers, David J. 187, 188
Chambers, Timothy 153, 160
Charlesworth, M. J. 139, 146
Chrysippus 19, 20, 126, 127
Cicero 13, 14, 18–20, 30, 43, 48, 126
Cleanthes 43, 129–31
cognitive science of religion 11, 26, 27
comprehensive greatness view 63–71, 76, 99, 106, 112
conceivability 8, 9, 94, 187–9, 202, 203
cosmological argument 11, 28, 35, 123, 127, 129, 132, 185

Darwin, Charles 46
Davies, Brian 15, 119
deontic perfection 195, 196, 202, 203
Descartes, Renee 128, 133, 159, 186
design argument 11, 28, 35, 123, 185
devil parody objection 169–74
Diogenes the Babylonian 128
Drange, Theodore M. 131

epistemically possible scenarios 80, 94–9
extensity objection 64–6, 69–71
extensive equality 56, 57
extensive inferiority 56
extensive superiority 56, 57

Gassendi, Pierre 146, 159
Gaunilo of Marmoutiers 48, 107, 128, 134, 140–2, 152–60, 174, 178, 182
Geach, Peter 118
Gellman, Jerome I. 119, 120
Gödel, Kurt 159, 197, 200–4
great chain of being 3, 40–9, 70–3, 75, 76
great-making properties 13, 26, 30–3, 35, 53, 55–61, 64, 70–3, 75, 81, 82, 94, 99, 103–12, 120, 123, 136, 139, 143, 162, 166–8, 177, 201, 203
  absolute great-making properties 65–70
  relative great-making properties 65, 66
  See also omni God thesis
Grim, Patrick 67, 83, 88, 195; *See also* type-A arguments; Contarian argument

Hartshorne, Charles 29, 124, 131, 181–3, 186, 198
Harwood, Robin 32

Higden, Ranulf 47
Hill, Daniel J. 91
Hitler, Adolf 75

imaginability 189, 190
intensity objection 64, 66–70

Kant, Immanuel 1, 132–4, 146, 159, 182, 195
Kantian objection 132, 145, 158, 178
Kenny, Anthony 82
Kordig, Carl R. 195–7

La Croix, Richard R. 182
Leftow, Brian 15, 24, 119, 120, 124
Leibniz, Gottfried Wilhelm 47, 64, 186, 197–204
Lewis, David 47
linear model 3, 41, 42, 49–53, 59, 61–3, 70–3, 75, 76, 136
Lovejoy, Arthur O. 42, 47, 48

Mackie, J. L. 38, 68, 86, 117, 118
Malcolm, Norman 29, 124, 133, 134, 181–3, 186, 198
Martin, Michael 86
maximal excellence 183, 184, 194, 204
  real maximal excellence 205
maximal excellence account 104, 105
maximal God thesis 2–4, 90–4, 100–3, 106, 109, 115, 117–20, 180, 181, 204–7
  maximal greatness 110, 183, 184, 193, 194
  real maximal greatness 205
McGinn, Colin 132
Mersenne, Marin 186
Miller, Barry 132
Millican, Peter 3, 124
  Millican's objection 138–51
  See also principle of the superiority of existence; theory of natures
modal argument from evil 115
Monadology, *see* Leibniz, Gottfried Wilhelm; positive properties
Monologion, *see* Anselm of Canterbury
monotheism 3, 7, 11, 12, 14, 38, 109–11, 120, 192
moral argument 11, 28, 35, 123, 129, 132, 185
Morris, Thomas V. 50–3, 72, 75, 76, 116
Morriston, Wes 89, 90, 118, 119

Nagel, Thomas 196
necessary existence 9, 30, 35, 98, 133, 134, 182, 183, 189, 191, 193–5, 204
nothingness 33, 34
Nozick, Robert 131

omni God thesis 2, 25, 27, 36–40, 79–86, 90–4, 97–103, 106, 113, 115, 118, 120, 123, 207
ontological argument:
  classical ontological argument 4, 107, 123–33, 180–2, 205
  modal ontological argument 3, 12, 79, 116, 124, 125, 128, 134, 154, 159, 180–6
  See also possibility premise
Oppy, Graham 15, 159, 173, 174, 195, 200
ought implies can 195–7
overall greatness view 71–3, 76, 99, 106, 107, 112, 136

panentheism 3, 10–14, 38
pantheism 3, 10–14, 19–22, 38, 43, 192, 193
paradox of the stone, *see* type-A arguments
parody objection, *see* Millican, Peter; Chambers, Timothy
perfect being theism 2–4, 7–12, 14, 15, 27, 28, 30, 33–6, 38, 39, 40, 64, 65, 76
  arguments against, *see* type-A arguments; type-B arguments; type-C arguments
  arguments for, *see* cosmological argument; design argument; moral argument; ontological argument
  biblical foundation 23, 24
  bottom-up view 32, 33
  case-by-case approach 88–90
  historical origins 15–22
  top-down view 32
  See also monotheism; cognitive science of religion
perfect being thesis 10–15, 18, 23–38, 40–2, 45, 46, 52, 63, 69, 72, 73, 76, 123, 126, 204, 205, 207; *See also* omni God thesis; maximal God thesis
phylogenetic tree 43, 46
Plantinga, Alvin 29, 88, 157, 183, 184, 186, 204, 206
Plato 10, 15–18, 22, 42, 131

Polytheism 3, 8, 10–14, 22, 38, 110, 111, 192, 193
positive properties 197–203
possibility premise 4, 180, 181, 184–8, 190–206
principle of the superiority of existence 135–42, 144, 161, 166, 171
Proclus 22, 23, 44, 48, 49
Proslogion, *see* Anselm of Canterbury
Pruss, Alexander 189–94

radial model 3, 42, 52, 53, 60–4, 69, 70, 76, 94
reductio ad absurdum 83, 125–7, 129–31, 154, 156
Reese, William L. 29, 181
Rogers, Katherine A. 72

Śamkara, Adi 190, 191
scala naturae, *see* great chain of being
Seneca 21
Sextus Empiricus 43, 44, 65, 66, 127–30
Simplicius 18, 130
Stoic philosophy 13, 18–21, 65
  Stoic argument 127–9
Summa Theologiae, *see* Aquinas, Thomas

Teresa, Mother 75
theory of natures 134–7
Tillyard, E. M. W. 46, 47
tokens 48, 49
Trakakis, Nick 119
type-A arguments:
  argument from moral admiration 83, 88
  Cantorian argument 37, 67, 83
  paradox of the stone 37, 67, 83, 88, 100, 113
type-B arguments:
  argument from experience 68, 84, 85, 88
  argument from God's inability to sin 37, 67, 68, 84, 88, 101, 113, 115, 118
type-C arguments:
  argument from divine hiddenness 38, 68, 86–9
  argument from evil 38, 68, 85–8, 101, 103, 113–15, 119, 120
  argument from the imperfection of the actual world 87, 89

uniqueness of God 109

value commensurability 9, 51–3, 60, 61, 71–3, 75, 76
  universal value commensurability 50, 62, 63, 70, 76

Wantzel, Pierre Laurent 95
Wierenga, Edward 15, 21, 24, 44, 124
Worshipworthiness, *see* maximal excellence account

Zeno of Citium 18, 19, 30, 65, 127–9
zombie argument 188, 189

Printed and bound by CPI Group (UK) Ltd, Croydon, CR0 4YY